Cold War
in the Balkans

Cold War in the Balkans

American Foreign Policy and the Emergence of Communist Bulgaria, 1943-1947

MICHAEL M. BOLL

THE UNIVERSITY PRESS OF KENTUCKY

Scholarly publisher for the Commonwealth,
serving Bellarmine College, Berea College, Centre
College of Kentucky, Eastern Kentucky University,
The Filson Club, Georgetown College, Kentucky
Historical Society, Kentucky State University,
Morehead State University, Murray State University,
Northern Kentucky University, Transylvania University,
University of Kentucky, University of Louisville,
and Western Kentucky University.

Editorial and Sales Offices: Lexington, Kentucky 40506-0024

Library of Congress Cataloging in Publication Data

Boll, Michael M., 1938–
   Cold war in the Balkans.

   Bibliography; p.
   Includes index.
   1. United States—Foreign relations—Bulgaria.
2. Bulgaria—Foreign relations—United States.
3. World War, 1939–1945—Bulgaria.   4. United States—
Foreign relations—1945–1953.   5. United States—
Foreign relations—1933–1945.   I. Title.
EL83.8.B8B65   1984   327.730497′7   84-7438
ISBN 0-8131-1527-2

Contents

Preface

The contemporary American student of the Cold War possesses advantages denied his colleagues of even a decade past. In the last few years, a wealth of materials on American policy as made by both the Department of State and the Department of War has become available in the National Archives and the National Records Center. Equally important, serious and, on the whole, creditable scholarship dealing with the early postwar period has appeared in the various East European states, greatly facilitating the inquiries of students able to read the requisite languages. Bulgarian scholarship well illustrates this development, and even a brief perusal of such journals as *Istoricheski pregled* (Historical Survey), *Voennoistoricheski sbornik* (The Military-Historical Collection), and *Izvestiia na instituta po istoriia na BKP* (The news from the Institute for the History of the Bulgarian Communist party) reveals a wealth of secondary sources little used in the West.

When combined with the numerous collections of documents published by both the Bulgarian People's Republic and the Soviet Union, these articles provide the scholar with detailed information on the aims and intricacies of American policy in a key East European state at the war's close. The dynamics of political and economic interaction between Bulgaria, the Soviet Union, and the United States in this formative period can be examined without resort to ascribing abstract motives for American policies. Numerous memoirs written by the more important Soviet generals and diplomats show that the uncertainties about East Europe's likely postwar future were not confined to American policy makers. Although the present study concentrates on Bulgaria, the rich materials available for this small state suggest that earlier assumptions that America lacked a policy for postwar Eastern Europe south of Poland will require significant reappraisal.

This examination of American policy toward Bulgaria in the early Cold War began as part of a project in a National Endowment for the Humanities Seminar directed by Thomas Paterson at the University of Connecticut one year after I had spent time studying in Bulgaria under an IREX grant. Although it is primarily a historical study, I also have been guided by practical considerations that confront anyone working

directly with American foreign policy past or present. Having served
as an analyst for Radio Free Europe in Munich, and later as a Foreign
Service officer in Washington, I acutely felt the need for specific
studies that might form the background and sketch the parameters of
possible change in contemporary American policy toward Eastern Europe. Thus the questions I posed to guide my research transcend those
normally associated with a strictly historical study of a time long past.
When I spent a year on the policy-planning staff of the Pentagon in
1980–81, the goal of understanding the opportunities of the present in
terms of the successful or abortive policies of the past assumed a more
urgent dimension. It is my hope that this book will be of assistance to
historians and diplomats alike by offering an interpretation of how the
current situation in the Balkans came to be.

It is difficult to single out those individuals and institutions most
responsible for education and insights accumulated in more than a
score of years. I owe a debt to Thomas Paterson for his enlightened
guidance of my initial inquiry and to George Herring for aiding in
publication of the results. John Taylor and Robin Cooksin of the National Archives were most helpful in identifying materials needed. I
wish to acknowledge the assistance of Stanford University, the Hoover
Institute, the National Records Center in Washington, Ivan Duridanov,
who ran the Summer Seminar in Sofia in 1979, and Philip Bokov of
the Bulgarian Embassy in London, who years ago gave me my first
textbook in the Bulgarian language. The Bulgarian Embassy in Washington, a much smaller installation than the corresponding facility in
London, was of less help, sending me another copy of Georgi Dimitrov's collected speeches on freedom and democracy regardless of
what information I requested.

Cyril Black of Princeton University was most kind in answering a
number of inquiries dealing with the involvement of American diplomats in Sofia in the period under consideration. Charles Burdick of
San Jose State University and Hugh De Santis of the State Department
provided encouragement and suggestions. Several other friends, members of East European Communist parties, provided special insights
into the evolution of Balkan Communism, but they must remain unnamed. My students at San Jose State University have been instrumen-
tal during the past decade in maintaining the scholarly atmosphere so
necessary to prevent snap conclusions and partial inferences when
dealing with topics concerning the Soviet Union and Eastern Europe.
Finally, I wish to thank my wife, Margaret, without whose encourage-

ment and sometimes benign neglect this study would have not seen the light of day.

Portions of Chapter 1 and Chapter 3 appeared in *Diplomatic History* and *East European Quarterly*.

SAN JOSE, CALIFORNIA

Introduction

The mid-1940s were formative in the emergence of an intense East-West rivalry, which has diminished little to the present day. Reflecting upon the defeat of Hitler and its implications, Joseph Stalin informed a visiting American senator in the fall of 1945 that "we shall have to find a new basis for our close relations in the future. And that will not be easy."[1] That such a basis remained undiscovered has inspired a plethora of studies of postwar international diplomacy, each seeking to attribute fault or ignorance in varying degree to the policies pursued by the victorious powers once the common goal of defeating the Axis brought into the open rivalries among the Allies. With such a wealth of scholarly effort, it may appear somewhat presumptuous to offer yet another analysis, the more so in that the present study focuses upon a narrow sector of what quickly became a global struggle for power and prestige. And yet there are compelling reasons to turn from more general examinations of the period to a more confined area of Great Power dispute. Concentration upon the broad spectrum of American-Soviet relations threatens to leave the student of the period with general assumptions and platitudes, frequently unconnected with a specific field of competition and often focusing on supposed aggressive traits of Joseph Stalin. As Vojtech Mastny perceptively noted, "such readings of Stalin's aspirations, though not necessarily wrong, may be misleading. While plausible with the benefit of hindsight, they do not always conform to the contemporary evidence without important qualification. In any case, they mark the beginning rather than the end of serious research."[2] The same might be said for the numerous and often contradictory observations on American policy in the same period. Recent works by such scholars as Thomas Paterson and Hugh De Santis delineate important variations of opinion among U.S. policy makers in the immediate postwar period, with each point of view contributing an unquantified input into the overall policy process.[3] And as evidence of diversity grows, the student of the Cold War becomes more overwhelmed than enlightened, forced to qualify each assumption about the supposed influence of the policy maker involved or the region under discussion. Arguments which hold that a Soviet operative principle was the avoidance of free elections which might return a non-Communist majority in Eastern Europe are refuted by the experience of early postwar Hungary. Assumptions that there was no

consistent U.S. commitment to democratic reorganization in Eastern
Europe south of Poland are denied by the lengthy and often rancorous
American involvement in postwar Bulgaria. In each area of postwar
East-West rivalry, the Great Powers were forced to modify at least
their tactical approach to the issues in question, recognizing the
nuances and special conditions obtaining in countries whose futures
they sought to influence or determine. And as George Kennan remarked in the early days of the Cold War: "It is axiomatic in the world
of diplomacy that methodology and tactics assume an importance by
no means inferior to concept and strategy."[4]

The history of American foreign policy toward Bulgaria in the wartime and postwar period is important both in charting the local disputes
that contributed to the growing suspicion of evil Soviet intentions and
in identifying the basic American policy goals that unfailingly under-
lay each specific dispute between the Allies. The absence of any deep
American interest in prewar Bulgaria, the minuscule economic ties
between the two nations before 1941, and the somewhat contingent
fashion by which Washington became deeply involved in the alternative futures of postwar Bulgaria allow clear insight into the more
general principles guiding American participation in postwar East European reconstruction. To a large degree, American involvement in
Bulgaria was fortuitous, the result of accidental opportunities in combination with an abiding desire among both military and civilian planners to expand American influence wherever a possibility might present itself.

In 1943, Bulgaria alone among Hitler's East European satellites had
refused to declare war upon the Soviet Union, maintaining regular if
somewhat strained diplomatic relations with its giant Slavic neighbor.
As the discussions between the American leaders of the Office of
Strategic Services (OSS) and the heads of the Soviet NKVD confirmed, the Soviet Union had yet to develop plans for invading the
southern Balkans, preferring to lend support to an inspired American
plan designed to force Bulgaria into accommodation with the West. In
the ensuing twelve months, an OSS project for Bulgaria's surrender
gained support from the Joint Chiefs of Staff, the State Department,
and President Franklin D. Roosevelt, as detailed schemes both for
Bulgaria's participation in the war against Germany and for Bulgaria's
reintegration within the democratic family of nations poured from the
various military and civilian bureaus in Washington. Once the Teheran
Conference had laid to rest the British plan for an invasion of Europe's
"soft underbelly," and following a specific British disclaimer as to the

eventual fate of Bulgaria, America remained virtually alone in her commitment to the democratic future of this small state.

The shifting fortunes of war, the reluctance of the wartime Bulgarian cabinet to desert Hitler in the face of the German occupation of Hungary, and the unexpectedly rapid advance of the Soviet armies through Rumania in the summer of 1944, however, converted Bulgaria into a test case for postwar U.S.-Soviet accommodation in the Balkans. Although evidence suggests that the Soviet declaration of war on Bulgaria in September 1944 was made primarily on military grounds with little or no thought of postwar political objectives, the very presence of an occupying Soviet army undercut American expectations of relying upon the Bulgarian army as a basis of Western influence. Yet Bulgaria retained a central position in America's postwar planning as Washington refused to concede that the already acknowledged Soviet preeminence in Rumania ought be extended to Sofia. Thus Bulgaria assumed a significance transcending her intrinsic importance to either America or the Soviet Union, and a tripartite control commission became the medium in which the ability of the Great Powers to resolve differences of policy within a confined geographic space might be tested. Within the parameters of this control commission, the distinctive goals of American and Soviet postwar planning slowly emerged.

If America's commitment to Bulgaria's democratic future remained strong throughout the period under discussion, the means by which this policy was furthered varied within the broader context of East-West relations and the shifting balance of power among the competing Bulgarian political parties. The refusal of the Soviet chairman of the control commission to convene regular meetings while the war against Germany continued was grudgingly tolerated as long as successful Allied cooperation against the common enemy dominated American thought. Yet even in this initial phase there were limits to Washington's acquiescence in activities likely to preclude the eventual emergence of a free Bulgaria. In the spring of 1945, confronted with the reality of a Bulgarian electoral campaign that threatened to set a totalitarian pattern for all of Eastern Europe, the Truman administration invoked the right of consultation promised at the Yalta Conference, producing the first postponement of elections in Soviet-liberated Europe. With the termination of the German conflict, America's tactics, but not her resolve, shifted once more as Secretary of State James Byrnes adopted a strident and confrontational approach to the growing prospect of total Soviet domination. At Potsdam and at the London Foreign Ministers' Conference, Byrnes refused to accord recognition to the increasingly unrepresentative Bulgarian regime, demanding the readmission of opposition parties to the cabinet before Bulgaria would be reintegrated into the postwar family of nations. Maintaining wartime restrictions upon Bulgaria's economic exchanges with the West, Byrnes demanded and received a Soviet pledge to transform the malfunctioning control commission into a truely tripartite body that might allow significant American influences in Bulgaria's subsequent evolution. Not until the much-maligned Moscow Foreign Ministers' Conference of late 1945 did Byrnes modify his intransigent position, opting for a compromise that promised at least minimal accommodation among the feuding Bulgarian political parties. When this tactic failed in the face of concerted Soviet resistance, the wily Byrnes shifted to a new approach. Relying upon the perceptive and detailed reports from Maynard B. Barnes, America's political representative in Sofia, Byrnes attempted to exploit the growing disagreements between the Bulgarian Communists and their domestic allies, hoping to reopen the possibility of expanding the undemocratic coalition. Only with the failure of this approach in the late spring of 1946 did America acknowledge that chances for influencing Bulgaria's future had all but evaporated. Believing that persistent American involvement had at least ensured the survival of the Bulgarian opposition, and heartened by the fall 1946 parliamentary elections which returned anti-Communist candidates in large numbers, Washington signaled a willingness to extend de facto recognition to the still objectionable Bulgarian government. By now, fears of Soviet expansion beyond the confines of Eastern Europe became more and more dominant in American thought, and a decision was reached to concentrate future American efforts on preserving democratic order in Western Europe. With great reluctance, President Harry Truman extended recognition to Sofia in 1947, expressing America's deep interest in Bulgaria's future development and sorrow that efforts to enhance democratic order had come to naught. Even at this late stage, the decision for recognition arose from an expressed American desire to retain at least some influence in Sofia once the control commission ceased its functions.

If the history of American policy toward Bulgaria reveals a shifting array of tactics designed to secure unchanging objectives, the same conclusions cannot be ventured for the policy pursued by Moscow. The numerous Soviet and Bulgarian memoirs and documents confirm the absence of detailed political objectives during the initial stages of the Russian occupation; the primary goal was the integration of the strong Bulgarian army into the continuing effort against Germany. Once firmly in occupation, it was natural that the Soviet High Command extended full support to those indigenous political parties willing to sacrifice Bulgaria's pressing economic and social needs to the overriding military objectives. Thus an alliance soon developed between the Bulgarian Communists, who were fanatically committed to victory over fascism in all its forms, and the occupation regime, an alliance that complemented and transcended a natural ideological kinship. It would be naive to assume that this linkage was inevitable, and its logic must be sought within the dominant military objectives of the advancing Soviet army. Relations between the Soviet government and the Bulgarian Communists had experienced numerous ups and downs during the preceding decade, and as late as September 1944, Stalin expressed interest in reaching an accord with the last bourgeois government in Sofia if only that cabinet would bring the Bulgarian army to the Soviet side. Any suggestions of inevitable friendship between the Soviets and their Bulgarian comrades must explain both the extensive purge of Bulgarian emigrés during the 1930s and the subsequent terror inflicted upon the domestic Bulgarian Communists in the final years of the next decade.

Even though the Bulgarian Communists quickly showed themselves to be pliant tools in pursuit of larger Soviet goals, Moscow maintained a willingness to sacrifice their basic political interests on behalf of larger Soviet objectives. Thus in the fall of 1945, Moscow consented to basic reforms in the structure and functioning of the Allied Control Commission, which promised to augment Western influence before completion of the Communist drive for total power. Perhaps hoping to assuage growing American fears of Soviet expansionism until a final agreement was reached on Soviet participation in the occupation of Japan, the Soviet Union accepted two postponements of Bulgarian elections despite the clear gain such elections offered the domestic Communists. Only after the London Foreign Ministers' Conference demonstrated an American refusal to accommodate Soviet objectives in the Far East did Moscow adopt a firm attitude toward Bulgaria which never again would vary. Reforms promised for the control commission died stillborn, and subsequent American protests about Soviet activities in Bulgaria were curtly denied. Even the apparent compromises of the Moscow Foreign Ministers' Conference, allowing minimal expansion of the Bulgarian government, were derailed through a quickly arranged trip by Deputy Soviet Foreign Minister Andrei Vyshensky to Sofia. In this manner, Stalin served notice that neither

domestic objections to Soviet-Communist dominance nor protests from
the West would henceforth be considered. The Communist future of
Bulgaria was assured.

The history of this period suggests that only one important participant in Bulgaria's postwar evolution never varied in its tactics or
overall objectives: the Bulgarian Communist party. Relegated to the
sidelines of Bulgarian politics in the 1920s, with many of its elder
spokesmen in wartime exile within the Soviet Union, the party resolved to exploit the entry of Russian troops into Bulgaria to the
fullest. Forming the backbone of a small if determined resistance
movement during the war and entering the coalition government of
September 1944 with only four positions, the Communists waged an
unflagging struggle for total control. Pushing themselves forward as
the most trustable Soviet allies at a time when pacification of Bulgaria
assumed importance because of the continuing military drive through
Yugoslavia and Hungary, the Communists quickly entrenched themselves in key positions of military, political, and economic control. It
was to the Communists that the Red Army turned in its drive to reform
the Bulgarian army into a reliable supporter of the war effort, and it
was Communist direction that ensured mobilization of Bulgaria's declining economic assets. When the military objectives of defeating
Germany were replaced by a growing Soviet drive to consolidate their
newly won empire, the Bulgarian Communists remained indispensable
and entrenched. In 1946 the Communists clearly articulated their goal
of achieving "People's Power" during the hotly contested elections
against the weakened opposition. In 1947, the People's Republic of
Bulgaria was officially declared, marking the termination of an unchanging three-year campaign.

The history of American policy toward Bulgaria in this seminal
period is thus the story of the interaction of the changing or constant
tactical and strategic objectives of these main participants. It is the
history of the early Cold War not as fact but as process.

1 Wartime Planning for Bulgaria

Bulgaria on the eve of World War II was a small Slavic state often described as the "key to the Balkans." Located along the Black Sea and bordering on Greece, Yugoslavia, Turkey, and Rumania, Bulgaria possessed a population slightly in excess of 6 million and embraced just over 103,000 square kilometers, its borders having been determined by the Treaty of Neuilly at the close of World War I. Bulgarian politics had experienced a stormy path in the interwar period under the guidance of its monarch, King Boris, who had established tight control over domestic and international policy following a palace coup in 1935. Isolated from normal diplomatic intercourse because of her defeat as an ally of Germany in 1918, Bulgaria, like many of her Balkan neighbors, drifted toward the Axis camp in the 1930s. This trend was apparent in both her foreign trade and her foreign policy.

Aware that a small Balkan state must operate within the confines of Great Power politics, King Boris attempted in the initial stages of World War II to avoid outright hostilities while maintaining close relations with both Italy and Germany. Although certain peculiarities of Bulgaria's existence such as the known pro-Russian (not pro-Communist) proclivities of the population and the bitter territorial disputes with her neighbors helped shape Bulgarian policy, in the last resort both the king and the Council of Ministers realized that the fortunes of the larger European states would determine Bulgaria's future. Thus King Boris carefully measured the war's progress, attempting to avoid direct conflict with either of the European blocs. In 1940, this cautious policy induced a number of Great Powers to intervene in an effort to chart Bulgaria's future. Among them was the United States. By now, both Bulgaria's strategic location and her large and well-respected army made her a tempting prize of international diplomacy.

America's concern for Bulgarian politics arose early in World War II from the desire to enhance the prospects of British resistance to German domination short of an actual commitment of American forces. The lack of any significant cultural ties or economic relations between Washington and Sofia in this period necessitated the submergence of Bulgarian relations within the broader perspective of denying Germany new conquests in the yet unresolved future of southeastern Europe and the Middle East. Thus America's first intervention into Bulgarian internal affairs came at the specific request of London. Hard-pressed by the seemingly unending German victories, Great Britain sought American diplomatic pressure to forestall the accession of Bulgaria to the Axis Pact, a feared first step in an eventual German invasion of Greece. In January 1941, President Roosevelt responded by sending his personal representative, future OSS Chief Bill Donovan, to several Balkan states with a promise of American assistance for nations fighting Nazi expansion. In the third week of January, Donovan flew to Athens to assess Greek preparedness and to receive a detailed report from the British military attaché on the political and military situation in Bulgaria.[1] On January 20, Donovan arrived in Sofia and the Bulgarian cabinet resolved that concerted German pressure to adhere to the Axis Pact no longer could be resisted.[2] Unaware of this momentous decision, Donovan made the rounds of high Bulgarian officials in his quest for continued Bulgarian neutrality. The following day, he conveyed his president's firm belief in an eventual German defeat to the Bulgarian foreign minister, Ivan Popov. The United States, Donovan cautioned, would aid Greece in resisting any German invasion through Bulgaria. That afternoon Donovan repeated America's dire predictions as to Germany's eventual fate to War Minister Teodosi Daskalov.[3] Later the same day, Donovan visited Prime Minister Bogdan D. Filov, who recorded in his diary: "He was very militant and did not want to hear of peace until the Germans are finally crushed." That evening, the shaken Popov informed the prime minister that Donovan's strident attitude confirmed his own distaste for Berlin and that on no account would he approve the Axis Pact. Confronted with a demand to sign, Popov stated, he would choose suicide.[4]

The culmination of Donovan's policy of "gentle persuasion" came the next morning in an audience with King Boris. America, Donovan related, was aiding Great Britain by all means possible, certain of a final British victory. Bulgaria, he informed the startled King appeared to be on the verge of joining Germany—an event that would range Sofia against America. In weak rebuttal, Boris reiterated his oft-stated opinion that Bulgaria as a small nation must stall for time in the face of a confusing welter of Great Power politics.[5] Following this conference, Donovan departed for Belgrade.

The importance of Donovan's journey to Bulgaria in 1941 must not be underestimated in assessing the OSS chief's subsequent belief in Bulgaria's potential as an eventual Allied partner. The King, Donovan confided to the British ambassador, was an honest if confused idealist who sincerely wished to avoid bringing Bulgaria to the German side. Should Bulgaria be forced to join Germany, the King would assent but with the hope that America would not condemn her for it.[6] This belief in Bulgaria's unwillingness to participate in the strategic plans of her Teutonic neighbor received reinforcement following Pearl Harbor when Bulgaria, under renewed German pressure, declared war on America and Britain. In the final meeting with the U.S. ambassador, Foreign Minister Popov expressed the "deep sadness" of his government in this unwished turn of events, stating that the break was the result of German insistence and against Popov's own advice.[7] Well aware of Bulgaria's position, Washington delayed her own declaration of war against Sofia until June 1942.

During 1942 both America and Bulgaria pursued national interests having little to do with one another. Washington was concentrating on operation Torch, the planned landings in North Africa. Bulgaria, in turn, continued to exploit the tranquil conditions in the Balkans that had followed the 1941 defeat of Greece and Yugoslavia, focusing energies upon occupation and administration of the newly won territories of Thrace and Macedonia. Only in the spring of 1943 with the intense discussions between Washington and London as to the preferred invasion route into occupied Europe did America once again turn attention toward Bulgaria. Renewed interest in Sofia's possible defection from Axis control was matched by Tsar Boris's growing desire to leave the war under the best possible conditions. Switzerland and Turkey quickly became the centers of a new American effort toward Bulgaria, with both the OSS and the Department of State being the initial American participants.

In the spring of 1943, the U.S. intelligence chief in Switzerland, Allen Dulles, established contact with the Bulgarian consul in Geneva, M. H. Milev, in an attempt to ascertain Bulgaria's conditions for an armistice. Milev reported to Sofia that Dulles possessed a large staff so as to facilitate contacts with enemy states and that discussions already were in progress with the Rumanians and the Hungarians. The Bulgarian ambassador in Switzerland, former Prime Minister Georgi K'oseivanov, initially refused all suggestions of discussions with the Americans, but by the summer of 1943 he informed Sofia: "It would be useful for us to know what the Americans are thinking and what their intentions are with respect to Bulgaria, and, at the same time, to explain our problems."[8] In August, K'oseivanov returned to Sofia to report on his contacts. The Americans, he informed Filov, refused to concede Bulgaria's control of territories captured with German assistance as the price of an armistice.[9] This issue of territorial acquisitions was to remain an important barrier to Bulgaria's withdrawal from the war.

While Allen Dulles was fostering ties with Milev and K'oseivanov, Tsar Boris dispatched his own special envoy, L. Pulev, to contact former U.S. ambassador to Bulgaria, George Earle, then in Ankara. Berlin, however, discovered this mission before initiation of discussions. Undaunted by this temporary setback, Boris authorized a well-known Bulgarian industrialist, Georgi Kiselov, to establish contact with the American consulate in Istanbul.[10] On May 20, 1943, U.S. Consul Burton Berry filed a lengthy report on these discussions. Boris, Berry cabled, was determined to avoid active warfare with troops of the United Nations short of a direct attack upon Bulgarian soil. The December 1941 declaration of war against America, Kiselov confirmed, was deplored by most Bulgarians and resulted solely from German pressures. Should a United Nations force invade Bulgaria, the inevitable Bulgarian defeat would destabilize existing order and produce a Communist dictatorship. Pleading that he was acting on his own initiative, Kiselov asserted that Bulgaria sought exit from the conflict although the terms of unconditional surrender were unacceptable given the absence of actual fighting. A separate peace ran the risk of inviting a German occupation. Despite these caveats, Sofia would consider any tolerable solution that would allow retention of the 1941 frontier.[11]

The Pulev and Kiselov missions reflected Boris's growing disillusion with his German ally. In late March 1943, Boris informed his prime minister that "in the last analysis the German cause is already lost." In June, the depressed tsar told Filov that at his recent meeting with Hitler the conclusion had been reached that an Allied invasion of the Balkans was probable. Bulgaria, Hitler demanded, must further expand its military readiness. In mid-July, Boris read Filov a letter from the former Bulgarian ambassador to London which recommended a combined British-Bulgarian effort to drive German forces from the Balkans.[12] At approximately the same time, Boris reportedly authorized the socialist leader, Krastiu Pastouchov to construct a list for an anti-German cabinet so that Bulgaria might renounce her past allegiance to Berlin; such a list was drawn up.[13] By midsummer 1943, a convergence of American and Bulgarian policies had become apparent.

The growing Bulgarian interest in seeking accommodation with the West was but one factor in developments that eventually would deeply involve American planners in charting both the wartime and postwar future of this state. In the late spring and early summer President Roosevelt, flush with success from the victories in North Africa, revealed a renewed flexibility in considering limited Allied activities in the southern and southeastern Mediterranean. Despite staunch resistance from the American Chiefs of Staff to any diversion of military resources that might imperil the planned invasion of Western Europe the following spring, Roosevelt agreed in mid-May 1943 that General Dwight D. Eisenhower might exploit the invasion of Sicily by such operations "as are best calculated to eliminate Italy from the war and to control the maximum number of German forces."[14] That same month, Roosevelt directed the military chiefs to consider the possibility of attacking Germany by way of Bulgaria, Rumania, and Turkey.[15] In mid-July, reviewing a recent message from Winston Churchill which included a proposal from General Jan Smuts that capture of Rome might create new opportunities for Allied advanced toward the Balkans and the Black Sea, Roosevelt thought that "something of that kind can be undertaken." By the end of the month, Churchill was informed that an Italian collapse might prompt consideration of plans to seize Corfu and the Dodecanese in tandem with the dispatch of limited assistance to Greece, Albania, and Yugoslavia. While maintaining his firm commitment to the invasion of Western Europe, Roosevelt continued to entertain a deep interest in expanding the scope of the Allied threat to the more exposed regions of Hitler's Europe. Given the known limitations of available men and equipment, however, any such plans necessarily would rely upon the participation of indigenous forces within the Balkans willing to war for Allied objectives. As Roosevelt noted at the fall 1943 Quebec Conference which reaffirmed the priority of the West European invasion, he was "most anxious to have the Balkans [sic] divisions which we have trained, particularly the Greek and Yugoslav, operate in their own countries."[16] Although the president's general notions of a possible Balkan strategy failed to spark the interest of his military planners at Quebec, it did receive the careful attention of the Office of Strategic Security Services, which already had drafted a detailed plan to induce several Balkan governments to abandon their German ally and join the Allied cause.

Roosevelt's speculations on possible use of local forces in the Balkans were the inevitable result of renewed military operations by the Allies in the summer of 1943. On July 10, Sicily was invaded, and nine days later a major American bombing assault destroyed the railyards and port of Rome. On July 25, Radio Rome announced that fascist dictator Benito Mussolini had been ousted from power, with King Victor Emmanuel II reassuming full authority. On August 3 the new Italian regime made its first peace overtures.[17] This disruption of Axis unity in southern Europe and the expected upheavals in the Balkans, where Italy maintained twenty-five occupation divisions, offered a unique opportunity to exploit the use of local forces consistent with Roosevelt's objective of threatening Germany without a major commitment of Allied troops. OSS Chief Donovan had been recruiting agents for almost a year in a plan to bring the large Bulgarian army to the Western side, and the time seemed ripe for a formal proposal.[18]

In early August, General Donovan submitted a memorandum to the U.S. Chiefs of Staff entitled "O.S.S. Plan to Detach Bulgaria from the Axis." It stressed the vast importance of recent Italian events as they affected Bulgaria, whose queen was Victor Emmanuel's daughter and whose population included large pro-American and pro-Russian groups. Arguing that the defection of Italy might force Germany to form a new defensive line running from the Po Valley through the Dalmation coast to Transylvania and the Carpathians, Donovan pointed out that such a withdrawl would place Bulgaria outside the German protective perimeter. This move would facilitate the defection of Bulgaria with her seven hundred thousand "well-equipped soldiers" and would be of "inestimable value" to the Allies. Such a defection, Donovan continued, could be brought about through concerted influence upon the tsar or by establishing ties with the Bulgarian General Staff or the church.[19] The following day, August 3, Chief of Staff George Marshall detailed the OSS plan to a full meeting of the Joint Chiefs, agreeing at the request of General Henry H. Arnold to submit the memorandum to the Joint Staff planners for consideration.[20]

The speed with which Donovan's memorandum was treated reflected both the timely nature of the proposal and the tight schedule of the Joint Chiefs. At that very moment, the Chiefs were deeply involved in preparations for the upcoming Quebec Conference (Quadrant) for which they shortly departed. Thus initial review of Donovan's proposal was assigned to the appropriate subcommittee.

Consistent with the continuing military apprehension over any proposal that might diminish available resources for the future invasion of Western Europe, the subcommittee of the Joint Staff planners concluded on August 18 that although Bulgaria's defection would be desirable, it ought not be undertaken if it involved extensive American commitments.

One possible exception was noted, however: the forthcoming Quadrant Conference might opt for a revision of existing American plans for the Balkans. That same day, the Joint Staff planners approved the subcommittee's recommendation.[21] On August 24, the Joint Deputy Chiefs informed Donovan that no action should be taken that might entail military, economic, or political commitments to Bulgaria.[22] Clearly, Donovan faced a formidable task if this plan for Bulgaria's defection was to become part of a new American approach in south-eastern Europe.

Well aware of the existing military consensus that troop assignments to the Balkans were forbidden and cognizant that no Balkan mission could be planned without at least tacit Soviet approval, Donovan had prepared his rebuttal to the expected War Department decision before he received the Joint Deputy Chief's report. Having opened discussions directly with Secretary of State Cordell Hull and with the Joint Chiefs, Donovan sent a second memorandum on August 20 promising to clear his proposed operation with Moscow through General John R. Deane, the American military attaché. As the OSS leader realized, final disposition of his efforts would lie with President Roosevelt, and Donovan now hastened to Quebec to acquaint the president personally with his proposal. In a paper delivered at the Quadrant Conference entitled "A Proposal to Accentuate Our Present Subversive Efforts in the Balkans, Donovan requested permission "in agreement with Great Britain and the U.S.S.R. to bring to bear upon Bulgaria, Rumania and Hungary certain subversive pressure which may induce those countries to withdraw from the war, or at least to cause difficulties for the Axis." The centerpiece of this project, Donovan revealed, was the "K Project," which revolved about Angel Kouyoumdjisky and his suggested mission. Although plans were also under consideration for a possible defection of the other two Balkan states, Donovan concentrated on gaining the president's approval for the Bulgaria program.[23] Once Roosevelt approved, the Joint Chiefs quickly fell into line. On September 7, the OSS was officially authorized by the Joint Chiefs, with the expressed approval of Secretary Hull, to proceed. As Donovan noted in his assessment of the now expanded Bulgaria project, the goal would be to discover what the Allies must do to obtain "(a). Active military operations against German forces by the Bulgarian Army, (b). Bulgarian withdrawal from military operations against the Allies, (c). the organization and direction of guerrilla warfare in Bulgaria against German forces, (d). Any other form of action against the Germans."[24] To further these objectives, Kouyoumdjisky, who had been made an American citizen the preceding April and was now a colonel in the U.S. army, departed for the Mideast in charge of a special "Financial Commission." A telegram from the Joint Chiefs to the commanding U.S. general in Cairo, Ralph Royce, stressed that Kouyoumdjisky's "mission is regarded by the Joint Chiefs as of considerable importance."[25]

The newly won support of the Joint Chiefs was a crucial step in elevating one of many OSS operations in the Balkans into a plan whose success would involve America in both the wartime and postwar future of southeastern Europe. In sharp contrast to Hungary and Rumania, where American efforts to arrange Axis defections soon failed because of an inability to guarantee the absence of Soviet occupation, Bulgaria alone offered an area of operation in which both Russian and British claims were minimal. Success of Donovan's operation promised to allow the numerous supporters of the Atlantic Charter within the State Department a field of practical exercise. It was assumed, correctly, that little Soviet objection would be forthcoming because Russian troops were still far from the Bulgarian borders and Bulgaria had taken great pains to maintain neutrality toward her larger Slavic neighbor. Bulgaria alone of the Axis partners had refused to declare war on the USSR.[26] The situation with respect to British interests in Bulgaria was somewhat more complex but appeared capable of resolution given the support Donovan now received from Roosevelt, Hull, and the Joint Chiefs.

British postwar planning for Eastern Europe, as it emerged in the first years of the war, called for groupings of states within regional confederations. The issue of such confederations had been broached with the Soviet foreign minister Vyacheslav Molotov, during negotiations over the proposed Anglo-Soviet treaty in the spring of 1942. While not rejecting such plans outright, Molotov replied that "the Soviet government had certain information to show that some federations might be directed against the Soviet Union," a clear hint of eventual Soviet disapproval. In June 1942, Sir Orme Sargent, deputy undersecretary of state, prepared a detailed paper on a possible confederation in southeastern Europe. Although the possibility of an anti-Soviet posture in such a grouping was recognized, Sargent thought that possible allocation of strategic basis to the Soviets in Bulgaria and Rumania might soothe anticipated Soviet objections.[27]

Continued Soviet apprehensions about London's promotion of regional groupings premised on anti-Soviet feelings received confirmation in a Foreign Office draft of March 1943 dealing with Bulgaria: "Although we cannot say so at present, our idea for the future of Bulgaria is that she should be forced to form an integral part of whatever federal scheme may emerge in the Balkans after the war. The enthusiastic pro-Russian and pan-Slav feeling of the majority of Bulgarians makes Bulgaria a potential bridgehead for Russian penetration of the Balkans, and we are therefore anxious to incorporate her in a wider federation, the predominant bias of which will be neither pan-Slav nor pro-Russian."[28] This goal of denying the Soviets postwar dominance in Bulgaria was to be facilitated by a regional confederation including the non-Slavic states of Greece and Turkey.[29]

In the spring and summer of 1943, London received unmistakable indications from the Soviet ambassador to Britain, Ivan Maisky, and from Molotov himself that the Soviets continued to object to postwar confederations in southeastern Europe.[30] When discussions on the eve of the 1943 Quebec Conference confirmed American refusal to support any major Balkan invasion, Britain disclosed a greater willingness to divest herself of responsibility for Bulgaria's future. In mid-August, the Foreign Office informed the American State Department that London was not committed even to the survival of a postwar Bulgaria and that His Majesty's government would take no part in any negotiations with Boris:

> His Majesty's Government therefore cannot have any dealings with King Boris whose fate they regard as a matter of indifference, any more than they can have with the present government. The King is a man of no little ability and cunning, but morally weak and incapable of courageous decisions, a true son of his father. Any attempt to give him support in the hope of detaching Bulgaria from the Axis would probably fail and we should . . . merely compromise ourselves in the eyes of our Balkan allies and the world besides laying up for ourselves incalculable difficulties in our plans for the future of South Eastern Europe.[31]

Although this specific British disclaimer received in August 1943 suggested little resistance to the OSS plan, the existing relations between U.S. and British intelligence operations in the Balkans required important modifications. In September 1942, the OSS and the British Special Operations Executive (SOE) approved a "treaty" relegating the Americans to a subordinate role in Mideast operations.[32] Headquarters lay in Cairo under the overall command of British General Henry Wilson, and to date America had been content with British domination in Balkan activities. This policy would need to be changed. On September 25, 1943, President Roosevelt authorized Hull to propose American political representation on the Administration of Territories Balkan Committee in Cairo.[33] This was only the initial indication of a move Hull and Roosevelt undertook to ensure the unrestricted success of expanded OSS Balkan operations.

On October 22, while Secretary Hull was attending the Moscow Foreign Ministers' Conference, Roosevelt dispatched a carefully worded letter to Churchill. Complaining about the chaotic conditions prevailing in the Balkan operations, FDR proposed a complete reversal in the heretofore secondary OSS position: "In the present confused condition, the only hope I see for immediate favorable action is the presence of an aggressive and qualified officer. The only man I can think of now who might have a chance of success is Donovan. . . . If we decide to send him, all agencies of ours now working in the Balkans should be placed under his direction and the resources we put into this effort should be at his disposal. *I feel this is an urgent matter.* If you are inclined to agree to my idea, I will discuss the possibilities with Donovan at once."[34] When the startled Churchill, as yet unapprised of Donovan's OSS plan, responded that such a reversal of authority would place in question the more than eighty British missions operating in the Balkans, the stage was set for Donovan's withdrawal from British supervision. U.S. activities dealing with Bulgaria and Rumania now moved from Cairo to Istanbul.[35] The British head of the SOE in Cairo for Bulgaria, Rumania, and Hungary recalled when finally informed of Donovan's activities, "It was obvious also that somewhere the wires had got badly crossed, as the O.S.S. representatives at Istanbul were supposed to tell our people there about what he was doing. As it was, we had heard nothing of Kouyoumjisky's approach either in Istanbul or in Cairo. We told General Donovan this in no uncertain terms, adding that this was not what we understood by collaboration. But he thought that peace feelers were not covered by our agreement to work together. It was an angry exchange, and perhaps we were in the wrong."[36]

If freedom from British restrictions was the negative moment in America's Bulgarian venture, the coordinated positive phase was gaining active cooperation from the USSR. On October 23, one day after Roosevelt's letter and immediately following a report by British Foreign Secretary Anthony Eden to the Moscow Conference on the disposition of Bulgarian units, Secretary Hull requested permission for General Deane to address the meeting: "General Deane said that the United States Chiefs of Staff considered that there was great opportunity in the Balkans, particularly during the winter months to intensify sabotage and disruptive work in order to undermine German military strength. He said that the Office of Strategic Services had the equipment and trained personnel to carry on this work and was prepared to penetrate the area by air and other means. He said that the American military authorities hoped this would be agreeable to the Soviet Government and he wished to assure them that the purpose of these operations was purely military." When Soviet Foreign Minister Molotov requested more details, Deane, well aware that much more than military operations was planned, responded that it would be difficult to give specifics because "all such operations were of necessity opportunistic." Offering no objection to Deane's suggestions, Molotov suggested that a final decision be delayed pending further information.[37] Such detail, naturally, could be given only by Donovan himself because it was not Moscow's acquiescence but her active cooperation which was sought.

In addition to Molotov's willingness to learn more about General Deane's Balkans plans—a willingness that prompted Washington to prepare a visit by Donovan to Moscow—the conference marked the demise of the British plans of a southeastern European confederation. On October 26, Molotov informed the conference delegates of Moscow's veto:

> The Soviet Government considers that the small countries will require some time which cannot yet be definitely calculated and which will not be the same for all of them, to enable them fully to oriente themselves in the new situation created as a result of the war and in the re-created relationships with neighbouring and other States, without being subjected to any outside pressures to join this or that new grouping of states. The premature and possibly artificial attachment of these countries to theoretically planned groupings would be full of danger both for the small countries themselves as well as for the future peaceful development of Europe.
>
> For these reasons, the Soviet Government considers it premature . . . now to plan and thus artifically to encourage combinations of any States in the form of federation and so forth.[38]

The collapse of British plans to submerge Bulgaria within a postwar confederation reinforced the more militant British approach to Sofia indicated in the August 1943 Foreign Office message to Washington. At a meeting of the British Defense Committee held in mid-October, Churchill demanded that a purely military solution be developed through massive air assaults upon the Bulgarian capital, adding, "We cannot tolerate any longer these activities of Bulgarian jackals however much they may be under the heel of the Germans." The proposed daylight attacks were to be followed by nighttime sorties and were to include the dropping of leaflets citing the fate of Hamburg and Hanover.[39] In December, Churchill's option for a purely military solution, devoid of specific plans for postwar Bulgaria's future, were formalized into the new British strategy. In a memorandum of the British Chiefs of Staff prepared for the second Cairo Conference, the new goals were described as follows: "We consider that our object in the Balkans should be to bring about the surrender of Bulgaria and open a short sea route to Russia. The surrender of Bulgaria is most likely to be achieved by: (a) Air action, (b) Russian diplomatic and subversive action, (c) The psychological effect of Turkey becoming an active ally of the United Nations."[40] This new emphasis upon a military approach found an immediate place in the tactical plans of the commander in chief of British Air Forces Mid-East, Sir John Slessor, who informed the British Chief of the Air Staff: "[The] best service we in this theatre can perform for OVERLORD is really to create Hell in the Balkans by every measure, air, land, and sea."[41] This significant shift of emphasis from postwar planning to the military demands of the moment in support of OVERLORD left the American plan for Bulgaria's future as the only articulated option.

In December 1943, General Donovan arrived in Moscow for a two-week visit. According to the lengthy report filed by U.S. Ambassador W. Averell Harriman, the OSS chief immediately visited Molotov to explain planned OSS activities. The Soviet foreign minister at once arranged meetings between Donovan and his opposite number in the NKVD, including General Deane in the conversations. It was agreed to collaborate closely, establish reciprocal liasion representatives in Washington and Moscow, exchange information, and carry on joint operations. All this, Harriman noted, "was approved and authorized by the highest Soviet authorities." The Soviets seemed to want the United States to take the initiative but would assist if presented with a specific proposal. Donovan presented his recommendations for the Balkan venture, forwarding a copy of proposed U.S.-Soviet cooperation to the Joint Chiefs, with an informational note to Secretary Hull. Soviet concurrence in the Bulgarian initiative was immediately expressed in a lengthy article in the party journal, *Pravda*. As Harriman reported: "I said [to Molotov] that we both read with interest the *Pravda* article on December 27 concerning Bulgaria since our talk and that we had been struck by the similarities of views expressed in that article with those expressed by General Donovan. In reply to my inquiry, Molotov indicated he was in general agreement with the article."[42]

The *Pravda* article, "The Crisis in Bulgaria," was indeed a clear reflection of Soviet support for Donovan's plan. Written by the personal confidant of Stalin and head of the Bulgarian emigreś in Moscow, the future head of the Bulgarian state, Georgi Dimitrov, it condemned the ruling Bulgarian government for maintaining an alliance with Germany despite the numerous Axis reversals of 1943, which fore-shadowed the eventual German defeat. Bulgaria's desire to retain captured territories was dismissed as a valid excuse for remaining within the Axis Pact because "it is clear to everyone who has not lost his reason that following the unavoidable destruction of Germany, there will not remain one stone on another of the so-called 'united' Bulgaria." The national interests of Bulgaria could be assured, Dimitrov argued, only by an immediate break with Germany and discussions with Bulgaria's Balkan neighbors as to future disposition of disputed lands.[43]

While America was pursuing its new Balkan policy in the fall of 1943, major if ambiguous change was occurring in Bulgaria. On August 28, Boris—the single most important figure in the American plan—died in mysterious circumstances following a trip to Germany. Because the heir to the throne, Simeon, was seven years old, a regency was formed consisting of former Prime Minister Filov, the dead tsar's brother Prince Cyril, and former War Minister General Nikola Mikhov. By mid-September, a new cabinet was proclaimed, led by former Finance Minister Dobri Bozhilov.

In its first months, the Bozhilov government gave every sign of continuing Boris's policy of increasing Bulgaria's distance from German designs. Despite concerted pressure from Berlin, the Bozhilov cabinet refused to break diplomatic relations with the Badoglio government in Italy and spurned recognition of the newly formed Mussolini regime in Salo until September 28. Even then, the representative of King Victor Emmanuel remained in Sofia until the following May.[44] Sava Kirov, the new Bulgarian foreign minister, was widely regarded as pro-Western; Filov noted in his diary that Kirov believed Germany had already lost the war.[45] In October, a confidential German assessment of the new government dismally concluded: "The Regency and the Government have established themselves anew on the foreign political course of the [deceased] King. In this regard, it must again be mentioned that it was the former Bulgarian policy to henceforth hold back support from Germany in the war, to act only so far as necessary, and above all, not to upset the English and Americans."[46] And yet Bulgaria's continued stress upon her own national interests was not necessarily a direct step toward leaving the war. Uppermost in the mind of Regent Filov was the wish to ensure retention of the territories of Macedonia and Thrace, lands captured from her Balkan neighbors. On September 23, Filov confided to his diary that with fellow Regent Mikhov, "we established that it will be necessary to begin a system of energetic work in three directions: (1) to prove by all means that we took only our land; (2) to assert that we will defend and that we will fight for our unity as we have done up to now regardless of who will be the victors in the world conflict; (3) to begin inquiry about some war profiteers who irritate public opinion greatly."[47] In mid-October, the "defeatist" Foreign Minister Kirov was replaced by Dimitur Shishmanov, who was judged "very satisfactory" by the German Foreign Office.[48]

In October and November, Hitler arranged personal interviews with the regents and with Bozhilov and Shishmanov. The just-concluded Moscow Foreign Ministers' Conference, Hitler informed Bozhilov, assigned the Balkans to the Soviet sphere of influence, and smaller Axis partners had no reason to expect a positive interim solution short of total victory. Hitler added, "It is really laughable that some people wish to believe that England would be able to put up a barrier to the advance of Bolshevism in the event of a German defeat."[49] Any course except full support of Germany could only bring ruin to civilization in general and the Bulgarian way of life in particular. Yet despite such dire warnings, both Bozhilov and Filov resolved to continued exploratory contacts with the Americans.[50]

Angel Kouyoumdjisky and his "Financial Commission"—the backbone of General Donovan's plan to effect a reversal of Bulgaria's Axis commitments—arrived in Cairo in late November to receive a briefing from General Deane who was fresh from Moscow. A promise was extracted from Deane to guarantee American subsidies for the Bulgarian army equal to those provided by the Germans once the defection had been arranged. The issue of Macedonia and Thrace, Deane warned, ought not to be negotiated until the final peace settlement. Three days later, Donovan gave Kouyoumdjisky his final instructions, introducing him to OSS staff in Cairo. On December 1, 1943, Kouyoumdjisky arrived in Istanbul and immediately opened clandestine contacts with past friends and associates in Sofia through OSS channels. Donovan's expressed belief in the depth of Kouyoumdjisky's influence in Bulgaria received prompt confirmation; even Prime Minister Bozhilov was quickly informed of his presence in Istanbul. By the second week of his sojourn, Kouyoumdjisky had received an invitation from the Bulgarian ambassador in Turkey, Nicolas Balabanov, also an old friend, to meet at once in Ankara.[51]

The initial meeting of the old friends quickly established that Balabanov also believed it time for Bulgaria to seek exit from the war, a task he hoped Kouyoumdjisky could facilitate. Kouyoumdjisky requested Balabanov to ask Bozhilov to send two friends of Kouyoumdjisky at once to Istanbul for discussions: M. Gouneff, governor of the

Bulgarian National Bank, and General Vasil Poppoff, governor of the Dobruja. According to the lengthy report later filed by Kouyoumdjisky with Secretary Hull, Balabanov pledged to telegraph the request posthaste along with his own personal recommendation.[52]

Materials discovered in the Bulgarian Archives of the Foreign Ministry contain Balabanov's report of December 18 to Sofia in which he informed his superiors that Kouyoumdjisky "has reason to think that he is able to save Bulgaria both economically, politically, and partially *(otchasti)* territorially."[53] As indication of his influence, Kouyoumdjisky told Balabanov he personally had arranged to halt the bombings of Bulgaria for a week.[54]

The reference to territorial issues in Balabanov's message suggests that Kouyoumdjisky exceeded his instructions. In a series of articles written after the war, Balabanov recorded that at a meeting with Kouyoumdjisky he was given to understand that "if Bulgaria were to side with the U[nited] S[tates], not only would the present borders be preserved, but they would be broadened in certain areas and there would even be a chance to save the dynasty."[55] The main thrust of the meeting, however, focused upon the agreed primacy of the Bulgarian army. As Kouyoumdjisky reported in a separate document, "I wish to note that in a conversation that I had with the Bulgarian ambassador in Ankara, Mr. Balabanov, he told me that the army will be ready to march with the Allies without condition if Bulgaria is guaranteed that communism will be avoided in the country."[56] Kouyoumdjisky's mission was definitely on the main track.

While awaiting a response from Balabanov and Sofia, Kouyoumdjisky established contact through Balabanov's niece with the leaders of three Bulgarian opposition political parties, who, pleading inability to cross the heavily patrolled Bulgarian-Turkish frontier, formulated a code by which they might regularly communicate with Kouyoumdjisky.[57] In early January, Kouyoumdjisky and his mission were recalled to Cairo to explain their activities to the poorly informed and outraged British. Upon return to Istanbul, Kouyoumdjisky was met by an urgent call from Balabanov, which stated that the ambassador had been summoned to Sofia. Informing Kouyoumdjisky that Bulgaria was prepared to shift allegiances to the Allied side, Balabanov asked if the dispatch of two *authorized* representatives would be in order. Kouyoumdjisky, whose initial request had been for two *unofficial* delegates, promised to seek Washington's approval.[58] The OSS plan appeared to be ahead of schedule.

Balabanov's recall to Sofia was in part prompted by the ongoing governmental crisis caused by the devastating Allied bombing of Sofia in mid-January. Regent Filov, unaware of Soviet support for Dono-van's project, had approached the Soviet representative in Sofia, Aleksandr Lavrishchev, requesting Russian mediation with the West to halt such raids, only to receive a surprising rebuff from the heretofore accommodating diplomat. The USSR would intercede before the Americans and British, Lavrishchev stated, only if Bulgaria withdrew her occupation troops from Greece and Yugoslavia. Filov now hoped that Balabanov might use his excellent contacts with his Soviet counterpart in Ankara, Sergei A. Vinogradov, to investigate the shifting Soviet attitude. Shortly after his return to Turkey, Balabanov called upon Vinogradov, receiving an equally disappointing response. The Soviet representative informed him that Russia was unable to understand Bulgaria's blindness as to the inevitable German defeat, cautioning that Sofia ought not simply to wait for the coming catastrophe. Bulgaria's postwar prospects would be greatly enhanced, he concluded, if Sofia were "timely" in her separation from Germany.[59]

The pressure exerted upon the Bulgarian cabinet by Lavrishchev and Vinogradov was the lesser part of a Soviet strategy designed to force Bulgaria out of her alliance with the Axis and into an accommodation with the West. In early January, the Soviet Embassy in Sofia informed Prime Minister Bozhilov that construction of boats and barges by the Germans in the Black Sea port of Varna was contrary to Bulgaria's professed neutrality in the Nazi-Soviet conflict. When the surprised Bulgarians rejected the warning, Lavrishchev arranged a second meeting at which he termed the Bulgarian response "unsatisfactory."[60] On January 22, a written protest was sent from Moscow once again emphasizing the Soviet position on such construction, ending with the warning: "The Soviet government expects the Bulgarian government to quickly take measures to end construction of military vessels used by the Germans in military actions against the USSR."[61] On January 27, the USSR joined the United States and Britain in forwarding a pointed message to Sofia, demanding cessation of all aid to Germany, renouncement of the Axis Pact, and recall of occupation armies from foreign soil.[62] Caught between the threat of renewed Allied bombings and coordinated Soviet pressures, the Bozhilov government informed Balabanov that contacts with the American mission in Turkey were to be expanded.

On February 5, back in Turkey, Balabanov again sought out Kouyoumdjisky for urgent discussions. Informing the OSS agent that in Sofia he had talked with the regents, the prime minister, the foreign minister, and heads of the larger political parties, Balabanov stated: "In consequence, the regency, including all the members of government, authorized me to state to you, Mr. Kouyoumdjisky, that they understand the need to change their existing policies and to extricate themselves from the Axis."[63] When asked by Kouyoumdjisky about the views of the all-important Bulgarian military, Balabanov replied that the army followed the government and would present no problem.[64] At a meeting the following day, the two men reached full agreement, with Balabanov promising to request the immediate dispatch of two authorized representatives for talks with the Allies. Balabanov was presented with a five-point memorandum which listed the conditions and topics for discussion for the anticipated delegation. True to the terms of his own mission, Kouyoumdjisky noted that the delegation "at the first interview will only discuss the conditions of the Bulgarian government for placing the army at the disposal of the Allies to aid in driving the enemy from Bulgarian territory and continuing the war with the Allies against Germany."[65]

The successes of the Kouyoumdjisky mission were at once reported to Washington, catapulting the impatient executive branch into immediate action. On February 9, President Roosevelt sent a personal letter to Churchill, informing him of reports that a high-level Bulgarian delegation was expected in Istanbul and suggesting that bombing of Bulgaria be temporarily suspended. In the subsequent exchange of six letters, the two heads of state agreed on Cairo as the preferred place for the meetings.[66] Informing the Soviet Union was left to the State Department because Secretary Hull was already in the midst of discussions with Moscow about how unconditional surrender would be applied to Bulgaria.[67] On February 10, Harriman was asked to inform Soviet officials that a Bulgarian delegation was anticipated.[68] A week later, Vinogradov told Balabanov that the Soviets were well aware of U.S.-Bulgarian contacts.[69] On February 25, FDR confirmed to Churchill that the USSR would authorize its representative in Cairo to attend the upcoming negotiations.[70] The Soviet envoy informed his Western colleagues in Cairo that his role would be restricted to hearing what the Bulgarians might say and reporting to his government: "He definitely denied that he had any instructions in either case to present any views.[71] Thus, as expected, the Soviet role in the Bulgarian surrender would remain passive. In the first week of March, Churchill told Roosevelt that the minister resident at Allied Headquarters, Harold MacMillan, would represent Great Britain at the Cairo talks.[72] On March 11, a personal message from Secretary Hull sent at the specific request of President Roosevelt was delivered to Balabanov in Ankara. The Americans, Hull noted, would, with the British and Soviet representatives, await the Bulgarian delegation in Cairo.[73] By now,

Kouyoumdjisky and his mission had already departed for Egypt, and the OSS plan to detach Bulgaria from the Axis seemed on the verge of fruition.

Agreement as to the place of meeting and the acknowledged subordinate role of the Soviet Union in discussions required the Americans to take the lead in drafting an instrument of surrender. In this undertaking, both the Joint Chiefs and the State Department took an active part, forwarding the finished plan to the American representative on the European Advisory Committee in London in accord with agreements reached at the Moscow Foreign Ministers' Conference of 1943. The goal of a postwar, pro-Western Bulgaria was ensured in draft recommendations foreseeing no change in Bulgaria's socioeconomic structure, proposals designed to return Bulgaria to representative and democratic government, and reliance upon the Royal Bulgarian Army, which was expected to fight side by side with Allied troops.

In August 1943, following receipt of Donovan's initial plan, the recently established Civil Affairs Division of the War Department authorized the first study of military government for Bulgaria. The resulting document, which ran to nearly forty pages, foresaw joint American-British occupation with the personnel of the two states to be represented in "approximately equal numbers." Detailed recommendations were presented for stabilizing the domestic political and economic situation, including prescriptions for administration of private property, religious institutions, cultural societies, and the like. A section was devoted to establishing a viable exchange rate between the dollar and the inflated Bulgarian lev.[74] In February 1944, the director of the Civil Affairs Division, General J. H. Hilldring, presented his department's final recommendations for the Bulgarian surrender to the Joint Chiefs. This document, designated WS-58, received final JCS approval in early March. Predicated upon the principle of unconditional surrender, the terms allocated to America and Britain alone "the right to occupy with any forces at their disposal and in any way they deem necessary, and to utilize in any way they deem appropriate any or all parts of Bulgarian territory."[75] In the final draft sent to London under the symbol WS-58b, America and Britain were charged with sole control over Bulgaria's return to a peaceful postwar status: "The Government of the United States and the United Kingdom, acting in the interest of the United Nations, should reserve full freedom of action in case Bulgaria's obligations under the terms of surrender are not fulfilled."[76] A second document, WS-59b, also forwarded to London, reaffirmed exclusive Western responsibility for imposing surrender terms, with the detailed armistice provisions being perceived as "an adequate legal basis for the principal security, political and economic controls which the United Nations will need to impose on Bulgaria at the time of surrender and thereafter."[77]

State Department deliberation over the preferred, pro-Western armistice terms for Bulgaria also began in late 1943 with an incisive assessment of Bulgaria's territorial claims to Macedonia and Thrace.[78] In February 1944, the Interdivisional Country and Area Committee analyzed economic aspects of the proposed Bulgarian surrender, including suggestions for stability. Certain key features of Bulgaria's economic structure were identified for retention, price controls suggested, and the alternate disposal of accounts in Bulgariàs banks considered. Educational institutions and continued shipping on the Danube were to be supported.[79] Such proposals were subsequently combined with drafts from the Joint Chiefs and later dispatched to London for approval by the European Advisory Committee.

And yet the drafting of proposed armistice statutes by the State Department was but an initial stage in a continuing process of discussion and refinement which ran well into the summer of 1944. While awaiting arrival in Cairo of the Bulgarian delegation, the two most important departmental committees—the Committee on Postwar Programs and the Policy Committee—spent countless hours redrafting America's plans for Bulgaria's short- and long-range future. The final report of the Postwar Program Committee included a seventeen-point list of objectives under the heading "Long-Range Interests and Objectives of the United States." It was established as State Department policy that Bulgaria ought to expand her postwar world trade and that the United States should be prepared to conclude a trade agreement with her. Another goal was that "full encouragement should be given to democratic forces within Bulgaria and to the restoration of representative government."[80] The Policy Committee identified the goal of establishing "democratic government" as the central U.S. policy in postwar Bulgaria.[81]

Unfortunately for the Allies, the Western capitals were not the only ones aware of the Bulgarian peace overtures. Beginning in December 1943, a steady stream of reports to Berlin from Germany's Bulgarian ambassador, Adolf-Heinz Beckerle, revealed the ongoing talks in Turkey.[82] In March, the Bulgarian regents received an urgent request from Hitler to attend discussions in Salzburg. As with the earlier Hitler-Bulgarian meetings, transcipts of these talks have survived.

These talks, held on March 16 and 17 between the regents, Hitler, General Alfred Jodl, Field Marshal Wilhelm Keital, and Joachim von Ribbentrop, inspired a new caution among the Bulgarian leaders. Once again Hitler stressed the extreme threat a Soviet military victory posed to all European civilizations. Recounting the efforts of Soviet Foreign Minister Molotov to gain control over Bulgaria in November, 1940—an effort which, Hitler now revealed, had been blocked by the Reich—the Germans left little doubt as to Bulgaria's fate in the event of future Russian successes. In the face of such bleak prospects, Hitler demanded that Germany and all her allies devote full moral and military effort to the conflict.[83] And yet the message most important to the Bulgarians dealt with their own negotiations with the West. As Mikhov wrote in his diary: "The aim of the discussions was to suggest to us that conducting negotiations concerning peace and to ascertain the conditions of peace offered by the enemy is a major mistake. . . . Suddenly he [Hitler] stated that he had to solve a difficult problem with Regent Horthy [of Hungary]. (Later we learned what this meant)."[84] Two days after the regents' return to Sofia, Hitler's threat against those who negotiated with the Allies became manifest. On March 19, German troops occupied Hungary, later installing a pro-German puppet government.

The example of Hungary and the Western reluctance to discuss possible territorial concessions led the regents and cabinet to reconsider sending an official delegation to Cairo.[85] Instead, the "unofficial" contact through Kiselov was renewed, and on March 25, the U.S. consul in Istanbul, Berry, reported his return. Prospects for peace, Kiselov informed Berry, were not now especially bright because "(1) [the Bulgarian government] believes its action in sending delegates to Cairo would become known to the Germans who would use it as a pretext for occupying the country, and, (2) public opinion is not yet ready to accept . . . a break with Germany entailing the loss of Macedonia and Thrace." A month later, with no Bulgarian delegates yet in view, Balabanov confirmed Sofia's hesitancy in the face of the Hungarian example.[86]

By the late spring of 1944, the consensus of the War Department, White House, and State Department on behalf of the OSS plan was also in jeopardy—all eyes were on the upcoming invasion of France. A successful effort here would place Germany in much more direct peril than defection of her Balkan satellites. In April, the Combined Civil Affairs Committee recommended to the Combined Chiefs of Staff that the issue of armistice terms for Bulgaria ought no longer to be classified as urgent.[87] In May, President Roosevelt raised the issue anew with the American Joint Chiefs; the conclusion was drawn that "it now appears to be fairly clearly established that the US Government does not intent to participate in the occupation and control of Bulgaria in the post-surrender period in the same way that it will participate in such occupation and control in Germany."[88] In the face of diminishing agreement in Washington, Secretary Hull mounted one last effort. On May 12, a joint U.S.-U.K.-USSR appeal was released, calling upon the governments of Bulgaria, Hungary, Rumania, and Finland to cease collaboration with Germany and resist Nazism by all means in their power.[89] When no reply came from Sofia, interest in Donovan's plan waned. Unknown to Hull, a deep Bulgarian cabinet crisis prevented serious consideration of this final appeal—a crisis provoked by the Soviet attempt to force Bulgaria to the Western bargaining table.

In March, before the meeting between Hitler and the regents, the Soviet Union had informed the Bulgarian government that a satisfactory response to its January protests was still outstanding.[90] With the capture of Odessa during the spring Soviet offensive, Germany's use of Bulgaria's Black Sea ports assumed increasing importance. On April 17, Molotov told the Bulgarian Ambassador in Moscow that German use of such ports "is incompatible with normal relations between the USSR and Bulgaria, and further tolerance is not possible." In rebuttal to further Bulgarian denials, the Soviets presented their harshest demand, which, if fulfilled, would have required Bulgarian noncompliance with and exit from Axis commitments. Reviewing the recent history of Soviet protests and Bulgarian denials, Moscow now insisted that Bulgaria reopen the Soviet consulate in Varna and allow establishment of two additional consulates in Ruse and Burgas. Such an action would allow the USSR to verify the reported German activities.[91]

This new Soviet demand accompanied by the clear threat to disrupt relations ought to have induced Bulgaria to find immediate accord with the still patient West. Instead, it caused a major crisis in the already badly split Bulgarian cabinet at the crucial moment. In early May, the Bulgarian foreign minister visited the Soviet Embassy in Sofia on three occasions, seeking Soviet support for more lenient surrender terms if a delegation were dispatched to Cairo. According to the archival findings of the leading contemporary Bulgarian historian of this period, "D. Iakovlev [Soviet representative in Bulgaria] most definitely sought to destroy the illusion of the Bulgarian ruling circles concerning the existence of serious misunderstandings between the allies of the anti-Hitler coalition." He stated that issues " 'purely military' " dominated common policy—the desire to destroy Germany. " 'Do not imagine that before such a major task we would quarrel over some small political considerations or gain.' " Similar advice in response to similar requests for Soviet mediation was given by Soviet representatives in Ankara and Stockholm.[92]

Having failed to break the unity of East and West in support of

Allied surrender terms, the Bulgarian cabinet continued to temporize. On May 18, the Soviet chargé in Sofia handed Bozhilov a message threatening to break relations between the two states, a possible precursor to the much-feared declaration of war.[93] In the face of increased Soviet pressure, the Bozhilov cabinet resigned, thus delaying the dispatch of a delegation to Cairo for more than three months. Not until July would a new Bulgarian cabinet find itself able to draft a response to the Soviet demands, and by then Western interest in Bulgaria's fate was subordinate to the growing struggle in France. Despite Soviet cooperation, the OSS plan to detach Bulgaria from the Axis had failed.

Although withdrawal of the Kouyoumdjisky mission and the spring cabinet crisis in Sofia terminated immediate American interest in arranging Bulgaria's defection from the Axis, they had minimal impact upon the extensive plans for Bulgaria's postwar future. During the preceding nine months, Washington clearly had signaled her deep interest in Bulgaria's fate and had received at least tacit Soviet acknowledgment of American priorities. This period had witnessed a major effort by the State Department to draft documents of surrender which would allow Bulgaria's reintegration into the postwar family of nations consistent with American ideals and objectives. In the spring of 1944, Bulgaria still retained its unique status as the sole Balkan state in which American planners might expect eventual success in their efforts to provide for the future. With Soviet troops approaching the northern Balkans and the British redoubling efforts to ensure Western influence in Greece and Yugoslavia as a counterbalance to the anticipated Russian domination of Hungary and Rumania, Bulgaria alone held prospects of remaining a receptive area for democratic ideals long cherished in America. Thus the locus of planning shifted from the War to the State Department with little indication of flagging interest.

2 The Diplomacy of the Bulgarian Surrender

Although Secretary of State Cordell Hull's endorsement of the OSS plan to detach Bulgaria from the Axis in the fall of 1943 lent a sense of urgency to deliberations within his department about that nation's future, a Bulgarian surrender had been broached within the State Department's Post-War Foreign Policy Advisory Committee some eighteen months before. The major task confronting the civilian planners from late 1943 onward was to convert the plethora of ideas and suggestions into an agreement that could get Bulgaria out of the war while meeting both the needs of the War Department and the changing realities of the Balkan situation.[1] Despite President Roosevelt's normal reticence to involve the State Department too deeply in the intricacies of his own postwar "grand design," the exigency of the moment made the department the sole institution able to handle the now pressing need of drafting a surrender instrument for Bulgaria.[2] Well aware that Roosevelt wished to have the last word in all decisions regarding the war, Secretary Hull wisely sought White House advice on matters of possible dispute. The first such issue that arose when formulating the Bulgarian surrender terms was the precise meaning of unconditional surrender, a doctrine first publicly proclaimed at the Casablanca Conference in January 1943.[3] When Secretary Hull learned in early 1944 that a Rumanian peace delegation also was expected shortly in Cairo, the question of how to implement this doctrine within two documents of surrender assumed central importance.[4]

The doctrine of unconditional surrender had bothered Hull ever since its proclamation because the concept had not been cleared with the State Department.[5] This principle had been substantially modified when applied in the Italian surrender of 1943. The need to combine it with the OSS plan for Bulgaria, which anticipated minimal direct American activity, suggested the need for further modification.

The opportunity to raise the question with Roosevelt came during the December 1943 Donovan mission to Moscow. Upon completion of his talks with Donovan, Foreign Minister Molotov asked Harriman whether unconditional surrender should be applied to the smaller Axis satellites. Harriman, unclear about American policy on this point, quickly sought guidance from Hull,[6] who raised the issue with Roosevelt, cloaking his own reservations behind the new Soviet support for modification. Three days later, Roosevelt reconfirmed his preference for the principle, at least when applied to Germany: "The German people and Russia should also be told the best definition of what 'unconditional surrender' really means. The story of Lee's surrender to Grant is the best illustration. Lee wanted to talk about all kinds of conditions. Grant said that Lee must put his confidence in his [Grant's] fairness. Then Lee surrendered. Immediately Lee brought up the question of the Confederate officers' horses . . . . and Grant settled that item by telling Lee that they should take their horses home as they would be needed in the spring plowing."[7]

The questionable relevance of this homespun homily—Hull notes in his *Memoirs* that Roosevelt was not historically accurate—especially when the issue at hand concerned not Germany but the smaller satellite states, prompted Hull to exercise his own discretion when replying to Harriman: "I added that Harriman might inform Molotov that our Government would rather deal with the case of each individual enemy country as it arose because we did not consider it wise to attempt at this time to make any general public definition of 'unconditional surrender.' "[8] In March, Hull again stated his personal preference for more lenient treatment of the Axis satellites in a message to the American ambassador to London, John Winant, who shortly was charged with discussing the Bulgarian surrender terms with his British and Soviet colleagues. A general message, Hull suggested, ought to be transmitted to all East European satellites promising Allied flexibility in the event of rapid surrender.[9]

The dispute between Hull and the president over surrender terms for the Axis satellites also extended to the forum in which the terms were to be decided, the European Advisory Commission (EAC). Created at the 1943 Moscow Foreign Ministers' Conference as a three-power arena for discussion of future surrender documents and for determining possible areas of postwar Allied occupation, the EAC never gained the full confidence of the American president. Located in London, the commission was composed of the American ambassador to Britain, John Winant, the Soviet ambassador, Feodor Gusev, and Sir William Strang, the British undersecretary of state. From its initiation, it was agreed that no proposals would be tabled for discussion until they were approved by each constituent government, a rule intended to restrict the initiative of all delegates.[10] To add to the confusion, Ambassador Winant enjoyed a special relationship with the president which allowed him to use a White House code to bypass the State Department. Robert Murphy, the American political representative to the postwar Allied

Control Commission for Germany, has written that on such key EAC topics as ensuring Allied access rights to Berlin, Winant excluded the State Department from the discussions; the department files for 1944 reveal no communication from Winant on this crucial matter.[11]

The special relationship between Winant and Roosevelt was not the only problem Hull faced in directing the topics before the EAC. In December 1943, a special group known as the Working Security Committee was formed in Washington to clear messages to the EAC. Its ranks included representatives from the War Department's Civil Affairs Division and a navy delegate from the corresponding Naval Office for Occupied Areas. All proposals that touched on military matters were referred to the War and Navy departments for approval. Winant's staff in London also included representatives from these concerned military departments.[12] According to George Kennan, the War Department's Civil Affairs Division took particular pride in obstructing all proposals forwarded for consideration by Secretary Hull.[13] When one recalls that the main focus of the EAC was Germany and that Winant and Gusev sat on the commission in addition to their ambassadorial duties, the confusion attending the drafting of the Bulgarian surrender is understandable.

On March 4, 1944, the State Department sent Winant two lengthy documents that were to be the basis for the anticipated Bulgarian surrender. The first, WS-59, emerged in the Post-war Programs Committee in late February, and Winant was told that it had been approved by the Joint Chiefs of Staff. Consisting of twenty-seven articles, the document suggested severe restrictions upon future Bulgarian use of domestic radio and press and on financial transactions. The Bulgarian army was eventually to be demobilized and the production of war materials curtailed per the future instructions of the Allies. Territories captured after January 1, 1940, were to be evacuated but without prejudice to eventual disposition. Enforcement provisions contained in two articles requiring Bulgarian compliance with orders from any future occupation authority were strengthened by a general enabling clause that allowed the Allies to demand additional rights if necessary. Reflecting the existing status of the Hull-Roosevelt debate, the term *unconditional surrender* was prominently included. Since only America and Britain were at war with Bulgaria, the surrender document would be signed by a representative of the two Western powers. The costs of any occupation were to be borne by Bulgaria.[14]

The accompanying document, WS-59b, focused upon turning the proposed surrender terms into a comprehensive agreement. Preference was expressed for a single document with the reservation that changes might later be necessary. Because a Bulgarian delegation was shortly expected in Cairo, WS-59b suggested accepting an immediate surrender, especially if use of Bulgarian territory was promised so there would be no need for an extensive Allied expeditionary force. Modifications of WS-59b were to follow the guidelines already formulated by the Joint Chiefs in their proposals for a German surrender. The same day these documents were sent, March 4, Undersecretary of State Edward Stettinius informed Harriman that terms had been sent to Winant, requesting that Moscow inform its representative on the EAC to join the discussions.[15]

Because the United States had taken the initiative both in the Kouyoumdjisky mission and in transmitting documents to Winant, its representative became responsible for achieving consensus in the EAC. But on March 13, the first obstacle to rapid agreement emerged when Foreign Minister Molotov commented that such discussions were inappropriate.[16] A cable to Harriman and a meeting between the ambassador and Molotov revealed that although Moscow had no substantial objections to drafting terms for Bulgaria, the timing was considered unfavorable in view of the EAC's already pressing schedule in dealing with German matters.[17] Confused about this Soviet hesitation and aware that there was no preliminary agreement with Britian as to the benefits of including terms for unconditional surrender in the Bulgarian draft, Hull resolved to open direct discussions with London. By now, even the mercurial Kennan had voiced his strong objection to the term *unconditional surrender* when applied to the Axis satellites.[18]

The vehicle for U.S.-British discussions was a high-level mission led by Undersecretary of State Stettinius, which was scheduled to depart for London in the first week of April. Stettinius's mandate, which involved discussion of a broad range of problems dealing with the postwar world, was expanded to include exchanges concerning the future of the Axis satellites.[19] The Division of Southern European Affairs charged the mission to seek British advice both on terms necessary for ensuring Bulgaria's rapid surrender and on London's understanding of possible Soviet intentions toward Sofia. The background section dealing with American interests confirmed Hull's preference for flexibility, noting that all boundary questions ought to be postponed until the postwar period and suggesting that Bulgaria's northern border was acceptable as currently defined.[20]

Discussions on Bulgaria between Stettinius and British Undersecretary of State Orme Sargent commenced on April 18; the agenda included examination of the merits of unconditional surrender. Southeastern Europe, Sargent stated, held special significance for London because of British interests in the Middle East, which would be threatened by domination by "a rival Great Power."[21] The absence of significant Soviet power in the area, Sargent continued, could be ensured by promoting the speedy departure of Bulgaria from the conflict before Soviet forces reached the peninsula. To achieve an immediate peace, surrender terms far short of unconditional capitulation were preferred. In such a case, an Allied occupation might be avoided. If an immediate surrender was not forthcoming, an Allied control commission would be needed, and British troops would consider a token occupation. Occupation naturally would require some consultation with the Soviet Union but would not imply authorizing significant Russian influence in Bulgaria.[22] As Lord Hood, chief of the British Foreign Office's Department of Economics and Reconstruction, explained: "The situation in Bulgaria could not be considered parallel to that in Rumania where the British were willing to permit the Soviets to take over the whole responsibility of occupation and control. The British intended to take a considerable degree of responsibility in Bulgaria and had no intention of permitting the Soviets to dominate."[23]

The clear British interest in the rapid defection of Bulgaria combined with suggestions of a possible British occupation force if required reinforced Secretary Hull's goal of effecting a quick Bulgarian surrender on terms far short of unconditional surrender. When in early May the Soviet Union acknowledged the wisdom of starting surrender discussions within the EAC, the stage was set for an appeal to the Axis satellites.[24] On May 12, the three powers addressed a common public message to Hitler's allies in Eastern Europe, promising conditions short of unconditional surrender in event of East European positive responses.[25]

This new emphasis upon conditional surrender and the exchange of opinions with the British about arranging a rapid Bulgarian defection produced a new flurry of drafting activity in Washington. In June, the Interdivisional Country and Area Committees of the State Department wrote a new guideline for the Bulgarian surrender. The key issue, according to this document, was to identify terms that would bring Bulgaria to the negotiating table as soon as possible. The section entitled "Inducements for a Bulgarian Surrender," suggested that Bulgaria be offered the status of co-belligerency, a guarantee of independence and territorial integrity within the 1939 borders, a promise that no Greek or Yugoslav troops would be invited to join any occupation force, and the concession that the final territorial determination along the disputed Bulgarian-Rumanian frontier would be decided in accord with the expressed wishes of the region's inhabitants.[26]

In late June 1944, the State Department's Post-War Advisory Committee reported its approval of these recommendations to the Joint Chiefs. By now, the War Department had once again reversed itself as to the advantages to be gained from a rapid Bulgarian defection. In contrast to their April report, which had foreseen decreased significance in Bulgaria's entry into the Allied ranks, the Joint Chiefs now advised arranging the defection as soon as possible. On July 3, they approved the State Department recommendations, dispatching a letter of assent to Hull the same day. White House acceptance of the new flexibility toward Bulgaria was affirmed in a subsequent letter from Roosevelt's chief of staff, Admiral William Leahy.[27]

With a consensus on the general terms to be offered to Bulgaria, the stage was set to finalize an agreement within the EAC along the lines of Hull's earlier proposal for a conditional surrender. In July, Winant received the State Department guidelines, which confirmed that the May appeal to the satellite states "implied that an early capitulation of the Axis satellites would be rewarded by less severe terms than those which would be imposed if they refused to surrender before the defeat of Germany."[28] This document from State, which superseded all previous drafts, was limited to eight points, including provisions for an occupation in case of need and calling for evacuation of captured territory by the Bulgarian army without prejudice as to final disposition. The advantages of immediate surrender were reconfirmed with reference to the June draft from the State Department's Interdivisional Country and Area Committees with the sole exception that the offer of co-belligerency was not included because of the firm British objection. One week later, Winant informed Hull that a British proposal for surrender terms had been tabled and that the two documents could probably be merged. No difficulty was anticipated with the Soviet delegate because he already had expressed Moscow's willingness to allow America and Britain to handle terms for states with which the Soviet Union was not at war.[29]

By the end of August, the final American-British draft terms were essentially prepared. Following the guidelines developed in Washington with few additions, the thirteen articles demanded that Bulgaria sever all relations with Germany, comply with measures of demobilization as requested, and permit the Supreme Allied Command to have right of free movement on Bulgarian soil as needed. The enabling clause guaranteed that Bulgaria would accept any additional demands that might be necessary to ensure fulfillment of the surrender terms.[30]

The brevity of the draft terms, the enabling clause, and the memories of the confusion surrounding the Italian surrender the previous year prompted the Americans and British to label their document as terms for an "armistice." The final provisions that would transform the draft into one of a "surrender" would await the negotiations with the Bulgarian delegation in Cairo. As Hull remarked at a meeting of his Committee on Post-War Programs: "It would be inadvisable to have inflexible ideas regarding the treatment of Bulgaria. The primary objective was to get Bulgaria out of the war as soon as possible."[31] And yet the State Department had carefully drafted the general objectives America would pursue in Bulgaria after surrender regardless of any changes that might be negotiated at Cairo. These provisions had emerged from the Committee on Post-War Programs and consisted of seventeen points. They represented the heart of America's long-expressed concern with the future of postsurrender Bulgaria and were to play a major role in the subsequent disputes in the early stages of the Cold War.

America's central goal in Bulgaria was defined as the creation of a democratic, representative government and the nation's reentry into the mainstream of postwar international life. Considerable understanding for future border rectifications was expressed, including the possibility that Bulgaria would receive access to the Aegean Sea via free port facilities in the Greek city of Salonica. To ensure that Bulgaria's past economic dependence upon Germany would not be repeated, "Bulgaria should be encouraged to expand its world trade on a nondiscriminatory basis and within the framework of such international economic organizations as may be established." An independent if pro-Western posture would be furthered by American support for Bulgaria's participation in regional groups designed to "promote economic welfare and political security." In the transition period following surrender, "opportunity should be afforded . . . for the establishment of a provisional government representative of democratic groups in Bulgaria as the best means of insuring a permanent government of a representative character."[32]

The time and care given to drafting these guidelines for the future of Bulgaria reconfirmed America's abiding interest in this small Balkan state, a concern consistently displayed since approval of the Kouyoumdjisky mission. Although some of the initial documents were conceptualized within the broader confines of general policy toward the Axis satellites, Bulgaria retained a special distinction as the state in whose future America was determined to remain a main participant. The importance of Bulgaria becomes clearer when one reflects upon concurrent State Department planning for her northern neighbor. When discussing policy for Rumania, the State Department merely recommended that Washington ought not oppose Soviet acquisition of the provinces of Bessarabia and North Bukovina. With Soviet occupation of Rumania beyond American control, the State Department wisely limited its proposals for this nation's future to general principles which Moscow might accept. A department paper stated, "The United States should use its influence to bring about the replacement of the present totalitarian regime in Rumania by one which is more representative of the desires of the people. Beyond this, and in accordance with its established policy of non-intervention, the United States is not concerned with political developments in Rumania so long as they do not represent a menace to the security of other states."[33]

On August 29, 1944, the last potential obstruction between the American-British draft armistice and the Soviet Union disappeared. The Soviet representative in the EAC, Gusev, informed his colleagues that he would take no further part in the discussions.[34] Now all that appeared required to wrap up the Bulgarian surrender was the arrival of Bulgarian negotiaters in Cairo, a prospect that seemed likely because concerted and coordinated pressure had been exerted upon Sofia during the summer months.

Although the ease with which the British and Americans reached a common set of terms for Bulgaria marked a high point in Allied cooperation, it must be remembered that the future of Bulgaria held a decidedly lower priority in British than in American plans for the postwar Balkans. At the very moment when Winant and Strang were approaching agreement, the British Foreign Office was focusing renewed attention upon the troubled present and future of a more important British concern: Bulgaria's neighbor to the south, Greece. By the spring of 1944, relations between the internal Greek resistance movement, the EAM-ELAS, and the British-supported royalist Greek government in exile reached a new low. In April 1944, the official Greek armed forces stationed in Egypt mutinied, demanding the resignation of the exile government and accommodation with the resistance. About half of the Greek armed forces were subsequently rounded up by British troops and confined to detention camps for the duration of the war. Shaken by this unanticipated threat to postwar British interests in the eastern Mediterranean, Churchill instructed his foreign secretary, Anthony Eden, to prepare for a cabinet discussion to identify potential areas of British and Soviet conflict in the region.[35] This moment dates the beginning of the British effort to establish clear lines of demarcation in the Balkans.

On May 5, Eden approached Ambassador Gusev to suggest "casually" the possibility of reaching an understanding about the future of

Greece and Rumania. As Eden noted, the object of this conversation was "agreeing between ourselves as a practical matter that Rumanian affairs would be the main concern of the Soviet Government while Greek affairs would be in the main our concern, each government giving the other help in the respective countries."[36] On May 18, Gusev informed Eden that such an arrangement was acceptable to Moscow, but he inquired whether the American government had been consulted. The Soviet reluctance to proceed without the approval of Washington reflected Moscow's earlier commitments to the Donovan mission. Believing that Washington probably would raise no objection, Eden instructed his ambassador there, Lord Halifax, to raise the issue with the State Department.[37] Churchill then sent a personal letter to Roosevelt, setting forth the British proposal and disclaiming any desire to create spheres of influence in the Balkans.[38]

Eden's proposal engendered some division of opinion among the various State Department committees dealing with postwar planning, but Hull remained adamant against such efforts, which might lead to a fragmented postwar world. Two months earlier, the State Department had authored a report rejecting the need for spheres, and Hull now stood firmly on its conclusions.[39] When a follow-up letter from Churchill to Halifax suggested that Bulgaria be included in the proposed area of Soviet concern, the State Department committees rallied to Hull's position. On June 10, a letter from Roosevelt to Churchill, drafted by Hull, reiterated the State Department's firm objection. Yet two days later, while Hull was absent from the capital, Roosevelt dispatched a second letter, agreeing to try the British proposal for three months.[40]

The confusion attending this disagreement between Roosevelt and Hull soon prompted a personal inquiry from Stalin as to the true American position. Washington's response was so contradictory that neither the Soviets nor the British could interpret it.[41] On June 22, another letter from Roosevelt to Churchill confirmed the outstanding American objections to the British demarche. On June 30, Gusev informed the British that in view of the American position, the matter merited no further discussion. When Churchill cabled Stalin for reconsideration, the Soviet leader replied that the matter ought to be postponed until Washington consented. On July 15, the State Department informed Stalin directly of its "official" objections to the British proposal.[42] The first attempt to define Balkan spheres of influence had run its course.

While the issue of Balkan spheres was causing confusion in the Allied capitals, the Bulgarians were involved in a government crisis over the response to increased Soviet demands for cessation of aid to Germany. The immediate cause of the crisis was the Soviets' April 26 demand that Bulgaria reopen the Soviet consulate at Varna closed two years before and allow creation of two additional offices in Burgas and Ruse. Such Soviet observation points, Moscow stated, were required if the frequent Bulgarian denials of aid to the Axis were to merit belief.[43] The ensuing Bulgarian cabinet meeting revealed a deep split among the respective ministers as to how best to respond to the Soviet note. The agriculture minister, Ivan Beshkov, with support for two colleagues, suggested compliance with the Soviet request, with a face-saving counterdemand to include the expansion of Bulgarian consular activity in the Soviet Union. The opposing view, championed by Foreign Minister Dimitur Shishmanov, suggested a play for time. The Soviet request should be met only following the resumption of normal trade relations between the two nations. Given that the primary function of consulates was dealing with matters of trade, Shishmanov's position struck the assembled ministers as legally apt, although the Soviet response was expected to be unfavorable. With a fragile consensus to try this last-ditch effort, Beshkov and three fellow ministers promised their resignations in case of failure.[44] On May 6, the agreed-upon response was given to the Soviet embassy. Three days later, Moscow responded that such conditions were unacceptable.[45] A week later, a lengthy note from Moscow confirmed that Soviet patience was at an end: "The Soviet Government warns that in the absence of satisfaction . . . *it will consider it impossible to maintain relations with Bulgaria except as with a state which aids and intends to aid henceforth Hitler's Germany in the war against the Soviet Union.*"[46] With the Bulgarian cabinet now in total disarray and the resignation of four ministers on the table, the regency opted to form a new government.[47]

The new Bulgarian cabinet formed on June 1 pledged to diminish Sofia's ties with Germany while seeking an understanding with both the Soviet Union and the Western Allies. Its immediate objective was to avert direct Bulgarian military participation in the approaching battle for the Balkans. The new prime minister, Ivan Bagrianov, a member of the Bulgarian Agrarian movement and a minister in prewar Bulgaria, promised the regency he would avoid further involvement in the war while retaining the essence of the Bulgarian-German alliance. His mandate "to deal simultaneously both with Germany and with Russia" symbolized the complexity of the situation and an unrealistic belief in Sofia's remaining freedom of maneuver.[48] In early June, as a precondition for the entry into the cabinet of Purvan Draganov, former Bulgarian ambassador to Berlin and Madrid, a detailed program designed to avert a feared invasion was approved. Its stated goals were to avoid "at all costs" a conflict with Soviet Russia, to open negotiations with America and Britain for a withdrawal from the war, to remove Bulgarian occupation forces from some of the captured territories, and to settle the domestic Jewish question. This policy was to be conducted with subtlety and a craftiness such that "(a) new calamities are not created for the people; (b) a foreign occupation is avoided; (c) a coup d'etat with or without the influence of the Germans who are able to facilitate such a coup is averted."[49]

Realizing that the pursuit of such contradictory goals would require careful diplomacy and, above all, time, Draganov informed the Soviet Embassy of his intention to place Bulgarian-Soviet relations on a sound basis. Understanding and patience, he asserted, were essential for success.[50] At the same time, Draganov instructed the Bulgarian Embassy in Moscow to inform Molotov that "the response of the Government to the Soviet note [of May 18 demanding the immediate opening of the consulates in question] will be delayed still a few days due to the importance of the question and the conditions under which the government works."[51] On June 20, a message from Draganov to the Bulgarian consul in Istanbul authorized renewed contacts with the Americans designed to achieve a surrender. The terms proposed for such negotiations were carefully defined. Bulgaria would require American support for an outlet to the Aegean, retention of the major share of Macedonia and the existing western border and Dobruja, no occupation of Bulgaria, not raising the question of evicting the Germans from Bulgaria, and a rapid response.[52] The key to this convoluted attempt to placate the Soviets short of acceptance of their demands while arranging a surrender with the Americans now rested upon gaining a German commitment to diminished Bulgarian aid to the Reich and avoiding a Nazi-inspired coup from the more intransigent members of the Bulgarian right. Negotiations to achieve these objectives were already in progress.

Ever since receipt of the Soviet demands, the Bulgarian regent, Bogdan Filov, had maintained an open channel with the German ambassador, Adolf-Heinz Beckerle. As expected, Beckerle had strongly advised against compliance with Soviet demands for reopening consulates in areas where Germany maintained a major military presence.[53] The significance of the Bulgarian ports in the continuing German-Soviet conflict had been augmented by the 1944 Soviet spring offensive, which took Soviet troops to the Carpathians. On April 10, the major Soviet Black Sea port of Odessa had fallen, and the same month, the units of German Admiral Kurt Fricke's command had disembarked in Varna.

By mid-May, an average of eight German troop convoys were moving through Bulgaria each day because the Rumanian railroads were over-burdened.[54] By early June, Russian intelligence reported the presence of more than two thousand German soldiers in Varna alone, along with fifty to sixty warships including submarines.[55] When Beckerle sought advice from Berlin, Foreign Minister Joachim von Ribbentrop responded that Bulgaria should stall for time because the virtual absence of a Russian Black Sea fleet and the expanded strength of German units in the Balkans made a Soviet invasion of Bulgaria highly unlikely.[56] A quickly arranged visit of Regents Cyril and Filov to Berchtesgaden in the second half of May resulted in new demands from Hitler that Bulgaria increase its assistance to Germany.[57] These direct pressures were accompanied by secret messages from Berlin to Beckerle requesting full information on disposition of pro-German forces able to effect a coup.[58]

As the Bulgarian scholar Ilcho Dimitrov has noted, the advent of the Bagrianov cabinet in early June ushered in a decisive shift in Bulgaria's heretofore pro-German policy.[59] The visible distrust between Bagrianov and Regent Filov—the latter confided to his diary on June 15 that the prime minister was secretly acting against him—promised a degree of friction but did little to restrict a new policy of asserting the primacy of Bulgarian national interests even when these impinged upon past German commitments.[60] The new direction was confirmed with the entry of Draganov into the cabinet. When asked why he had accepted such a thankless position, Draganov philosophically responded: "I am perfectly well aware of the fact that we have only three more months liberty to enjoy in Bulgaria."[61] This new attitude was also evident in the changed position of the regents.

On June 1, Filov informed Beckerle that Bulgaria had decided to offer the Soviets a "small" concession by reopening the Varna consulate.[62] At a subsequent meeting attended by Draganov, Filov told Beckerle that a withdrawal of German units from Varna would best serve the Reich by diminishing the possibility of a new military front in the Balkans.[63] That same day Draganov cabled his ambassador in Berlin of the withdrawal request, stating that a conflict with the Soviets was neither in the German or Bulgarian interest.[64]

Expecting German acceptance, Draganov informed the Soviet chargé in Sofia, Stepan Kirsanov, on June 19 that he would travel to Varna to verify continuing Soviet charges of a German military presence.[65] Shocked to discover some sixty Axis vessels in the harbor, Draganov hastened back to Sofia to inform the Soviets that such activities were at odds with Bulgaria's pledges of neutrality and would not be allowed to continue.[66] Again pleading the need for time, Draganov told the Soviet chargé that a reply to the Soviet demands of May 18 was still being drafted.[67] Not until the second week of July, following renewed requests to Berlin, did Germany at long last consent to withdraw her vessels from the harbor.[68]

The belated German compliance with the Bulgarian request paved the way for a cabinet response to the still outstanding Soviet note. At the end of the month, Draganov delivered the official answer to Kirsanov, promising to reopen the Varna consulate "in the near future" and suggesting that the additional two consulates might best be accommodated by expanding the Varna consular district.[69] That day, Draganov sent a personal letter to Soviet Foreign Minister Molotov reaffirming Bulgaria's desire to maintain and strengthen friendly relations with Moscow but noting that "some" would react negatively to undue haste. Extreme caution was required to avert both domestic and foreign threats to the Bulgarian government.[70]

Unfortunately for the tireless Draganov, the "three more months liberty" so perceptively noted in June were rapidly drawing to a close. As he confided to his diary on July 21, "The catastrophe for Europe, Germany and Bulgaria is approaching. Events unfold, outstripping us, and we cannot do anything for the salvation of the state."[71] By now, the military situation in the Balkans and Bulgaria's continuing if diminished aid to the Germans were becoming increasingly important in Soviet military planning. On August 2, the Soviet High Command ordered the second and third Ukranian fronts to prepare an offensive in Bessarabia; their success might lead Soviet forces into direct confrontation with German units remaining in Bulgaria.[72] That same day, Turkey broke diplomatic relations with Berlin, threatening a possible attack on Bulgaria and Rumania from the south.[73] On August 12, the Soviet chargé in Sofia informed Bagrianov that the conditions for stable relations between the two countries henceforth would include new demands: "If Bulgaria intends somehow to get out of the blind alley, then now she must pose the question of severing Bulgaria from Germany. The Soviet government asks the Bulgarian government whether she is prepared to break with Germany. The Soviet government awaits a response . . . and hopes that the Bulgarian government will not prolong the decision on this question."[74]

Clearly the options for Bulgarian policy had significantly narrowed by the second week of August in the face of a continuing Russian advance toward the Balkans. Unknown in Sofia, however, Soviet operational plans to engage the German army on Bulgarian soil were as yet undrafted, permitting a final opportunity for the Bagrianov government to avoid invasion by ceasing all assistance to the Axis. But this alternative, too, was laden with peril. The Bulgarian minister of interior, Aleksandr Stanishev, informed the cabinet one day after receipt of the Soviet note of an impending pro-Nazi coup.[75] The eleventh hour for Bulgaria's future had struck.

From the American perspective, the unrelenting Soviet pressure upon Bulgaria which bore its first fruit in formation of the Bagrianov cabinet produced new hopes for a rapid accommodation with the West.[76] Upon the withdrawal of the Kouyoumdjisky mission in the spring of 1944, the American consul general in Istanbul, Burton Berry, became the main contact point for future Bulgarian peace feelers. On June 8, Berry informed Hull that recent talks with Bulgarian officials confirmed that a dramatic reorientation of Bulgarian policy was in process as evidenced by the new prime minister's first public address. A week later, Berry reported that the prominent places accorded former military officials in the Bagrianov cabinet implied the Bulgarian army would play a key role in formation of future policy, a situation fully consistent with the objectives of the Kouyoumdjisky mission.[77] Chances for peace, Berry advised, would be improved by an expressed American willingness to negotiate still disputed Bulgarian claims to areas such as Macedonia. In early July, Berry informed Hull that Bulgarian Ambassador Nicolas Balabanov was shortly expected with a new proposal for ending Bulgaria's role in the war.[78]

On July 20, Balabanov arrived in Istanbul and confirmed the Bagrianov government's wish to withdraw from the conflict but on conditions that might be of advantage to postwar Bulgaria. Sofia, the ambassador related, had already taken important steps to cut her ties with Germany and to provide evidence of her good intentions toward the West. The number of German troop trains traveling through Bulgarian territory had been reduced to one per week, Berlin had agreed to remove her naval presence from Bulgaria's Black Sea ports, domestic tranquillity had been achieved by the existing cabinet with even some Communist groups expressing support, and the removal of occupation troops from Serbia aside from small border detachments had been ordered. "Bulgaria is making every attempt to get out of the war short of sacrificing the nation's unity and vigor," Balabanov affirmed. It was now America's turn to state her position on the future of the Balkans with special reference to Bulgaria.[79]

A week later, Hull cabled his response to the new Bulgarian peace overture. Noting that Balabanov's list did not fulfill a complete break with Germany, Hull again suggested that Bulgaria be instructed to dispatch an authorized representative to Cairo as discussed during the

Kouyoumdjisky mission. Negotiators from the United States, Britain, and the USSR would await this representative.[80] On August 1, Georgi Kiselov, Berry's main contact, left for Sofia, where Hull's response was interpreted as an implied American willingness to consider Bulgaria's outstanding territorial claims in discussions before she left the war.[81] One day later, across the Atlantic, the Joint Chiefs of Staff gave their consent to the expected Cairo negotiations.[82] Winant, the American representative at the EAC, was advised to hasten discussions with the British on the final surrender terms, and Harriman was requested to gain Soviet acceptance of Cairo as the scene of the future peace parleys.[83] In early August, Kiselov returned to Istanbul with a pledge from the Bagrianov cabinet to dispatch an official delegation to Cairo.[84] It was to be led by Stoicho Moshanov, a prewar Speaker of the Bulgarian parliament and personal friend of the British ambassador in Turkey, Sir Hugh Knatchbull-Hugessen. In Bulgaria, Moshanov was well known as a firm anglophile.[85]

The selection of Moshanov as the central Bulgarian negotiator had been under consideration for some time. Shortly after formation of the Bagrianov cabinet, Moshanov informed the new prime minister of his deep belief that German prospects for victory had evaporated. On June 19, following a particularly harsh public address by Winston Churchill castigating Bulgaria's continued participation in the conflict, Bagrianov and Draganov invited Moshanov for discussions. It was suggested that Moshanov begin "unofficial" talks with the British in Ankara, seeking London's terms for leaving the war. When he was later told that his mission would not be disclosed to the Bulgarian regents, Moshanov refused to consider the matter further. Only with the heightened possibility of invasion provoked by the Turkish disruption of relations with Germany in early August were the regents brought into the discussions. On August 6, they approved Moshanov's mission.[86]

The continuing rivalry between the Bagrianov cabinet and the regency so evident in the initial talks with Moshanov cast its shadow on his mission. His instructions were only to inquire what conditions the Allies might offer in exchange for Bulgaria's exit from the war. No negotiating position or set of possible terms was entrusted to Moshanov. With such a mandate, Moshanov was able to exercise considerable leeway in selecting his opposite number. Thus in a sharp reversal from past Bulgarian practice, Moshanov, avoiding longstanding American contacts in Turkey, sought out his British friend, Ambassador Knatchbull-Hugessen. On August 16, Moshanov held his first meeting in the British Embassy in Ankara, a meeting attended by an unnamed American representative.[87]

Moshanov's unofficial status produced a new series of exchanges between Washington and London in an attempt to make sense of this new Bulgarian mission. The Bulgarian was duly informed that conditions would be presented only to authorized Bulgarian delegates and only in Cairo, a position Moshanov promised to communicate to Sofia while himself remaining in Turkey.[88] Three days later, Foreign Minister Draganov cabled his ambassador in Turkey, Balabanov, that Moshanov and the Bulgarian military attaché in Turkey, Colonel Zheleskov, were now fully authorized to negotiate the peace. Their objectives and conditions, Draganov stated, included withdrawal of Bulgaria from "active participation" in the war, avoidance of military action in Bulgaria proper, and some compromise on the territorial question of Macedonia which would permit significant postwar Bulgarian influence. Peace ought to be arranged short of a formal break with Germany because a total disruption of ties might call forth a concerted German effort to overthrow the existing Bulgarian cabinet.[89]

Before Moshanov could present his new credentials to the Allies, the rapidly changing fortunes of war once again forced a refocusing of Bulgaria's intricate foreign policy. On August 19, Bagrianov informed his cabinet that a conspiracy to effect a pro-German coup had been discovered, indicating the possibility of German occupation of Bulgaria.[90] The next day, the long-awaited Soviet offensive in the Balkans opened with a massive assault in eastern Rumania. The overthrow of the Antonescu government in Bucharest three days later and the movement of Soviet troops to the Bulgarian frontier announced that the hour of decision for Bulgaria had at long last arrived. The shocked regent, General Nikola Mikhov, noted in his diary: "This news was totally unexpected [because] the Germans always assured us we need not worry about the Eastern front and thus about our Northern border. We have nothing there such as a fortified line. It would be absurd to do battle in such conditions."[91] As part of the urgent reconsideration of policy, Moshanov was recalled to Sofia for consultation. That same day, August 24, the depth of the crisis was confirmed by a message from the Soviet chargé, Kirsanov, requesting transportation to Moscow.[92]

The Soviet offensive and the persistent rumors of planned pro-Nazi coups exacerbated the political rivalries within the government which had broken out anew following a major foreign policy address by Bagrianov in mid-August.[93] With the government in disarray, faced with the urgent need to appease Germany and the Soviet Union, both poised to strike against the faction-ridden Bulgarian regime, the task of delivering new instructions to Moshanov temporarily assumed a secondary position. On August 25, Bulgarian units began disarming German troops fleeing over the Rumanian border while an urgent Bulgarian cabinet meeting deliberated the future. The following day, Draganov informed the Soviets that Bulgaria was henceforth "strictly neutral" and that disarmed German prisoners would be treated in accord with existing international conventions. That day, a telegram on behalf of the Bagrianov cabinet to Berlin demanded that all German troops be withdrawn from Bulgarian soil.[94] The First Bulgarian Corps was recalled from duty in Serbia and plans made to withdraw occupation units from Macedonia.[95] Aware that the Bagrianov cabinet's goal of avoiding war now stood in shambles, the regents began open consultation with various domestic politicians to form a new cabinet. On August 28, Konstantin Muraviev, a leader of the old Agrarian party and former war minister in the short-lived Stamboliiski government of 1923, received permission to assemble a "cabinet of national salvation." It took power in early September.[96]

In the midst of this domestic and international confusion, Stoicho Moshanov made his way to Cairo for the long-promised armistice talks. To the surprise of the assembled Allies, Moshanov informed his interrogators at the opening meeting on September 1 that he lacked official authorization to negotiate an armistice. Such a mandate, he stated, would be forthcoming if requested from Sofia, but he would not seek it until a new cabinet, more representative of liberal politicians, was formed.[97] On September 2, the new Muraviev cabinet communicated an unasked-for authorization to Moshanov, only to be informed that Moshanov refused the mandate.[98]

The strange behavior of Moshanov has prompted considerable discussion among contemporary Bulgarian scholars as to his motive and goals.[99] Yet the most perceptive analysis was provided by the American representative at the Cairo talks, Harold Shantz. He cabled to Hull that he believed Moshanov had come to Cairo to arrange an "Armistice Conference" at which terms might be discussed and concessions received. Such an outcome, Shantz suggested, would have greatly advanced Moshanov's political future in postwar Bulgaria. When confronted with stiff Allied demands that showed little concern for Bulgaria's territorial claims, Moshanov opted to refuse conditions that might impinge on his political reputation.[100] On September 5, Moshanov received a confirmation of his authorization from Muraviev, but again he refused it.[101]

In calmer times, Moshanov's tactics, reminiscent of Trotsky's "no peace, no war," might have produced a new Allied compromise. There was, after all, considerable flexibility built into the American-

British draft terms. But time had run out. Buoyed up by the unexpectedly rapid collapse of Rumania, the Soviet High Command quickly made plans to exploit its successes by pressing the demoralized Axis forces by an attack into Yugoslavia by way of northern Bulgaria. On September 5, the Soviet Union declared war on the Muraviev government, crossing the Bulgarian frontier several days later. Only after an official Bulgarian declaration of war against Germany on September 8 did Moscow consider the frantic pleas from Sofia for an armistice. On September 9, Soviet troops ceased their advance southward, well short of the Bulgarian capital.[102]

The unanticipated Soviet occupation of northern Bulgaria terminated the Cairo discussions. The final report of the conference on September 7 simply noted that Bulgaria had asked for an armistice with the United States and Great Britain, the conditions for an armistice had been given to the Bulgarian delegation, and conversations for an armistice were ended because of the entry of the Soviet Union into the ranks of the belligerents.[103] Two days later, on September 9, the beleaguered Muraviev government collapsed in the wake of a domestic uprising and was replaced by a Communist-led coalition known as the Fatherland Front Government. On September 11, at the order of Soviet Marshal F. Tolbukhin and in the name of the new government in Sofia, Moshanov was informed that his mission had lost all meaning.[104]

The Soviet occupation of Bulgaria prompted a reconsideration of American policy if American interests in this state's future were to be secured.[105] The carefully drafted plans of the past twelve months had been premised upon a successful conquest of domestic power by the Bulgarian army and Bulgarian cooperation with the West to ensure fulfillment of the draft armistice terms. If such an arrangement were to falter, the alternative proposals foresaw the entry of a small British occupation force that would maintain Western dominance. But with Soviet troops in Bulgaria, some new means of asserting Western interests was required. At Hull's insistence, the draft armistice terms had included a degree of flexibility so as to meet any unforeseen contingencies. Now, paradoxically, flexibility would be needed to reach accommodation with both the new Bulgarian government and the occupying Soviet forces. Such negotiations promised to be even more frustrating and difficult than the already trying debates with the various representatives of the Bagrianov and Muraviev cabinets. To add to the confusion, the presence of the Soviet army now prompted the War Department to reaffirm its direct interest in the Bulgarian surrender.

On September 1, four days before the Soviet declaration of war, the British Chiefs of Staff suggested to their American counterparts the wisdom of including provisions for an Allied control commission in the Bulgarian armistice, a suggestion which the War Department found "unimportant."[106] But on September 8, in the face of the Soviet invasion, the U.S. Joint Chiefs suddenly reversed their position. Admiral Leahy pointed out that the Soviet declaration greatly complicated the situation, and General Marshall advised that the British proposal be accepted. The next day, the Joint Chiefs' decision was formally transmitted to both Secretary Hull and the British Foreign Office.[107]

The American and British Chiefs of Staff were not the only people deeply concerned with the uncertain prospect of Bulgaria's future. On September 9, Feodor Gusev informed the members of the EAC that he too had modifications to make in the still unsigned surrender document. Although Gusev acknowledged his earlier acceptance of the Western draft, the Soviet entry into the war now required Moscow's active participation in the continuing discussions.[108] Three days later, the Russians offered a detailed list of changes in the draft terms. Each of these necessitated involvement of the complex American chain of decision making for the EAC, but the suggested Soviet clause governing the proposed Allied control commission quickly assumed central importance. According to Gusev's instructions from Moscow, the proposed commission was to lodge unrestricted power in the hands of the occupying Soviet army.[109]

Since the cumbersome process of American interdepartmental discussion promised a delayed response from Washington, the British representative took immediate responsibility for objecting to this unilateral Soviet proposal. Having informed Winant that such a clause would place Bulgaria in the same position as Rumania—where Western interests had been acknowledged as greatly inferior to those of Moscow[110]—the British suggested a reformulation of the Bulgaria commission terms to redress the balance: "An Allied Control Commission, of which the Soviet member will be chairman, will be set up to regulate and supervise the execution of the Armistice terms and to communicate to the Bulgarian Government the instructions and further requirements of the Allies."[111] The purpose of this clause, Strang informed Winant, was to create a truly tripartite commission with each of the three powers having equality. A Soviet member would serve as permanent chairman, reflecting the presence of the Red Army, but the commission would not function at the dictates of the Soviet forces.[112]

The Soviet response to this proposal was immediate and unambiguous. Wisely stressing the main Allied objective of completing the destruction of German military capability, Gusev opined that in normal times, such tripartite control might indeed be acceptable. But at the present, when Bulgarian units were being reformed under Soviet supervision for the struggle against German troops in the Balkans, such a division of authority would work against the common interest. In conditions of war, the proposed commission would of necessity have to be subject to the demands of the Soviet commander in chief within the Balkan theater. Throughout the ensuing debate, Gusev remained intransigent in the face of Western objections.[113]

The Soviet demand for modification of several draft terms besides those concerning the control commission occupied the attention of both the State and War departments throughout September. The majority of the Soviet changes could easily be accommodated within the broad draft terms already approved, but the issue of the control commission promised a major dispute. On September 26, the U.S. Joint Chiefs recommended acceptance of the Soviet changes with the sole exception of the control commission.[114]

The evident stalemate in London and the delayed War Department appraisal of the Soviet suggestions prompted Winant to attempt a compromise. Acknowledging the force of Soviet arguments for military direction of postarmistice Bulgaria in view of the overriding demands of the war, Winant now suggested a two-stage implementation of the disputed control commission. The predominance of the Soviet High Command would be recognized only until the conflict with Germany ended. Thereafter, truly tripartite direction of the control commission would begin. He explained to Hull: "During the period of hostilities in Europe an Allied Control Commission will regulate and supervise the execution of the present terms under the general directions of the Allied (Soviet) High Command. Upon the cessation of hostilities in Europe and until the conclusion of peace with Bulgaria an Allied Control Commission will regulate the execution of the Armistice according to the instructions of the Governments of the United Kingdom, Soviet Union and the United States of America." On September 26, Hull warmly endorsed Winant's proposal, authorizing him to press forward with this compromise draft. In early October, the Joint Chiefs added their concurrence.[115]

Had the gods been friendly, Winant's successful effort to gain acceptance of his proposal from the welter of American bureaucratic entanglements would have been greeted by concurrence from his fellow EAC representatives. But such was not to be. Gusev remained adamant concerning Soviet dominance in the control commission, a position that would give Moscow the same freedom of action in Bulgaria as proposed for Rumania. In early October, Gusev left London for Moscow with the issue unresolved and with Soviet forces daily increasing their penetration of Bulgarian political and military life. Both Prime Minister Churchill and Foreign Secretary Eden were scheduled for high-level discussions in Moscow in October, so the American plan for the control commission was entrusted to their care. Eden promised Winant that he would take this issue up with Molotov in the forthcoming negotiations.[116] For the moment, the Americans could only wait and hope as the venue of debate shifted from the British to the Russian capital.

The details of the October 1944 British-Soviet Conference in Moscow and the infamous "percentage" division of the Balkans are too well known to require discussion here.[117] The task of translating the percentages reflecting future Russian and British control into policy fell to Foreign Secretary Eden and his Soviet counterpart, Vyacheslav Molotov. At their October 10 session, Molotov revealed an intrasigence worthy of Gusev when broaching the question of Bulgaria. If the Western proposal for a truly tripartite Bulgarian control commission was accepted, Molotov remarked, "There might be confusion which would lead to friction." Soviet dominance, he maintained, was consistent with the 90 percent control Russia required in Bulgaria. Throughout the week-long discussions, acerbic debate about Bulgaria's future was supplemented by exchanges of letters. On October 13, Eden informed Molotov that the American delegate to the European Advisory Commission, Winant, had rejected any revision of the clause that would grant permanent dominance to Russia. The following day, Molotov refused to modify the Soviet position. Anxious lest the negotiations terminate in anger at a time when Britain faced major problems in Greece with the Communist-led EAM-ELAS yet concerned about compromising his commitment to defend the American position on tripartite control in Bulgaria, Eden included in his next letter a specific disclaimer on binding Washington to any agreement he and Molotov might forge. He also accepted Soviet wording for the disputed clause concerning the control commission and secretly agreed that British and American representatives would not take their seats in the commission while the war against Germany continued.[118] As sent to Winant, minus Eden's secret agreement, the clause read: "For the whole period of the armistice, there will be established in Bulgaria an Allied Control Commission which will regulate and supervise the execution of the armistice terms under the chairmanship of the representative of the Allied (Soviet) High Command and with the participation of representatives of the United Kingdom and the United States. During the period between the coming into force of the armistice and the conclusion of hostilities against Germany, the Allied Control Commission will be under the general direction of the Allied (Soviet) High Command."[119]

As anticipated, the Eden-Molotov agreement for greatly reduced Western participation in the disputed Bulgarian control commission caused immediate consternation among American diplomats. On October 4, President Roosevelt had pointedly cautioned Stalin against reaching any decisions that might exclude American influence from any point on the globe.[120] When the revised clause reached London, Winant, yet uninformed of the secret promises, telegraphed Hull that one "might suggest that our friend Eden was having his pants traded off." But on further reflection, Winant realized that Bulgaria was relatively insignificant to Britain when compared to interests in Greece and Yugoslavia.[121] Churchill would later inform Eden that "having paid the price we have to Russia for freedom of action in Greece, we should not hesitate to use British troops to support the Royal Hellenic Government."[122] Aware that a Bulgarian peace delegation was already on the way to Moscow and faced with the actual presence of Soviet troops in Bulgaria, few alternatives were available to Winant and Hull. As Eden had perceptively remarked: "What will happen if we stand firm and a complete deadlock is reached? This might result in no armistice being signed. In that case Bulgarian troops would remain on Yugoslav and Greek territory, and Russian troops would continue to occupy Bulgaria. We should have no say in events and the Russians would doubtless ask us to recall our Mission which is just going in. We should certainly gain nothing from this course of action."[123] The sole course left was temporary acquiescence.

When the final draft of the Bulgarian armistice reached London, Winant was instructed by Hull to present identical letters to Gusev and Strang affirming that America's acceptance was provisional, being granted only in view of the arrival of a Bulgarian delegation in Moscow.[124] Thus the struggle for American interests in Bulgaria, now more than a year old, was projected into the postsurrender period. On October 28, the long-awaited and still unsatisfactory armistice with Bulgaria was signed.

The temporary American acceptance of Soviet domination within the proposed Bulgarian control commission reflected the renewed importance of the Balkan military theater and not a diminished concern among State Department planners for Bulgaria's postwar future. Aware of President Roosevelt's preference for subordinating potential and actual rivalries to the more immediate goals of Germany's defeat, Hull's civilian staff informed their Soviet colleagues that at termination of the European war America would demand equal treatment within an truly tripartite control commission. Having taken pains to draft a surrender that would establish democratic government in the sole Balkan state receptive to American influence, the State Department naturally refused to acknowledge a permanently preponderant role to the recently arrived Soviet invaders. The struggle for Bulgaria's future thus entered a new phase in an unanticipated setting replete with Soviet occupying units as the American representatives to the Bulgarian control commission received orders to proceed to Sofia. Yet despite uncertainties, American policy for postsurrender Bulgaria as approved by Secretary Hull and President Roosevelt two months after the Soviet invasion remained true to earlier goals of a democratic future.[125] Thus a primary task for the American delegation to Sofia was to gather sufficient and accurate information on the new Bulgarian situation to allow continued and effective American involvement. With the Soviet penchant for secrecy and in the face of a Communist-led government rapidly consolidating its political power, such an assignment was to prove most difficult.

3 Perceptions of Revolutionary Bulgaria

In the thirteen-month period from initial approval of the OSS plan in the fall of 1943 to the actual occupation by Soviet troops, U.S. postwar planning had been premised upon a Bulgaria administered by the two Western Allies dealing with a friendly cabinet in Sofia dominated by the Bulgarian army. The events of September 1944 abruptly ended assumptions. By the time of the October 28 armistice, a heretofore little-known revolutionary coalition, the Fatherland Front, sat as the government in Sofia. Equally unsettling, the Soviet High Command now dominated both military and political affairs in Bulgaria, reforming the Bulgarian army into an effective force capable of both domestic control and assistance in the continuing drive to expel the Germans from the Balkans. The very chronology of this radically altered situation aroused Western diplomats' suspicions about Moscow's likely goals. The Soviet declaration of war with little advance warning followed by a successful coup d'etat a mere four days later by a leftist Bulgarian alliance in which the Communist party played a conspicuous part prompted unsure speculations as to the future. In starkest terms—although the issue was not formulated in this fashion until later—the question was whether the Soviet invasion and subsequent leftists uprising constituted coincidence or conspiracy.[1] Initially both the State and War departments hesitated to pass firm judgment, but by early 1945 reports from Sofia revealed the pernicious alliance between the Soviet representatives and the new Fatherland Front government. In this three-month period immediate American uncertainties increasingly were replaced by the conviction that Bulgaria would soon once again be a satellite state, but this time in the service of the USSR. As Maynard B. Barnes, the U.S. political representative in Sofia, communicated in early January 1945: "Numerous observers of the political scene here see in the National Committee of the Fatherland Front which is dominated by the prison-hardened and Russian-trained female secretary, Zola Dragoicheva, the instrument that is being fashioned to turn Bulgaria into a Soviet state."[2] As the realities of the new situation were communicated to Washington along with similar reports from other outposts in Hungary and Rumania, a more defensive policy began to emerge in hope of maintaining at least a modicum of Western influence in southeastern Europe in the period from the armistice to the eventual peace. Barnes's prolific reports from Sofia were significant in alerting diplomats in Washington to the changing situation in East-West relations in the period before the Yalta conference. It is to this brief period, crucial for the formulation of Washington's subsequent policy toward Sofia, that the historian must turn in an effort to analyze the degree to which dire predictions of Soviet behavior were grounded in correct understanding of the matters at hand and not merely in the anti-Communist prejudice of the observers. It is not surprising that the plethora of documents, memoirs, and secondary accounts that have appeared in the thirty-five years since the Bulgarian armistice allows greater insight into the evolution of socialist Bulgaria than was possible for American diplomats suddenly thrust into the confusing dynamics of postwar Bulgarian politics. What is surprising, however, is the high degree of accuracy contained in American reports when viewed from the perspective of the 1980s. Even the initial hesitation to assume an identity of interests between the Bulgarian Fatherland Front and the invading Red Army finds affirmation in the initial and cautious Soviet policy on the eve of and during the Fatherland Front revolution.

The Fatherland Front, which assumed power on September 9, 1944, possessed a brief if turbulent history. Its birth was an appeal for unity among center and leftist Bulgarian parties drafted in 1942 in the genre of the common front appeals of the 1930s by the Bulgarian Communist party. By 1943, a loose grouping of Communists, military representatives (Zveno), Social Democrats, and Agrarians—all members of movements with deep roots in prewar Bulgarian politics—had formed, with each group retaining freedom of independent action. That same year, the Central Military Commission of the Bulgarian Communist party, orginally created shortly after the German invasion of the USSR, reorganized into the People's Revolutionary Army of Liberation (NOVA). All existing resistance groups were invited to enter this army, and the nation was divided into military zones, each subordinated to the General Staff concealed in Sofia.[3] Through organizational discipline, size, and functioning military staff, the Communist party dominated this amorphous alliance from the start.[4] The Fatherland Front made some progress toward drafting a common platform in 1943 and 1944, but it became a cohesive opposition group only on the eve of the coup of September 1944.[5] Even the Communist party, a model of unity when compared to fellow Fatherland Front groups, possessed an oft-divided leadership, with a Bureau-in-Emigration under veteran Georgi Dimitrov located in Moscow and a Politbureau and Central Committees functioning in Bulgaria. Communications between the top party bodies was often severed during the war years.

The key that elevated the Fatherland Front to the ranks of a potential contender for power was the Bulgarian cabinet crisis following the successful Soviet invasion of Rumania in August 1944. On August 23, the day the Rumanians withdrew from the war, a gathering of the National Committee of the Fatherland Front resolved to meet with the Bagrianov government to demand a transfer of power into their hands.[6] When Dimo Kazasov, a member of the Fatherland Front with close ties to the military, approached the prime minister, he was greeted with the cry, "God sent you"—a somewhat misplaced assumption. The following day, Bagrianov received a delegation of the Fatherland Front, indicating his readiness to resign. In the ensuing discussion, however, the leader of the Agrarian section of the Front broke ranks, informing the prime minister that a coalition with non-Front members, including even Bagrianov, might be acceptable. Hoping to strengthen his own faltering position by admitting some Front representatives, Bagrianov now announced that only the regency could decide the composition of a new government. On August 27, the regents invited representatives of several political factions for discussions but refused to receive the Fatherland Front delegates except as individuals. Unwilling to chance an additional breach of discipline, the Front delegations withdrew.[7]

While the non-Communist members of the Fatherland Front celebrated their partial victory in receiving official recognition as a possible future government—Kazasov recalled that August 23–24 marked the first time the Front had gained public acknowledgment, including reception by the cabinet—the Bulgarian Communists began a call for tighter discipline. On August 26, one day before the abortive meeting with the regents, the Politbureau authorized dispatch of a circular to all party groups calling for preparation of an armed uprising. The news of Soviet victories to the north certainly played some role in the timing of this appeal, but the Politbureau had been debating such a course for the past three days. The absence of any word from Georgi Dimitrov and the Bureau-in-Emigration in Moscow left the Politbureau uncertain about future Soviet military policy, as was clearly reflected in the circular, which proclaimed that "the fate of Bulgaria today depends *exclusively* on the people and the patriotic army." While calling for popular power, the circular emphasized the need to strengthen district committees of the Fatherland Front and to create additional committees in populated places and in factories. In the main, the appeal was cautious, consistent with the advice sent by Dimitrov in early August: "To proceed to an uprising only when there will be the possibility of combining action from within and without the state."[8] Unknown to the Bulgarian politbureau, Dimitrov himself remained painfully uncertain as to Soviet plans for Bulgaria until early September. A close friend of his in Moscow later recalled: "When it became known that a Bulgarian delegation had left for Cairo [the Moshanov mission of September 1, 1944] to request the English to enter into Bulgaria as confirmed on Radio Khristo Botev and the Bulgarian section of Radio Moscow, G. Dimitrov was asked: 'What is happening?' He did not answer at once, but after several days said: 'Comrade Stalin emphatically told me that no other feet will step into Bulgaria except the feet of the Red Army.' Then the necessary calm came among us."[9]

On August 27, Dimitrov sent a message to the chief of staff of the partisan army affirming the preparatory nature of the present phase of the struggle. All progressive and anti-German forces were to be invited to rally to the Fatherland Front. The soldiers and officers of the Bulgarian army as well as the civilian population should be called upon to open a struggle both against remaining German troops and for creation of a Fatherland Front government: "Take steps at once to secure the free appearance in public of the National Committee [of the Fatherland Front], its parties, groups, an uncensored press, and the liberation of political prisoners."[10] Only the last of six injunctions called vaguely for the people and the Bulgarian armed forces to pass to the side of the Red Army, about whose plans Dimitrov was uncertain.

Dimitrov's message is frequently characterized in Bulgarian historiography as a crucial link in the Bulgarian party's plan to mount an insurrection.[11] Except that Dimitrov began his communication with a call merely for "rallying about the Fatherland Front," current evidence reveals that this message did not arrive until September, by way of liberated territory in Yugoslavia. On August 29, the Bulgarian Politbureau sent a letter to Dimitrov, stating that his communication of August 20 had just arrived from Moscow. "We are still trying to create links with you," the message concluded.[12] Thus in the crucial party policy debate accompanying the demise of the Bagrianov cabinet and concerning the possibility of partial Front entry into a new government, direct information on Soviet intentions was lacking.

The possibility of Front representation in the Bulgarian government, broached by Bagrianov, was confirmed by his designated successor, Konstantin Muraviev, who opened negotiations directly with the Communists. In the days immediately before the formation of the Muraviev cabinet on September 2, the new prime minister met with Communist representatives, promising them three seats in the new government. This new cabinet, Muraviev stated, would fulfill the basic demands of the Communists by nullifying Bulgaria's 1941 accession to the Axis and Anti-Cominten Pacts, rupture of relations with Germany, and a declaration of war on Berlin. According to Tsola Dragiocheva, long-time Politbureau member and key participant in determining Communist strategy, Muraviev's offer of cabinet representation did not extend to the other Fatherland Front parties—a disruptive strategy similar to that attempted by Bagrianov, but with the Communists now identified as the favored group.[13] On the night of September 2, the Muraviev cabinet took power, announcing that negotiations with the Fatherland Front (no longer the Communists alone) would continue and that three seats would be held vacant for them.[14]

Confronted with the possibility of legally joining the new cabinet, albeit in a minority position—an offer the French and Italian Communist parties accepted in the spring of 1944 in their respective countries—but cautious as to Muraviev's true intentions, the Politbureau assembled on September 2 to discuss future policy. A report was presented by party members fresh from meetings with Muraviev, and a decision was reached to hold out for a purely Fatherland Front government. By now, Soviet troops were approaching the Rumanian-Bulgarian border, and the increasing panic evident in official circles augured well for a political atmosphere supportive of a sudden coup even without Soviet assistance. It was resolved to began a general uprising on September 6, a date selected to coincide with an already planned strike by Sofia transportation workers and a September 7 strike in the industrial city of Pernik. Additional support for immediate action arose from apprehensions over loyalist troop movements ordered by the government to defend the capital against a possible German attack. Sofia was designated as the revolutionary center because of the presence of two thousand party members augmented by three thousand adherents of the party's youth organization. According to Politbureau assessments, the potential insurgent forces consisted of twenty thousand partisans, with ten thousand organized into battle groups.[15]

Although some of the battle units had been secretly concentrated in Sofia, the odds against a successful uprising must have seemed staggering to the Politbureau members. The first Sofia division had just been repositioned in a siege deployment about the capital, and the General Staff of the Bulgarian army had moved its headquarters to Sofia. Forces loyal to the government in Sofia and its immediate environs numbered one hundred thousand, supported by fifteen thousand police and gendarmes. Although the presence of Soviet troops just over the frontier promised further to undermine waning military morale, little or no prospect existed for a rapid Soviet march to the distant Bulgarian capital even if war should be declared. The difficult logistics involved in gaining Soviet support give credence to Drag-oicheva's subsequent affirmation that the planned uprising was essentially a domestic initiative designed to exploit growing internal political confusion but without Soviet support: "The Politbureau did not suppose that the Soviet Union would declare war on Bulgaria very soon . . . ; we departed to the decisive assault, relying mainly on the forces of the party and the Fatherland Front, counting on the People's Liberation Army to prove its ability and preparedness to struggle for life and death against the fascist enemy." When, on September 5, the Soviet Union declared war but failed to cross the northern frontier, the Politbureau quickly reconvened to assess this new factor in its already formulated revolutionary plans.[16]

The Soviet decision to declare war on Bulgaria was made only in late August, largely in response to the military opportunities opened by the rapid collapse of Germany's Rumanian front. The possibility of war with Sofia certainly occurred to the Soviet General Staff by mid-summer and Bulgaria's domestic situation was discussed by the military commanders of the Soviet Third Ukranian Front and Georgi Dimitrov. Actual plans for an attack, however, date from the last week of August.[17] On August 22, while the battle for Rumania still raged, General A. I. Antonov, chief of the Soviet General Staff, urgently summoned Marshal G. K. Zhukov to Moscow. Arriving the next day by plane, Zhukov was ordered by the State Committee of Defense (GKO) to prepare the Third Ukranian Front for war with Bulgaria. Taking time to receive a briefing from Dimitrov on the likelihood of Bulgarian resistance, Zhukov departed for the front in the last days of August. By then, the Soviet campaign in eastern Rumania had successfully separated the German units in the Balkans from their comrades in Transylvania and the Carpathians, and Soviet command of air and sea was assured.[18] By early September, the Third Ukranian occupied positions along the Bulgarian border, including three armies and two mechanized corps. On September 3, a total of twenty-eight Soviet divisions and numerous support groups were in position, awaiting orders to advance.[19] The potential adversary, the Bulgarian army, was estimated at five armies and two corps, in total about 450,000 men supported by five air regiments consisting of 410 planes. Because the Bulgarian forces were largely deployed in the central and western parts of the state, two border brigades and two infantry divisions were directly in the path of a possible Soviet advance, with two additional divisions located in secondary defensive positions in north-central and northeast Bulgaria.[20] Although the Bulgarian order of battle suggested a Soviet victory, information on the likelihood of concerted resistance was scarce despite some initial contacts with members of the Bulgarian Communist party who had crossed the border in early September bringing intelligence on the Bulgarian army.[21] Marshal Zhukov concluded after his inspection of the new front that "the situation faced by [Marshal] Tolbukin's [commander of the Third Ukranian Front] forces had not been studied thoroughly enough. Bulgaria was somewhat off to one side from the main highway of the war, and was not formally our enemy, so that we were more familiar with the German forces than with the Bulgarian army." Not until September 4 were operations plans completed, with a tentative jump-off date set for six days later.[22]

Military uncertainty played its part in the Soviet reluctance to mount an immediate offensive, but hope that the new Muraviev government would peacefully offer assistance to the Soviet cause was also important.[23] It should be recalled that the Bulgarian Communist party conducted negotiations with the prime minister up through September 4 in an effort to gain legal authorization for a Fatherland Front government. Negotiations between Soviet and Bulgarian diplomats also continued, culminating on September 3.[24] That day, Muraviev instructed the chief secretary of his foreign ministry to inform the Soviet Embassy that a strict policy of neutrality would henceforth be followed by the Bulgarian government.[25] The Soviet representative, D. G. Iakovlev, in turn, demanded that all German naval and air personnel be interned at once and a detailed list be forwarded to Soviet representatives. The careful Bulgarian response promised the internment but offered only to release details on those German internees who had fled into Bulgaria from Rumania.[26] Aware that German units already were withdrawing from Macedonia, Serbia, and Bulgaria proper, the Muraviev cabinet sought time so as to fortify the capital before making a total break with the Reich. On September 4, Bulgarian units in Macedonia were ordered back inside the border in anticipation of a German attack. That evening, Muraviev informed his cabinet that the Germans had disarmed five Bulgarian divisions along the Serbian frontier. The new minister of war, General Ivan Marinov, immediately ordered a Bulgarian armored brigade to take up a blocking position against an anticipated German thrust toward Sofia, while bringing the already present First Infantry Division to a high state of readiness. Muraviev also informed his cabinet that negotiations with the Fatherland Front were still in process.[27]

The German disarming of Bulgarian units in Serbia now inspired the

Muraviev cabinet to break diplomatic relations with Berlin in preparation for a declaration of war. On the night of September 4 several of the assembled ministers demanded an immediate war declaration but were restrained by the war minister, who reported that the capital would be exposed should the Germans advance from positions in Yugoslavia. To complicate the already strained situation, the cabinet was informed that a new pro-Hitler conspiracy had just been discovered within the Bulgarian army. As it had often done in the past, the cabinet resolved to stall for time in the face of divergent threats incapable of simple resolution. But on this occasion, time had at last run out. On the evening of September 5, while deciding the needed interval before declaring war on Germany, the Muraviev cabinet learned that Moscow had declared war. The badly shaken gathering debated until two the following morning, reaching a consensus that by September 8 loyal units would be in position to ward off a German attack. That day, Bulgaria would declare war on Germany. The Soviet Embassy was immediately informed of the decision, an armistice sought, and Soviet patience requested. That same day, September 6, the cabinet attempted to reopen discussions with the Fatherland Front.[28]

The news of German action against Bulgarian units and the Soviet declaration of war prompted the Bulgarian Communist Politbureau once again to reasses its plans for an uprising. On the night of September 5, the Politbureau resolved to begin the revolution in Sofia on the night of September 8–9 despite continuing uncertainty as to whether Soviet troops would soon enter the country. Early the next morning, the General Staff of the Insurgent Army finally distributed a call to arms. Only on September 7 did the party leadership discover that a Soviet invasion was imminent, a conclusion drawn from leaflets dropped that day by Soviet planes.[29] As Tsola Dragoicheva would later recall: "The appeal of Tolbukhin was an indication for us that units of the Red Army would at any moment enter into the Bulgarian land."[30]

On September 8, the day Bulgaria declared war on Germany, Soviet units crossed the northern frontier. By now, Prime Minister Muraviev's request for an armistice had been transmitted to Moscow, and Stalin, aware of the impending Bulgarian declaration of war on Germany and the prospects for an uprising by the Fatherland Front, commanded the Third Ukranian Front to advance only 180 kilometers into the northern reaches of the country. As General S. M. Shtemenko, chief of the Operations Department of the Soviet army, later recalled "Stalin told him [Zhukov] about the events in Bulgaria and the doings of the insurgents, saying that a popular uprising was imminent and that the time had come for the Muraviev government to make some basic decisions that it should have a care for the future."[31] Thus, at the very moment of invasion, opportunities still existed for the Sofia government to rectify its past mistakes.

All prospects for a lightning Soviet thrust to the capital in defense of the anticipated Fatherland Front uprising were nullified by the removal of key divisions from the Third Ukranian Front on the eve of the invasion, a further indication that the long-term political future of Bulgaria was distinctly secondary in Soviet planning to the present military opportunities. As Sergei Biriuzov, Marshall Tolbukhin's chief of staff and later chief Soviet representative to the Bulgarian control commission recalled: "We, of course, were not able to render Dimitur Ganev [a delegate from the Bulgarian Communist party who visited Tolbukhin's headquarters on September 9, 1944] and his comrades our assistance for the defense of Sofia because at this time our force had been diminished (at the order of the Stavka, the Forty-sixth Army and the Seventh Mechanized Corps had been sent to the Second Ukranian)."[32] A day before the uprising, Stalin, content with Muraviev's declaration of war and unconcerned with the brewing Communist-led uprising, ordered that the Royal Bulgarian Army be allowed to retain its weapons when the armistice was signed.[33] As further confirmation of Moscow's disinterest in the prospects of a socialist Bulgaria, the chief of the main political administration of the Soviet military, General-Colonel A. S. Shcherbakov telephoned General-Colonel Zheltov, chief of the Third Ukranian Front's military council, to demand a policy of strict political noninterference by the Red Army. Zheltov quickly responded that existing directives ensuring no political interference in domestic matters was being followed.[34] Thus, aside from the evident political confusion attending the Soviet invasion, the domestic revolutionary forces were left largely on their own both in toppling the Muraviev government and in defending any gains achieved against a possible German assault on the capital. Not until six days after the Soviet invasion and four days following the successful coup in Sofia did the Soviet High Command order the Thirty-fourth Rifle Corps into the capital. Main Soviet forces continued to bypass Sofia far to the north, moving to the Yugoslav border in preparation for the liberation of Belgrade.[35]

The details of the successful Fatherland Front uprising have already been related in scholarly studies and require but brief review.[36] On September 6, the long-awaited strike by transportation workers threw the capital into confusion, augmented one day later by a coal miner's strike in Pernik and riots in Pleven. In the early hours of September 9, the War Ministry in Sofia was taken without bloodshed by insurgents, and later that morning Kimon Georgiev, the new prime minister, announced formation of a Fatherland Front government. Among the designated sixteen ministers, only four belonged to the Communist party although their responsibilities included the key departments of Interior and Justice. The ministries of War and Foreign Affairs were assigned to followers of Zveno, perhaps in recognition of the crucial influence still possessed by the Bulgarian military. Prime Minister Georgiev, as well, was a Zveno member.[37] In his first order, War Minister Colonel Damian Velchev commanded all insurgent units to enter regular army ranks in preparation for a joint offensive, under Soviet direction, against the common Axis foe.[38] One day later, the first reorganized Bulgarian units took up positions along the Yugoslav border. On September 17, the Bulgarian army was officially subordinated to Tolbukhin's Third Ukranian with General Biriuzov designated as the liasion with the Bulgarian General Staff.[39]

Combat with the German forces remaining in the Balkans now became both the primary goal of the Fatherland Front and the best means to assure Soviet support for the new government.[40] According to Soviet estimates, the Germans and their allies maintained twenty-one divisions, seven brigades, and some twenty-five smaller units in Yugoslavia, Albania, and Greece in early September.[41] In the remaining months of the war, Bulgaria mobilized 450,000 officers and men, with more than 200,000 assigned combat duty under Soviet direction in Serbia and Macedonia.[42]

The need to maintain this sizable military effort in a small country already in the throes of economic and political chaos engendered a dynamic domestic situation in which the consolidation of Fatherland Front rule became a central Soviet objective. By September 1944, Bulgarian industrial production stood at half prewar levels, and grain production had dropped by two-fifths. Inflation had reached disorganizing proportions, accompanied by aggravated class and urban-rural conflict.[43] Even among the new leaders of the Fatherland Front government, strong voices argued that an immediate return to peace was essential for the reconstruction of the economy. General Biriuzov recalled that at his first meeting with the Bulgarian minister of war, he was informed that the army was incapable of future action.[44] It was logical that the occupying Red Army, whose presence in Bulgaria was the result of military opportunities, would throw its weight behind those willing to exert all efforts on behalf of the war effort, supporting any domestic repression required to stabilize the home front. In September, the Red Army issued a general proclamation to the Bulgarian people which pointedly stated: "No transgressions of order, arbitrariness or unlawfulness will be tolerated, and such [acts] will be considered as deeds against the Red Army."[45] Thus from the beginning, the occupying Soviet army cast close glances at the willingness of the new government to maintain domestic order while assisting the war effort, identifying those individuals and groups most supportive of larger Soviet objectives. In short, Soviet policy immediately after September 9 embraced general assistance to all efforts to stablilize the political and social situation in Bulgaria while specifically aiding those elements of the Fatherland Front deemed most trustworthy. Although it may not have been certain from the start, the Bulgarian Communist party was to become the sole repository of Soviet trust in the end. It was into this highly fluid world that the American political and military missions entered in November 1944.

The chief American political representative to Bulgaria, Maynard B. Barnes, arrived in Sofia on November 19. A longtime veteran of the Department of State, assigned his first foreign mission in 1919, Barnes was at the climax of a distinguished twenty-five career in which he had held important positions in several prewar Balkan states including two years in Sofia and a term as assistant chief of the Division of Near Eastern Affairs.[46] A man of strong feelings, Barnes had little doubt that America was to play a major role in returning Bulgaria to a postwar democratic position. He later explained his initial assumptions to George Kennan's class at the National War College: "For example, we started the negotiations with Bulgaria—we, the United States—for an armistice. We started them in August, 1944. We were the ones who brought Bulgaria to the point where she sought an armistice. Russia was still hundreds of miles away. We and the British had gone in and blown Sofia not to bits, but we had destroyed twenty-five percent of it."[47] Rarely at a loss for words, Barnes quickly informed the Soviet chariman of the control commission, Biriuzov, of his apprehensions about likely Soviet policy:

> They were very frank talks, and one day he [Biriuzov] said to me, "Barnes, why is it you are so hostile to Russia and to our interests in Bulgaria?" I said, "well, I don't think that is the right way to put it. It is not that I am hostile, but let me tell you of my own personal experience." I then told him that I left Paris in 1941, and from the United States . . . I went to Reykjavik. I said, "if you had spent six months in Reykjavik, you would understand how deep my feelings must be." We had to go there because we had to

find ways of getting across the Atlantic. Anyway, from Reyk-
javik I went to Dakar. We went there to get some ships away
from the French . . . [and] it was necessary to fly to Miami, than
all down through the Caribbean, ending up in Natal. . . . I said,
"General, you see all of that was imposed on us by the fact that
Italy had cut the Mediterranean in two. Now what the hell is
going to happen to us when Russia does the same thing, and that
is why you are in Bulgaria. You have an explanation now of what
my feelings are and why.[48]

Following this exchange, neither Biriuzov nor the contemporary historian can have any question about Barnes's view concerning Soviet
responsibility for the deterioration of East-West relations. Although
Biriuzov's more subdued exterior prevented a similar response his
memoirs leave no doubt that Barnes's distaste for him was fully re-
ciprocated: "Barnes was a typical American bourgeois; expansive and
assertive."[49]

In political dealings Barnes held authority over all other American
representatives, including those assigned to the control commission as
authorized in an executive order issued by President Roosevelt in
1942.[50] Unlike the heads of the Soviet and British delegations, Barnes
was not included in the membership of the commission despite his
superior position. The reasoning behind this strange exception derived
from an American suspicion that Soviet leadership in the commission
would preclude all ties with the Bulgarian government except at the
behest of the Soviet chairman. By remaining outside the formal structure of the Control Commission, Barnes was free to approach the new
government on his own initiative.[51]

Although Barnes was undoubtedly familiar with the numerous policy suggestions for Bulgaria drafted during 1944, his final instructions
included a lengthy statement of American goals approved by the State
Department Policy Committee in November and sent to the president.
Among the five points, the key political purpose of the State Department representatives in the Balkans was identified as "the right of
peoples to choose for themselves without outside interference the type
of political, social, and economic systems they desire so long as they
conduct their affairs in such a way as not to menace the peace and
security of others."[52] Given the growing Soviet dominance in Bulgaria, Barnes had his work cut out for him.

The head of the American military delegation and official representative to the Allied Control Commission was Major General John A.
Crane. His knowledge of Bulgarian affairs had been gained during

prewar tours as military attaché in Istanbul and Sofia. Since Barnes and Crane had served together in Bulgaria during the 1930s, Barnes requested Crane's appointment "so as to be assured of a congenial colleague."[53] Crane, who arrived in Sofia on November 26, was initially authorized a support staff of eleven officers, one warrant officer, and thirty enlisted men.[54] A letter of instruction from the War Department specified that the primary purpose "of the Allied Control Commission is the regulation and control, under the general direction of the Soviet High Command, acting on behalf of the Allied Powers, of the fulfillment of the Armistice with Bulgaria." In his position as American representative, Crane could expect to make frequent tours outside Sofia to ensure compliance with the armistice. Additional instructions on American policy would be communicated "from time to time" by the U.S. chief of staff. In political matters, the authority of the State Department as represented by Barnes was to be respected.[55] In addition to his major function as representative on the Control Commission, Crane's responsibilities included the supervision of an extensive intelligence and reporting system.[56]

The man destined to be the American nemesis during the ensuing several years was General-Colonel Sergei Biriuzov, the chief of staff of Soviet Marshal Tolbukhin's Third Ukranian Front. A forty-year-old career officer, Biriuzov had entered the Red Army during the Russian Civil War, receiving his education at a makeshift workers' university and subsequently at the prestigious Frunze Institute. In political knowledge Biriuzov was vastly inferior to both Barnes and Crane because of his limited exposure to the realities of Bulgaria. He later confessed: "I myself also felt deeply the scarcity of my knowledge about Bulgaria. When I began to think about it, then I recalled the usual information taught in one's school days—about the majestic mountains, the picturesque rivers, the forests in which ran the noble deer, roe, badgers and fierce boars."[57] Biriuzov's lack of political training in general and his limited understanding of the domestic Bulgarian situation in particular provides additional evidence that military objectives remained uppermost during the initial stages of the Bulgarian occupation. He arrived in Sofia before Barnes and more than a month before the signing of the Bulgarian armistice. By the time the Americans arrived, Biriuzov's staff consisted of four generals, one rear admiral, more than one hundred officers, and a large group of civilians: a total of 270 people.[58]

The initial three months of interaction between the American representatives and the large Soviet mission were crucial in providing some assessment of the changing Bulgarian situation to an anxious State Department yet uncertain of Soviet intentions. The numerous cables from Sofia to Washington touched on many issues, but three general themes dominate the transmissions, each complete with supporting evidence. These were that the Allied Control Commission was not functioning with Western participation, but had become an adjunct to the Soviet High Command; the Bulgarian provisional government of the Fatherland Front was a façade behind which the Bulgarian Communists, with Soviet aid, were achieving domination; and the Soviets and their Communist allies were converting the Bulgarian army into a pliant tool on behalf of socialist objectives. It would be largely upon the perceptions contained in these reports that the State Department would formulate a specific set of policies designed to promote Bulgaria's postwar democratic future.

In early December, Barnes reported on the activities of the control commission: "Certainly to date, the ACCION Bulgaria insofar as it may be said to have any reality, is in no way a cooperative body—it is nothing more than a section of the headquarters of Marshal Tolbukhin's Sofia Chief-of-Staff, who, at the same time is the commanding officer of Russia's 37th army." A week later, Barnes again informed the secretary of state that the Allied Control Commission existed in name only and was actually part and parcel of the Russian military command.[59] In these two reports, Barnes had grasped the essence of the control commission despite his restricted sources of information.

The organic linkage between the Soviet command and the Soviet-dominated control commission arose naturally from events preceding Barnes's arrival in Sofia. The Soviet Third Ukranian Front entered Bulgaria on September 8, 1944, and it was to this group that the provisional Bulgarian government formed on September 9 dispatched an armistice delegation.[60] Fearful that German units retreating from Greece might launch a strike against Sofia, General Biriuzov left for the Bulgarian capital on a mission to ensure close cooperation between Soviet and Bulgarian military forces.[61] On September 17, the provisional Bulgarian government placed its army under the direct control of Tolbukhin, with Biriuzov to function as the sole liasion between the two armies.[62] Thus in the key activity of the period—warfare—Biriuzov established dominance over the new Bulgarian government. The pattern of Soviet military control in Sofia was determined.

Outside the capital, the Soviet occupation authorities established in each Bulgarian administrative district and major city as early as September 10 became the basis for subsequent orders by the control commission designed to ensure compliance with the October 28 armistice. There is little evidence of personnel changes in the districts after establishment of the control commission except for appointment of new regional Soviet military commanders during the month of November.[63] These Soviet regional authorities, in cooperation with local Communist-dominated political committees, maintained law and order, ferreted out "bourgeois-fascist" groups, and conducted security checks together with newly formed local militias. The best Bulgarian study to date of these administrative bodies fails to mention a change in purpose following establishment of the Allied Control Commission: "At the end of 1944 (November–December), the ACC and its empowered apparatus began to fulfill their function. And insofar as the commissions were led by high Soviet officers, their functions in essence were a natural continuation of the activities of the Soviet military command."[64] The exact nature and activities of these regional authorities were unknown to Barnes because U.S. representatives were unable to travel beyond Sofia without the approval of Soviet members of the control commission. An added, perhaps superfluous, Soviet order forbade citizens in the regional districts to spread "anti-Soviet rumors" or to relate information concerning disposition and strengths of Soviet forces.[65]

At the end of October 1944, General Biriuzov was informed by Tolbukhin that he would head the Allied Control Commission. Thus Biriuzov continued his direct ties with the Soviet military both through his rank and reporting channels and his simultaneous appointment as commander of the Soviet Thirty-seventh Division deployed in Bulgaria as a strategic reserve.[66] Although Biriuzov kept separate physical headquarters for each of his responsibilities, there are no indications that he discerned any distinctions between his roles.[67]

Biriuzov's main tasks, as he later described them, fell broadly into three categories. Administratively, the Allied Control Commission had to organize a reliable defense of the frontiers. As time would show, this "defense" increasingly was used to restrict the entry of Western representatives into Bulgaria, a task unlikely to lend itself to tripartite participation. With respect to military and political goals, Biriuzov saw his purpose as supervision of the Bulgarian transition from war to peace and purification of the Bulgarian military from fascist elements. Last, but not least, the economic mission of the commission was to study all capital investments and to transfer all industrial objects belonging to the enemy into the hands of the Soviet Union.[68] The latter objective achieved the greatest short-run success. In the first weeks following the armistice, 170 German enterprises located on Bulgarian soil, about 4 billion leva in capital, and 25 Hungarian enterprises were transferred to Soviet control, in addition to earlier assignment of German and foreign ships found in Bulgarian ports.[69]

The arrival of the American and British representatives to the control commission and the successful Soviet advance through Yugoslavia soon presented a new set of problems for the Soviet leaders. Aware that several parties within the Fatherland Front coalition were demanding a return to peacetime domestic conditions in the face of gigantic tasks of economic reconstruction and fearing Western support for such aims, Biriuzov added a political component to his direction of the commission designed to assist Communist calls for continued austerity until completion of the war against Germany:

> And above all, it was necessary somehow to discover in our work the main link. I saw it in the harsh struggle with the fascist aspirations of the reactionary bourgeois groups. We had no right not to aid the Bulgarian people quickly to crush these reptiles.
>
> We had no doubt that they [the Western representatives on the ACC] would try to hinder the establishment of democratic order in Bulgaria. Thus [we had to] knock the stick out of the hands of our "partners" which they, at every turn, tried to insert into the wheel of history.[70]

The executive staff of the Allied Control Commission, exclusively Soviet, consisted of a group of military and political advisers divided into a series of functional sections. These included military, naval, aviation, economics, military transport, signal, and security.[71] The normal daily flow of action involved discussions between Biriuzov and his chief assistant, A. I. Cherepanov, or with section heads, resolution of any existing problems, and sending a daily report to General Major Suchkov, who was charged with informing the Western representatives of decisions.[72] According to Barnes, however, little information ever escaped the closed circle of Soviet advisers.

Liaison between the Soviet executive staff of the ACC and the Bulgarian government was maintained through a special commissariat established on November 9 and attached to the Bulgarian Ministry of Foreign Affairs. Its task was to ensure compliance with the terms of the armistice and to study protests concerning nonfulfillment.[73] Since the Bulgarian minister of foreign affairs, Petko S. Stainov, was not a member of the reliable Bulgarian Communist party, and hence was suspected of maintaining ties with the West, Biriuzov took steps to ensure the absence of Western input in the process of Bulgarian compliance. Biriuzov informed the Bulgarian prime minister, Georgiev, by letter that "all appeals [*Vsiakakovi obrushteniia*] to the Bulgarian Government from other individuals of the Allied Control Commission, including the representatives of the Allied States are forbidden. The receiving and settling of issues which bypass the Directorship of the

ACC will be ignored by the Directorship of the Allied Control Commission.[74]

General Biriuzov's letter, which remained unknown to his Western "colleagues," precluded all effective communication between Barnes and either the liasion commissariat or individual members of the Bulgarian government about fulfillment of the armistice conditions. Since Western representatives were not present in the ACC sections and very few full ACC meetings were held, armistice enforcement and political reconstruction became a unique Soviet activity. By late December 1944, the British dimly perceived that some sort of secret Soviet-Bulgarian arrangement existed and took a somewhat unorthodox step to combat it. Having changed the letterhead on their stationery to read "The British Section *of* the Allied Control Commission," they attempted to communicate with the Bulgarian liasion group as if a member of the ACC directorship. On December 18, 1944, Biriuzov, not receptive to this touch of genius, informed the British mission that it was in violation of the armistice and demanded that the letterhead be changed back to "The Representative of the United Kingdom *in* the ACC."[75] This struggle between the British and Biriuzov engendered the first Western suspicion that Eden had undermined the armistice provisions in Moscow.[76]

Free from any checks or balances or from effective criticism, the Soviet members of the ACC continued to interpret the armistice as they saw fit. Not surprisingly, a number of their actions were directed not against alleged Bulgarian fascists but against the Western missions. The aviation section of the ACC concentrated upon controlling the flights of Western diplomats who were suspected of importing contraband and propaganda, believing that "from the first days of the ACC, they attempted by various means to transport into Bulgaria illegally their films, and even to deliver weapons and supplies for their agents." The administrative section of the ACC focused its attention on control of visas and worked closely with the Communist minister of the interior, Anton S. Yugov, concerned because "the English and Americans tried in those days to flood Bulgaria with all sorts of speculators, political and trade adventurists."[77]

Given the awesome, well-organized Soviet administration which confronted him and whose details he but vaguely knew, Barnes's frustrations over the malfunctioning of the ACC continued to grow. In late 1944, he informed Washington once more that his position was untenable. According to Barnes, the Bulgarian minister of foreign affairs had just expressed his regrets about a recent ACC decision not to restore postal relations between Bulgaria and the United States. The foreign minister registered surprise when informed by Barnes that the American mission had not been consulted on a matter that directly concerned American policy.[78]

Barnes's rage over the operations of the Soviet-dominated Allied Control Commission was shared by his military colleague, General Crane. At the initial ACC meeting, Crane was informed by Chairman Biriuzov that only Soviet delegates might deal with the Bulgarian government on fulfillment of armistice conditions. American and British activities would be restricted to presenting the views of their respective governments to the ACC so that the Soviet chairman "could press such points with the Bulgarian government *if he saw fit.*" At the second meeting in early December, Crane again was told that all decisions lay with the chairman or his deputy. In addition, Soviet officers must accompany inspection tours outside Sofia by American and British delegates. Crane angrily informed the War Department, "ACC Bulgaria is not yet operating as a Commission in any way. Everything done in its name is at Russian dictation without any reference to myself or [General] Oxley [Chief British military representative]." On December 13, Crane cabled that the deputy Chairman of the ACC, A. I. Cherepanov, refused to share information on orders given in the name of the tripartite commission: "He informed me that no orders had been issued by the ACC nor any action taken in his name. I know this not to be." To add insult to injury, Crane noted that he was unable to leave Sofia without an escort and that unaccompanied trips to the Sofia airport were prohibited.[79]

On December 27, Barnes and Crane invited both Biriuzov and his deputy, Cherepanov, to dinner in an attempt to ascertain firsthand the causes for deteriorating relations. In a wide-ranging conversation, Biriuzov expressed regrets for the limits on American travel, pleading that they were necessary because of suspicious activities by the British representatives. Biriuzov also apologized for his past failure to separate his function as ACC chairman from that of commanding general of Soviet forces in Bulgaria—a distinction long sought by the Americans.[80] At the next meeting of the ACC the following day, Cherepanov confirmed Biriuzov's pledge to separate the Soviet functions. Encouraged, Crane reported that this meeting was "the first to be held in a spirit of actual cooperation. . . . In addition, a schedule of ACC weekly or tri-monthly meetings will be established for the first quarter 1945." Unknown to Crane, however, Biriuzov had decided to suspend all ACC meetings despite Cherepanov's pledge. Restrictions upon American travel also remained in place. In February 1945, Crane reported the total absence of ACC meetings since December, dismally concluding: "At this end the existence of any American interest or sympathy is not apparent and American prestige here is at its lowest. Old friends of America here frequently state and with sadness: 'America has let us down and turned us over to the Russians lock, stock and barrel,' and this seems to be a fact."[81]

The implied criticism of Washington's policy contained in Crane's message in part reflected his recent discovery of details surrounding the secret Eden-Molotov discussions on Bulgaria at the mid-October Moscow conference. In January 1945, the British political representative, Willian E. Houstoun-Boswall, shared the secret with his American colleagues. The distraught Barnes quickly informed Washington: "The fact that in his letter of October 15 to Molotov, Mr. Eden said that he would not 'insist on the British and American representatives being seated in the Control Commission' before the conclusion of an armistice with Germany, would seem to justify the 'Soviet' as distinct from 'Allied' character of the operations of the Control Commission in Bulgaria to date."[82] Crane's report to the War Department was equally disheartened. Recounting that he had arrived in Bulgaria with only a copy of the armistice for reference, he had assumed that this document set forth the entire understanding with Bulgaria and had acted on that assumption. The just discovered secret understanding, however, apparently nullified all past efforts to achieve true tripartite control in Bulgaria.[83] Barnes and Crane refused to be consoled despite a disclaimer from Acting Secretary of State Joseph C. Grew, which noted that any secret British-Soviet agreement placed no restrictions on America, and a cable from George Kennan in Moscow, who had signed the Bulgarian armistice in October, which stated that it was his understanding that American representatives would take their seats in the commission as regular members.[84] Although abstract principles of legality supported the State Department's position, the reality of the situation in Sofia and the absence of effective means of rectification confirmed once again the Soviet domination of the Allied Control Commission.

In a message to the secretary of state soon after his arrival in Sofia, Barnes suggested that the current Bulgarian government, dominated by the Fatherland Front, was a prisoner of the Bulgarian Communist party. A month later, he reiterated his bleak warning and noted that true political power in Bulgaria lay in the National Committee of the Fatherland Front under its Communist chairman Tsola Dragoicheva. Important resolutions promising major political changes were increasingly coming from regional Fatherland Front committees.[85] Although history was to support the general outlines of Barnes's assessment, his restricted access to information prevented him from grasping the specific dynamics of the ongoing socialist reconstruction, especially with regard to areas outside Sofia, where the majority of the population lived and which were restricted for Western representatives.

The Fatherland Front, which seized power in Sofia on September 9, 1944, was a coalition of four Bulgarian political parties formed two years earlier. The largest party, the Agrarian, represented a solid tradition of rural politics dominant in prewar Bulgaria. The Social Democrats and the representatives of the military, Zveno, enrolled a more limited, specialized following. Only the Communist party, whose membership was between fifteen and twenty-five thousand on September 9, could claim close ideological affiliation with the most important occupying power. Among the sixteen ministers appointed in the new provisional government, only four were Communists. Communist dominance, however, was judged assured by retention of the key ministries of Justice and Interior, the latter being the most important. As the official history of the party notes: "During the practical decision of questions, the leading principle was the line of maximum unity of all truly democratic and patriotic forces, although the leading role of the Communist Party was maintained. For this purpose, it [the Party] retained for itself the directorship of the Interior Ministry upon which all depended for the internal order and security of the state."[86] The entrenched position of the Bulgarian Communists and their willingness to subordinate domestic interests to the military goals of the Red Army quickly made them indispensable allies of the Soviet authorities. As Biriuzov's deputy later recalled: "An inestimable help for us was the fraternal aid of the workers of the Central Committee of the BWP (k), the Fatherland Front, and the People's Democratic State apparatus. They knew well the true political features of all leading activists of the parties composing the Fatherland Front, and foresaw many of the maneuvers of the opposition, and the possible vacillations of the temporary allies of the Communist party. In a word, they were our political compass."[87]

Even before the arrival of the American mission, the Fatherland Front had taken measures to ensure formation of a people's democracy. In early October, the national police were abolished and replaced with a militia subordinated to the Communist minister of interior. More than thirty thousand police officials were fired; most were replaced by Communists or Communist supporters.[88] In the spring of 1945, assured of effective control over the means of coercion and of Soviet support, the provisional government issued its draconic law in defense of peoples' power. Under its provisions, the death penalty was prescribed for creation of or participation in conspiratorial organizations that aimed at overthrowing "people's power." Varying terms in prison awaited those who employed propaganda against the state, as well as anyone who did not surrender suspects. Possession of weapons and spreading rumors were proscribed. Harkening back to earlier Soviet codes, the new regulations assigned heavy penalties for frustration of industrial production and spoiling foodstuffs.[89] The backdrop for these new regulations was a massive war crimes trial in which the leading cabinet ministers of pre-September 9 governments were convicted and executed along with former members of the parliament. In total, nearly three thousand were condemned to death.

While the events in the capital offered ample indication that Bulgaria's political future would have little in common with the Atlantic Charter, changes outside Sofia were even more disheartening. The day after the September 9 coup, local committees of the Fatherland Front formed throughout Bulgaria. If Communist domination of the Front remained partially concealed in Sofia, the membership of local committees left no doubt as to where power actually lay. Of the 7,292 committees in existence during December 1944, the Communist party, with more than fourteen thousand members, possessed more than twice the representation of its closest rival, the Agrarians. Besides the many committees at the territorial level, counterparts existed in the ministries, enterprises, and various state institutions.[90] These groups exercised control and supervision over regional governments and economic institutions. Their key importance can be gleaned from a recent history of the Bulgarian Communist party:

> The committees of the Fatherland Front had the right to present candidates for appointment or to recall representatives from city and village municipal councils, regional administrations, and district directorships. They had responsibility for cleaning the state apparatus in the cities and countryside from fascists, and for filling it with employees loyal to people's power. They fulfilled an important economic function. They determined the size of the requisition and the work detail, organized the supply of provisions to the population, maintained social control over production and distribution, etc. The committees of the Fatherland Front were seen as the actual organs of Peoples Power in the entire economic, political and cultural life of the state.[91]

A continuing problem in completing major economic and political changes in the countryside was the domination of nonsympathetic, nonsocialist groups in the population. The most recent party history admits that in 1944, "the petit [*drebnata*] bourgeoisie, representatives of the lower-middle-class village and landowners and artisans, were the predominant part of the population."[92] Because resistance was both anticipated and discovered, the reformed militia units saw extensive duty. Their ability sometimes proved inadequate, however, and nearby Soviet troops were employed. In the Varna district, Soviet intelligence units were used to discover a group of administrators who had attempted to flee toward Turkey. In the large regional center of Sliven, officers from the local garrison resisting the authority of the Fatherland Front were disarmed by Soviet troops. In April 1945, in what appears as a major deviation from the normal low profile showed by the Soviet occupation forces in their "cleansing" of Bulgarian society, Aleksandr Cherepanov, General Biriuzov's main assistant, visited the city of Plovdiv to meet with the Fatherland Front. As a contemporary Bulgarian writer has noted: "At this meeting, General Cherepanov testified that in the name of the ACC, he and his co-workers wished to verify how the purifying [*chistkata*] of the state apparatus from fascist and pro-fascist elements was being fulfilled."[93]

Unable to travel outside of Sofia, Barnes and the American mission heard only vague reports of provincial changes. Yet these were sufficient to support the growing conviction of an evil plot designed to ensure total Communist domination.

In early December 1944, Barnes informed his secretary of state of a recent dispute within the Bulgarian army, prophetically noting that settlement to the advantage of the Communist would seriously hinder further efforts of democratic groups to influence state policy: "If the army, or that portion of it left in Bulgaria can be brought into line with 'the will of the people,' no serious obstacle to the completion of the September revolution should exist." A week later, still unclear as to the nature of the crisis that just had ended, Barnes grasped the significance of its resolution: "In view of the above [a reference to recent army reorganization] it would seem foodhardy to believe that democratic elements in Bulgaria may hope for support from the army in whatever resistance these elements may place against efforts of the Communist to gain political mastery in this country."[94] What was the background and nature of this upheavel whose result Barnes perceived without understanding its dynamics?

From the initial days of the Soviet invasion, control over the large Bulgarian army assumed a central position in the plans of the USSR and its local allies. Biriuzov, it will be recalled, first entered Sofia with the expressed intent of subordinating all Bulgarian units to the Red Army. Soviet officers were dispatched to Bulgarian units as advisers and instructors, with the goal of improving both the moral and physical capability of the new ally.[95] Use of Bulgarian contingents in the continuing struggle against the Germans was of great importance—339,000 Bulgarians were involved in the final phase of the war—but of equal concern was the army's support of anticipated socialist reconstruction. The latter task became a key goal of the Bulgarian Communist party.

Shortly after September 9, military committees were formed by the party at various levels within the army, functioning to instill a new sense of patriotic pride and to aid in removing officers targeted by the revolutionary government. According to an order issued by Major General Ivan Ivanov of the Communist-led partisan army, "Any officer who tries to undermine the prestige of the Fatherland Front [is to be] arrested at once and transferred to the corresponding authority. Anyone who opposes the decisions of the government and does not fulfill commands [is to be] . . . shot on the spot." To assist the military committees "inquiry commissions" were attached to division staffs, maintaining liasion with the regional Communist party and committees of the Fatherland Front.[96]

The purge begun by these committees soon reached every military level. All commanders were replaced as were all chiefs of staff in division districts, all division commanders, brigade commanders, and two-thirds of regimental, battalion, and company commanders. By the end of 1944, about eight hundred officers had been purged, including forty-two generals. Leaders of the prerevolutionary partisan movement, former political prisoners, and Bulgarians returning with the Red Army were set in their place.[97]

If the army purge was the negative moment in efforts to ensure control over the military, its positive counterpart was the swift adoption of the Soviet system of dual command. At the order of the party Central Committee on the very day of the September 9 uprising, the first political officers entered army ranks. On September 20, the function of the "assistant commander" was formalized and expanded by government order. According to the most authoritative recent study of this new institution, all assistant commanders were designated by the party Central Committee, the district and regional party committees, and the Communist Youth League although appointment technically lay with the government: "The fundamental task of the assistant commander set by the Central Committee of the BWP (k) was to introduce into the army Marx-Leninist ideology while eradicating the results and final remnants of bourgeois ideology and halting efforts for its revival. These tasks could be decisively determined only by members of the

BWP (k) and the assistant commanders were picked exclusively from Party ranks."[98]

This *gleichschaltung* in the Bulgarian army undoubtedly would have drawn protests from the American mission had it been perceived. It was followed closely and with concern by the non-Communist minister of war, Damian Velchev. As a representative of the Zveno party, a group representing former officers and nationalistic politicians, Velchev was compelled to retard the pace of military reorganization. On September 14, he issued an order restricting the arrests of army personnel.[99] One month later, Velchev emphasized the importance of considering an officer's war record and bravery when pondering his future use in the military.[100] Such limited intervention, however, failed to stem the increasing tide of arrests and replacements.

On November 23, the non-Communist members of the Council of Ministers met in secret to discuss the continuing military purge. Without informing their four Communist colleagues or the National Committee of the Fatherland Front—the political umbrella of the four coalition parties—the assembled ministers passed Resolution Four. Under this order, all officers, noncommissioned officers, and enlisted personnel currently under indictment might, if they wished, be detailed to the front for combat. Those subsequently wounded or decorated would be absolved of guilt. Prosecution of men at the front would be suspended.[101]

When the decision of the non-Communist ministers was discovered, an immediate motion of censure was passed by the Bulgarian Communist party Central Committee, and mass rallies of protest were organized. On December 7, 150,000 people assembled at party request in Sofia to demand that the resolution be canceled.[102] But since a quorum had been present at the clandestine gathering of ministers, the Communists realized that outside help was required. Shortly after discovering the offending resolution, leaders of the Bulgarian party rushed to the Soviet authorities, interrupting a meeting between Cherepanov and the chief Soviet political counsel, Lavrishchev.[103] General Biriuzov was absent from the control commission, visiting Soviet military units in the provinces. In the middle of the night, Cherepanov reached him by phone, relating that "in Sofia, conditions are at maximum tension."[104]

Biriuzov's response was prompt and to the point. Cherepanov was instructed to prepare a document in the name of the Bulgarian prime minister, Georgiev, which would include a demand to his fellow ministers to revoke the resolution in question: "Tell him to come to the ACC and give him the paper with an oral warning that this matter must not be delayed."[105] Biriuzov left at once for Sofia, meeting the surprised Georgiev to reconfirm his warning. Aware of the forces mobilized against them, the non-Communist ministers reluctantly revoked the resolution. The army, a major means of coercion and source of promotion and recognition, was safely under Soviet and Communist control.

The first three months following the October armistice clearly were of great significance in creating the impression of a Soviet–Bulgarian Communist–Fatherland Front conspiracy designed to reject all of America's careful plans for a postwar pro-Western, democratic Bulgaria. In his numerous reports to Washington, Barnes expressed increasing outrage and pessimism about activities he believed were designed to convert Bulgaria into satellite status. Although his cables frequently missed the nuances of the domestic political upheaval, the result of restrictions on American and British travel outside the capital, his basic insights are substantiated in history. Barnes's notion that a carefully drafted master design was guiding the evolution of Bulgaria into a Soviet satrap, however, was in error. He mentioned this idea to his counterpart, Biriuzov; apparently he saw analogies to the behavior of fascist Italy. In fact, Soviet policy was in a state of flux, initially premised upon the need for Bulgarian participation in the war and furthered by the pliability of the Bulgarian Communist party. Much remained to be considered and done before Communist domination of the Fatherland Front was guaranteed. Although a Soviet demand for a reorganization of domestic politics was evident in the three months following the armistice, no proof exists that Bulgaria, as it emerged in 1947, was the preordained goal of Soviet activities. Both the domestic and international situations were too fluid for final Soviet plans. By the end of 1944, non-Communist parties representing more moderate Bulgarian politics were also consolidating, and each, in turn, required a specific and well-chosen response. As time would show, 1945 brought considerable planning and speculation both in Moscow and Washington in an effort to establish clear objectives capable of guiding revolutionary Bulgaria toward various possible futures. The Soviet Red Army held the key to Bulgaria's future, but there remained much to be done and uncertainty as to what the future might hold.

4 Yalta and the Postponement of Elections

The final months of 1944 ushered in a period of renewed American uncertainty concerning Soviet policy in southeastern Europe during the remaining days of the war. Hugh De Santis titles his chapter covering this period "Distress Signals in Eastern Europe."[1] Even before the arrival of Maynard Barnes in Sofia, other U.S. representatives abroad cautioned that Soviet military victories portended harsher demands and more stringent rules against states occupied by the Red Army. In September, George Kennan, chargé in Moscow, warned: "People at home would find Soviet words and actions easier to understand if they would bear in mind the character of Russian aims in Eastern and Central Europe. Russian efforts in this area are directed to only one goal: power. The form this takes, the methods by which it is achieved: these are secondary questions."[2] The following month, Kennan reported indications of "a great pincers movement of Soviet military, political and cultural penetration through the Balkans."[3] In early November Edward Stettinius; acting secretary of state, informed diplomats overseas of continuing reports of Soviet intervention within the domestic affairs of occupied Rumania; these reports were soon confirmed by arriving U.S. political representatives in Bucharest.[4]

The angry, disheartened, and frequent cables flowing from Barnes in Sofia after his arrival in late November would, at first glance, appear to be a portion of this general expression of concern. But in fact, they played a much more important role. Bulgaria formed a unique part of America's initial plans for postwar southeastern Europe. Although the situation in Rumania generated concern, the United States had long acknowledged its lesser interest in that nation's future.[5] Neither Yugoslavia nor Greece was scheduled to possess control commissions or tripartite supervision, and the armistice for Hungary was yet to be concluded. Continuing disputes over the future of Poland remained of utmost importance in assessing Russia's willingness to abide by the spirit of general understandings as to the postwar future of Eastern Europe, but the absence of specific agreements and of an American mission reporting from Warsaw made determination of Soviet intentions there most difficult. Only in Bulgaria were U.S. and Soviet missions, each motivated by different conceptions of this nation's future, fated to engage in day-to-day interaction in support of increasingly divergent goals. Reconciliation of such disputes here might provide unique insight into the possibility of postwar harmony among the Great Powers. As the State Department's "Briefing Book" prepared for the Yalta Conference succinctly noted, "The present stage through which Bulgaria is passing is of great importance not only because of its probable future influence on the Balkans generally but also because Bulgaria in certain respects is the testing ground in the relations of the three principle Allies."[6] Such sentiments were fully consistent with the role and importance Barnes ascribed to his reporting station. "As matters go here," Barnes cabled in late December, "certainly will they go in Yugoslavia and probably also in Hungary."[7]

Confronted by the specter of augmented Soviet "military, political, and cultural penetration through the Balkans" as suggested by George Kennan, the State Department began preparations to safeguard long-expressed American interests in the region. On October 25, 1944, the Policy Committee carefully listened to a report by Ambassador Harriman, just returned from Moscow. According to Harriman, the recent conference between Churchill and Stalin "agree[d] that the Soviets should have a free hand in Rumania, Hungary and Bulgaria during the war."[8] In the ambassador's presence, a draft directive specifying abiding U.S. interests in Eastern and southeastern Europe was offered for discussion in the Policy Committee, receiving its final approval two weeks later. Although the committee remained unaware of the secret Eden-Molotov agreement precluding American participation in the Bulgarian Allied Control Commission during the war against Germany, Harriman's report inspired it to distinguish carefully between the interests of the United States and those of her Allies in the region. The resulting policy recommendation forwarded to the president on November 8 began with the admonition: "While the Government of the United States is fully aware of the existence of problems between Great Britain and the Soviet Union, this Government should not assume the attitude of supporting either country against the other. Rather, this Government should assert the independent interests of the United States."

The specific policy directives, subsequently forwarded to U.S. representatives in Eastern Europe, were divided into six sections. With an eye toward both Soviet and British pretensions of power, the first point confirmed U.S. policy in support of "the right of peoples to choose and maintain for themselves without outside interference the type of political, social, and economic system they desire, so long as they conduct their affairs in such a way as not to menace the peace and security of others." Additional directives affirmed equality of economic opportunity, the right of foreign news correspondents to enter and to transmit information without hindrance, freedom for American philanthropic and educational organizations to conduct their activities, general protection for American citizens and legitimate economic rights, and the longstanding U.S. demand that territorial settlements be reserved for the postwar peace conference.[9]

The drafting and approval of this Policy Committee document constituted a first stage in the determination to ensure protection of America's interests in the Balkans. Logically, such expressions of policy would require some means for implementation and guarantee of these interests, a task that was to prove difficult. By the start of 1945, such goals were tightly bound up with preparations for the Yalta Conference and specifically with the formation of an emergency high commission for Europe.

The genesis of the State Department's efforts to form a high commission has been tied to President Roosevelt's State of the Union Message of early 1945. According to Curtis Martin, the passage that lent support to already existing State Department intentions of ensuring a democratic evolution in postwar Eastern Europe was the president's pledge that "during the interim period until conditions permit a genuine expression of the people's will, we and our Allies have *a duty which we cannot ignore,* to use our influence to the end that no temporary or provisional authorities in the liberated countries block the eventual exercise of the people's right freely to choose the government and the institutions under which, as free men, they are to live."[10] Here, for the first time, the president spoke of an obligation to ensure the benefits of democratic government to liberated and former satellite states, benefits which reports from diplomats in Eastern Europe now suggested were increasingly problematical. Although the context of the president's words implied that Poland was his primary concern, the wording lent itself to the broader goal of promoting democratic reforms for all of Eastern Europe.

On January 8, 1945, John Hickerson, deputy director of the Office of European Affairs, sent a lengthy memorandum to the new secretary of state, Edward Stettinius, recommending formation of a "Provisional Security Council for Europe." The memorandum advised Stettinius to suggest to the president that such a council be formed at the upcoming Yalta Conference with the goal of ensuring the democratic transition of Eastern Europe back into the peace-loving family of nations. Among other tasks, the proposed council would supervise the reestablishment of popular governments and, in cases of dispute or contention, would investigate the situation at hand: "The Provisional Security Council for Europe shall have the authority to require in such a case the establishment of a coalition government broadly representative of all elements in the population." Eventual free elections might fall under the supervision of the council, whose membership would embrace the three principal Allies and France.[11] This membership might assure America of a majority in any future disputes over the course of the new East European regimes.

Two days later, a meeting of Hickerson, Leo Pasvolsky, special assistant to the secretary of state on international organizations, James Dunn, assistant secretary of state, and Charles E. Bohlen ordered preparation of a set of papers which might give birth to an "Emergency High Commission for Liberated Europe" as the proposed council was now to be called, and which would contain the principles that would guide its operation.[12] On January 16 the final documents were sent to Stettinius, and, upon his signed approval, forwarded to the president.[13]

Stettinius's accompanying recommendations to the president carefully avoided any suggestion of an expanded State Department role in the actual conduct of the war or in the postwar treatment of Germany, two areas in which even Secretary Hull had learned to tread with care. Instead, the proposed high commission would deal solely with the liberated and former satellite states of Europe.[14] An attachment to Stettinius's memorandum provided the details of the commission's structure and functions, including provisions for its demise once popular and stable governments functioned in Eastern Europe.[15] Since this attachment followed the discussions initiated by Hickerson, Pasvolsky, Dunn, and Bohlen, it dealt with the need for representative institutions and the possible requirement of supervised elections, thus precluding the need for a separate and detailed listing of policy principles for Eastern Europe. Thus a second attachment to Stettinius's memorandum entitled "Declaration on Liberated Europe" merely restated principles already expressed.[16]

Although the draft proposals for the suggested high commission reached the president's desk before his departure for Yalta, there was little indication that he gave them much attention. As Roosevelt's personal adviser, James Byrnes, later recalled, the president's schedule was hectic in the ten days between his inauguration and his trip to Yalta, greatly restricting his ability to study the mounting recommendations and papers submitted for his attention. Even aboard ship on the cruise to Malta, Roosevelt made only limited efforts to acquaint himself with potential policy positions.[17]

On February 1, at a meeting with his British counterpart, Anthony

Eden, held in Malta Harbor, Stettinius mentioned that his president had some reservations about the suggesed high commission and that the proposal ought temporarily to be considered "informal and unofficial as the President had not yet approved it."[18] Three days later, Roosevelt informed Stettinius of his objections to the plan, drawing attention to the failures of the European Advisory Commission in London and opining that future meetings of the foreign ministers might better handle such issues than another commission.[19] As a result, the proposal for creation of a high commission was omitted from the Yalta agenda.

Roosevelt's objections to the high commission meant that protection for democratic rights in Eastern Europe would have to be located entirely within the shorter "Declaration on Liberated Europe." This document, following an urgent redrafting and expansion, was presented to the president on February 5 in preparation for discussions scheduled among the Big Three for February 9.[20] In an attempt to provide enforcement short of formal creation of the rejected commission, the first redraft stated that in case of violations or disputes, the three Allies would "immediately establish appropriate machinery for the carrying out of the joint responsibilities set forth in this declaration."[21] When Soviet Foreign Minister Molotov subsequently objected to this wording, the term "mutual consultation" was substituted for "appropriate machinery."[22] Clearly, mutual consultation was more consistent with the president's desire to prevent the institutionalization of his still vague plans for ensuring postwar harmony among the Allies.

The approved "Declaration on Liberated Europe" in its augmented form retained many of the safeguards proposed for the high commission and reconfirmed the State Department's persistent interest in the affairs of Eastern Europe. The goal of Allied policy in the region was defined as "the establishment of order in Europe and the re-building of national economic life . . . by processes which will enable the liberated peoples to . . . create democratic institutions of their own choice." The plan for a high commission was replaced by a direct American commitment to participate in the evolution of the states in question:

> To foster the conditions in which the liberated peoples may exercise these rights, the three governments will jointly assist the people in any European liberated state or former Axis satellite state in Europe where in their judgment conditions require (a) to establish conditions of internal peace; (b) to carry out emergency measures for the relief of distressed peoples; (c) to form interim governmental authorities broadly representative of all democratic

elements in the population and pledged to the earliest possible establishment through free elections of governments responsive to the will of the people; and (d) to facilitate where necessary the holding of such elections.[23]

With slight changes, this paragraph was identical to a section in the proposal for the high commission and represented the main policy agreement between Roosevelt and his State Department advisers.[24] Although the precise machinery for intervention was left unspecified in deference to Roosevelt's objections, the declaration left no doubt about America's right to interfere in the domestic affairs of the liberated and former satellite states in conjunction with the other guaranteeing powers: "When, in the opinion of the three governments, conditions in any European liberated state or any other former Axis satellite state in Europe make such action necessary, they [the Big Three] will immediately consult together on the measures necessary to discharge the joint responsibilities set forth in this declaration."[25]

Although contemporary scholarship, most notably the recent study by Daniel Yergin, raises doubts about Roosevelt's commitment to this declaration, his subsequent speeches and actions gave the State Department little concern as to a possible divergence of interests. In his March 4, 1945, address to Congress, Roosevelt asserted that "final decisions in these areas are going to be made jointly." His special adviser at Yalta, later Secretary of State James Byrnes, informed a press conference upon his return from the Crimea that "where required, special three power commissions will be created to supervise the establishment of a government and to provide for the holding of free elections."[26] Such sentiments were consistent with the instructions Roosevelt gave Stettinius shortly thereafter: "I desire that you, as Secretary of State, assume the responsibility for seeing that the conclusions, exclusive of course of military matters, reached at the Crimean Conference, be carried forward. In so doing, you will I know, wish to confer with other officials of this Government on matters touching upon their respective fields. I expect you to report to me directly on the progress you are making in carrying the Crimea decisions into effect in conjunction with our Allies."[27]

Stettinius was not the only one who was given to understand the firmness of America's Yalta pledge to ensure democratic governance in Eastern Europe. In late February, Maynard Barnes inquired whether "the US really intends to make its influence felt in this part of the world, and, in particular, will it actively seek to assure a free expression of Bulgarian opinion in the forthcoming elections?"[28] The response from

Acting Secretary of State Joseph Grew left no doubt about the sanctity of the Yalta pledge: "The Department expects to see with respect to the former Axis satellite countries full implementation of the Crimean Declaration on Liberated Europe, announcing mutual agreement among the three principal Allies to concert their policies in helping these former enemy states to solve their pressing political and economic problems by democratic means, and where in their judgment conditions require, to assist these states to form interim governmental authorities broadly representative of democratic elements."[29] Within the week, Barnes informed the Bulgarian minister of foreign affairs "that the Declaration on Liberated Europe had been made by the three principal Allied powers in all sincerity and that it was the expectation of Washington that it would be carried out in its entirety in Bulgaria."[30]

The occasion for Barnes's sharply worded message to the Bulgarian foreign minister was the turmoil following an announcement by the minister of interior that early elections for a new parliament were in the offing.[31] By the spring of 1945, the four political parties that had joined forces in the Fatherland Front uprising of the preceding September were locked in an intense political struggle. The reconstituted Bulgarian Agrarian National Union (BZNS), the largest of the prewar parties, was leading the campaign for an autonomous existence against the Bulgarian Communists and their Soviet allies. Other coalition members, most notably the National Union–Zveno, were rapidly dividing into pro- and anti-Communist wings. The destruction of these parties would preclude representative elections as foreseen at Yalta, and Barnes had observed tbe domestic turmoil since arriving in Sofia. It was in the first days after the September 9 uprising that the differences so evident among the parties by the spring of 1945 initially emerged.

To the casual observer, the Fatherland Front coalition as constituted at its inception represented an equitable division of responsibility and power among its three largest components, Communists, Agrarians, and followers of Zveno. Each held four seats in the cabinet, with two minor posts assigned to the participating Social Democrats and two others given to independents. The Bulgarian Regency Council, still required because of the minority of the heir apparent, was retained but with its membership changed so that each of the three new regents was identified with one of the three main parties.[32] As a further symbol and guarantee of unity, a National Committee of the Fatherland Front existed to harmonize policies and platforms among the parties to the coalition.

If the visible, national institutions of the Front suggested a tranquil relationship, it was because the actual dynamics of political differentiation and competition proceeded at a much lower and hence more opaque level in the Bulgarian villages and small towns. In retrospect, it is clear that the Bulgarian countryside in the immediate postarmistice period functioned much as the Oder-Neisse territories in Polish history or the region of northern Transylvania in postarmistice Rumania. The Bulgarian rural regions provided the decisive arena in which the smaller but better organized Communists sought and found entrenchment, power, and patronage. The period following the September 9 uprising was a time of internal colonization with the Communists seeking administrative positions far out of proportion to their numerical strength. The key to this scramble for institutional power beyond the pale of the few large Bulgarian cities was under the control of the local committees of the Fatherland Front, which came to dominate the nation. In this competition, the Communists had a decisive advantage from the start.

The local committees of the Front had emerged even before September, with the Communists having the majority of members because of the conspiratorial nature of these institutions. If slightly under seven hundred such committees existed in early September, their number had grown to more than seven thousand two months later, enrolling twenty-five thousand members. Statistics confirm that at this level of cooperation, the disparity in membership between Communists and Agrarians was on the order of two to one. Zveno committee membership was one-thirtieth that of the dominant Communists.[33] It was to such committees that the government entrusted the discharge and appointment for all important bureaucratic posts in the realm of politics and economics, including even some positions in the larger cities below the ranks of the national bureaucracy. In the first month of the uprising alone, thirty thousand appointees of the old regime were replaced by individuals hand-picked by the local committees for their loyalty to the ideals of the revolution.[34] According to a law passed in November, all cities and villages were to be governed by municipal councils and by directors designated by the local Fatherland Front committees.[35]

Bare statistics poorly reflect the pace or political impact of the changes experienced in rural Bulgaria in the months immediately following the September 9 uprising. On September 16, for example, the five-man committee in the Razgradsko district (*okoliiski*) informed the National Committee of the Fatherland Front that it had resolved to dischrge all thirteen mayors then functioning in the district and to appoint their successors. A September 24 communication from the district committee in Pirdop noted that it had taken all authority, including control of the police.[36] By the end of the month, every mayor in the Novoselska district except for one village was a member of the Communist party appointed by the district committee. In the Blagoevgradska region (*oblast*) the vast majority of district directors and mayors were Communists, and in the Sofia region, of 12 district directors, 11 were Communists, as were 11 of the 12 mayors. Incomplete records as of December 31, 1944, show that of 84 reporting districts, 63 district capitals possessed Communist mayors, 11 were ruled by Agrarians, 2 by members of Zveno, 2 by Social Democrats, and 6 by independents. Village mayors were equally unrepresentative with the Communists holding 879 of 1,165 positions reported; their rivals, the Agrarians, held only 237.[37] This increasing disparity in the very areas where the Agrarians held their political base, the Bulgarian countryside, gave clear indication to the wary peasants of the likely political future years before Bulgaria officially joined the Communist camp.

Domination of local Fatherland Front committees offered great advantages in ensuring a permanent rural base of power and rewards for those who realized which direction the political winds blew as well as a means to protect Communist gains. The disbanding of the police in early September was accompanied by orders that local committees create a responsible militia. Military subcommittees of the Front functioning in district and regional committees also took a hand in maintaining the monopoly over the power of coercion rapidly falling under Communist control, keeping close ties with army units stationed in rural garrisons, "purifying" unreliable officers and soldiers, and working in conjunction with newly created army sections dealing with ideology.[38] Extreme problems in maintaining effective control would prompt the dispatch of Soviet representatives, sometimes accompanied by occupation troops, to assure a "peaceful resolution" of local problems.

Given the façade of unity symbolized by the existing membership of the Bulgarian cabinet and in the National Committtee of the Fatherland Front, the Bulgarian Communist party realized it had everything to gain by promoting unity of the Front even as the local committees further expanded dominance of the Communists throughout the state. Unity thus became a party hallmark, even as such unity was subverted outside the confines of the capital. The first party circular issued following the uprising called for creation of local Fatherland Front committees in every city, village, factory, and institution. Shortly thereafter, another circular insisted that supervision over all Bulgarian industry be transferred to such committees, including the right "to make recommendations for discharging or appointing workers, technicians, masters, etc."[39] Front committees quickly moved to take control of all economic life, forming subcommittee responsible for allocating scarce goods to consumers and raw materials to producers, a power fraught with possibilities for further increasing Communist dominance.[40] Given this visible expansion of authority and prestige and the continued presence of the Red Army, it is little wonder that party membership rose sharply from 25,000 in early September to over 250,000 by the year's end.[41] If left unchallenged, the specter of national unity and district subugation promised to erode support from all non-Communist members of the coalition. Since the Bulgarian Agrarian party boasted the largest prewar following of all Bulgarian movements, it quickly became the main bulwark against total Communist domination.

The Agrarian party, more correctly entitled the Bulgarian Agrarian National Union (BZNS), traced its beginnings to the late nineteenth century and had produced its most notable leader in Alexander Stamboliiski, whose brief tenure as prime minister in 1923 left an enduring if ambiguous legacy. In the turbulent politics following his violent overthrow, the Union split first into factions and then into antagonistic groups. As Nissan Oren aptly noted: "The internal politics of the Agrarians in the period between tbe overthrow of Stamboliiski and the coming of the People's Bloc is utterly confusing."[42] The Pladne Agrarians, destined to play the major role in post-1944 Agrarian politics and named for their newspaper of the same title, emerged in this period, achieving some political significance in the 1930s. But as Bulgaria began her fateful drift toward membership in the Axis Pact, the known pro-Western proclivities within the Pladne leadership resulted in increased repression. By 1941, many of the better-known Pladne leaders—men such as Dr. G. M. Dimitrov—were in exile, leaving guidance of Pladne to lesser-known individuals such as Nikola Petkov. It was Petkov who, despite the lack of a large personal following, led the remainder of Pladne forces into the Fatherland Front, being rewarded with four cabinet positions for his party including his own appointment as minister without portfolio. These Pladne Agrarians now began the painstaking process of resurrecting and reunifying the broader prewar Agrarian movement. But it was not Petkov but the more outspoken and flamboyant G. M. Dimitrov (usually referred to as Gemeto both because of the Bulgarian pronunciation of his initials and to distinguish him from the Communist leader of the same name) who quickly emerged as the most important Agrarian leader.

Gemeto had entered Agrarian politics in the stormy period following the 1923 coup against Stamboliiski, founding the newspaper

Pladne in 1928. With the dissolution of all political parties in 1934, Gemeto was thrown into jail, subsequently released, and, on the eve of the war, jailed once more. A fierce opponent of Bulgaria's increasingly pro-German foreign policy, Gemeto, in a last gesture of defiance, signed a protest letter to King Boris on the eve of his accession to the Nazi alliance and then fled the country with the aid of British intelligence. During the remaining war years, Gemeto led the Bulgarian National Committee in exile, working closely with the British in the Near East. Immediately following the September 1944 uprising, Gemeto prepared his return to Bulgaria, crossing the frontier on September 23.[43] Upon his return, he plunged into a frenzy of organizational activities.

The initial groundwork for uniting the various Agrarian factions and for bringing a sense of unity of purpose to Agrarian representatives in the local Fatherland Front committees had been undertaken by Petkov before Gemeto's return. On the very day of the uprising, a group of Agrarians led by Petkov dispatched a circular calling for unity among the Agrarians and creation of a new party. The general platform would follow rules adopted in 1933 just before the abolition of Bulgarian political parties. This first circular advised the Agrarians to focus their efforts on establishing party committees at the district and provincial levels. Shortly thereafter, the new Agrarian newspaper, *Zemedelsko zname,* began a campaign for Agrarian unity, under the joint editorship of Petkov and M. Genovski. The second circular, issued the same month, insisted that Agrarians expand their participation in the burgeoning Fatherland Front committees. As Mito Isusov, a respected Bulgarian historian concluded, the unity among the Agrarians at the local level was quickly accomplished but not without raising deep concern among the Communists. The circulars contained the traditional slogans of "Peace, Order, Law, and Freedom," watchwords pregnant with potential problems for a revolutionary regime intent upon prosecuting a foreign war. More threatening, the first circular refused to eschew the Agrarian belief in eventual domination among the Bulgarian peasants, who still formed the majority of the population. A Bulgarian Agrarian Union was necessary, the circular proclaimed, "as the one sole organization of the Bulgarian peasantry."[44] The suggested draft program for the reunified Agrarian Union with its call for "full restoration of democracy and making the fatherland a truly democratic, free, and independent state" promised concerted resistance to any attempt to convert Bulgaria into a Soviet satellite.[45]

The threats of a truly independent Agrarian party evident in early organizational efforts were quickly confirmed at the October 14–15

Party Congress called by Gemeto immediately following his return. Although Petkov was absent, serving on the armistice delegation then in Moscow, his efforts for unity brought success as two hundred delegates from all the prewar Agrarian factions convened the founding congress of the Bulgarian Agrarian National Union (BZNS).[46] A Managing Committee of forty-eight members was created, bringing together representatives of the diverse Agrarian currents and electing a smaller Standing Committee to preside over party affairs. The Standing Committee was dominated by Gemeto, Petkov, and the Agrarian minister of agriculture, Asen Pavlov. Gemeto was also elected chief secretary of the Union.[47]

The elevation of Gemeto to positions of power in the reconstituted Union served unambiguous notice to the Bulgarian Communists that an intense struggle for the future of the nation was at hand. In Gemeto, the Agrarians possessed an individual with firm roots in the prewar Agrarian tradition and a convinced follower of the democratic ideals held by the Western Allies. In his October 15 speech to the founding Agrarian Congress, Gemeto refused to acknowledge any special rights for the Bulgarian Communists, avoided mentioning future relations between the two parties, and gave strong emphasis to the revolutionary role of the Bulgarian peasantry. In the words of a contemporary Bulgarian historian, Gemeto advanced the "mistaken mechanical and metaphysical program according to which 'it is necessary for the BZNS to have the largest share in the Administration because it is the strongest party which represents and rests on the peasants who are three-fourths of the population.' " It simpler words, Gemeto stood by the notion that the majority should rule. Two months later, addressing eight thousand party members at a second party congress in the city of Stara Zagora, Gemeto reaffirmed his commitment to the independent policies of his party and their hopeful future, shouting to the crowd, "Long live the future independent Agrarian Bulgaria."[48] Touching upon relations with the Communists, Gemeto boldly reminded the assembly that it had been the Agrarian Stamboliiski himself who had invited the Communists to collaborate with him in the prewar period and that he, Gemeto, had warned the leaders of the Bulgarian Communists in 1939 that support for the Nazi-Soviet Pact would divide the futures of the workers and peasants. As reported by the official Agrarian paper, Gemeto's speech was met with a quarter-hour of applause.[49]

Gemeto's public assertions reflected his personal conviction that continued organization of the Bulgarian peasantry would soon place the Agrarians in a dominant national policy position. Shortly after his return to Bulgaria, Gemeto had informed a key member of the Communist Politbureau that if terror were used against the Agrarians, he personally would withdraw the Agrarians from the cabinet, this dooming the existing coalition. When Traicho Kostov then suggested that Gemeto himself might take the position of prime minister as a reward for maintaining the unity of the Fatherland Front and avoiding such crises, Gemeto responded that the National Committee of the Front possessed no legal standing and that he would never join it as a prerequisite for entering the cabinet.[50] Shortly thereafter, Petkov, just returned from Moscow, informed Gemeto that his outspoken opposition to Communist domination in Bulgaria had already come to the attention of authorities in Moscow. The Soviets, Petkov told Gemeto, were demanding that Gemeto be replaced in the Agrarian leadership: "The Russians want to split our party. Central Europe belongs to the Soviet sphere, they said, and our party could only hope to survive if it purged itself of Doctor Dimitrov and other anti-Soviet elements."[51]

Despite such threats: the revived Agrarian movement continued to expand its influence throughout Bulgaria. By the new year, the party had gained nearly 100,000 new recruits, with the largest concentrations naturally being in the rural areas. More than 17,000 members resided in the Plovdiv region, 15,500 in the Varna region, and nearly the same number in the Sofia and its environs. In February 1945, the alarmed Sofia District Committee of the Bulgarian Communist party reported that Agrarian influence had become equal to Communist in the majority of surrounding villages. In eleven villages, Agrarian influence was deemed superior.[52]

If the expansion of Agrarian independence formed the main area of Communist concern, similar tendencies among other coalition partners were also apparent. On October 1, 1944, a national congress of individuals associated with the political movement Zveno formed a new political party—the National Union–Zveno. The common platform of the Fatherland Front received approval, and a special committee was designated to formulate separate objectives worthy of membership support.[53] By December 1944, the party newspaper, *Izgrev,* asserted that official membership was over 250,000. Although the figure remains in dispute, it is clear that a new mass party had emerged.[54]

The potential problem faced by Communists when viewing this new party stemmed from two sources. First, adherents of Zveno occupied several of the most important positions in the cabinet, including those of prime minister, minister of war, and minister of foreign affairs. Expressions of partisan or parochial goals by such highly visible leaders would bring instant ministerial disputes and perhaps resignations. Second, the social composition of the expanded Zveno membership suggested to Communist analysts, the emergence of a new vehicle through which conservative opinions might be pressed upon the revolutionary government. According to Zveno statistics, of 1,600 members in the Sofia organization, 548 were civil servants, 172 merchants, 156 members of the professional middle class, 124 pensioners, 120 landlords, 111 artisans, 84 teachers, and 66 advocates. In Plovdiv, merchants, pensioners, and the service middle class also dominated, a pattern repeated in Ruse and other cities. The obvious attraction of the new party for the Bulgarian middle classes inspired a recent Bulgarian historical account to state that "as soon as the idea of the reorganization of Zveno into a political party arose, apprehension was expressed that such a party might turn into a covert [*prikrit*] party for Bourgeois contrarevolutionary forces."[55]

The evident cracks within the unity of the Fatherland Front quickly prompted the Bulgarian Communists temporarily to postpone their call for national elections until their control might be more firmly established. The September 17 platform of the Fatherland Front coalition had promised dissolution of the parliament and the "holding of free elections," and as late as December 1944, the Communist Central Committee resolved "to set a course for conducting elections in the nearest future."[56] Although time would show that the postponement was only temporary, with the call for elections arising again three months later, the interim was used to open a concerted campaign against the rising non-Communist opposition. A prominent position in this campaign was assigned to the major Communist daily, *Rabotnichesko delo*. Hopes that the Communists might split the rapidly expanding Agrarian party and conduct elections while the presence and prestige of the Red Army remained crucial factors were in part inspired by growing rivalries within the Agrarian movement. According to a Communist Central Committee report, "the moment was ripe" for action against G. M. Dimitrov (Gemeto) because sufficient of his enemies within the party were already offering their services.[57] Thus, on December 4, *Rabotnichesko delo* opened the campaign with an editorial asking whether Gemeto and his followers were for or against the unity of the Fatherland Front; it repeated the question twice more in the next several days.[58] Not one to be stilled, Gemeto authored a rebuttal in the Agrarian paper, *Zemedelsko zname*, in which he charged that the ongoing, Communist-inspired reforms in the Bulgarian army were socialistic in nature and constituted a major threat to Front unity.[59] *Izgrev*, the official Zveno organ, also charged that Communist rejection of War Minister Velchev's order granting relief from prosecution to officers volunteering for duty at the front was an effort by the Communists to seize political power.[60] A week later, *Rabot-nichesko delo* responded that charges advanced by both *Zemedelsko zname* and *Izgrev* were threats to the revolution and the recent conquests of freedom.[61]

The verbal assaults fired by *Rabotnichesko delo* against the opposition were soon supplemented by more direct action throughout the Bulgarian countryside. All Communists were directed to hold meetings on Christmas eve at places where the evil activities of the Agrarians and followers of Zveno might be exposed. As a recent Bulgarian study concludes, "Within the state, there was not a single village or square in which the hellish [*puklenite*] intentions of Gemetoists and their supporters such as the followers of [War Minister] Velchev were not revealed."[62] As a final blow to Gemeto's hopes for prominent Agrarian participation in postwar Bulgaria, Soviet ACC Chairman Biriuzov personally intervened in early January, demanding that Gemeto resign his positions of leadership within the party. Failure to abide by this demand, Biriuzov concluded, would result in the dissolution of the Agrarian party, a power which resided within the rights of the control commission.[63] By now the political struggle had become so intense that Maynard Barnes felt compelled to request advice from his superiors in Washington as to how he should handle a possible request from Gemeto for political asylum in America.[64]

On January 18, Gemeto convoked the executive organs of the Agrarian party to deliver a last report. More than 755,000 members were now registered, he stated, with an additional 230,000 enrolled in the Agrarian youth movement. Pleading that personal sacrifice must be made in the interest of party unity, but without publicly referring to Biriuzov's threats, Gemeto submitted his resignation as party secretary. Both that day and the next, the offer was refused. Finally, a compromise was achieved whereby Gemeto would take a "leave of absence" for reasons of health; Nikola Petkov would assume his responsibilities in the interim. When at a large gathering of Agrarians in Pleven two days later, Dobri Terpeshev, a Communist member of the cabinet, asserted that Gemeto would soon suffer the fate of former Prime Minister Filov, who was at that moment awaiting execution, the crowd roared its disapproval, and a riot by the assembly against the local militia soon followed.[65] Yet two days later, when Gemeto was in bed with pneumonia, Petkov assumed the post of Agrarian chief secretary.[66]

Communists hopes that the removal of Gemeto and the elevation of Petkov might clear the way for rapid elections quickly dissolved as the latter also indicated a desire to lead his party on an independent path.

At Petkov's direction, the executive board of the Agrarians called for an end to the purge against followers of Gemeto and agreed to indicate their continuing respect for their past leader by publishing his most controversial public speech.[67] The Agrarian Supreme Union Council officially asserted that the policy pursued by the party in the past months was correct both in basic principles and tactics.[68] In the face of such resistance, the Communist Central Committee, meeting in late February, concluded that "the party will conduct a struggle against Gemeto and the Gemetoists to the end, until all his supporters are fully exposed and removed from the Fatherland Front."[69] When the First Congress of the Fatherland Front met in March, dominated by Communist representatives sent by the local committees, it condemned all efforts to destroy the Fatherland Front and "recommend[ed] to the National Committee [of the Fatherland Front that it] assist in . . . cementing unity while nipping in the bud all efforts to counterpose peasants to workers or workers to peasants [while] exposing the hostile and antipopular aims of such attempts."[70]

In conjunction with the national appeals for unity and against the followers of Gemeto, the Communists, through their majorities in the local committees, began a purge of recalcitrant members suspected of aiding the opposition. On February 26, the regional committee in Pleven resolved to conduct a no-holds-barred struggle "against the main agents of fascism in the state and in the Pleven region, the Gemetoists, and all their followers in the BZNS and FF wherever they are." The Varna regional committee voted to liberate itself from "fascist elements and the consequences of Gemeto."[71] All through the month, the Communists organized joint meetings with other political groups at local levels designed to identify and purge supporters of the "evil" Gemeto.[72]

Close observations of the Bulgarian political struggle prompted Maynard Barnes to alert his superiors in Washington that concrete intervention was required if hopes for Bulgaria's future were to be sustained. In early March, Barnes informed Washington of predictions that elections would soon be held. He was certain that in a free election the Agrarians would carry the day, polling 60 percent of the vote. The danger, Barnes advised, lay in the possibility of a Communist move to block oppositional expressions through the imposition of a single electoral list. The use of such lists would mean that "the Bulgarian people will once again be deprived of the right to express their will in general elections, and a new clique . . . will have tricked the people into ceding their sovereign rights." The means to thwart this Communist design, Barnes advised, was to aid the Agrarians by confirming that "it really was intended at Yalta to assure elections in ex-satellite countries that would permit the democratic elements of each country freely to express their will." A discussion of the merits of a single electoral list was scheduled for the March Congress of the Fatherland Front, but Barnes cautioned that a defeat for the Communists on this point was unlikely. "As the Communists have gained a superior position in the local and district Committees of the FF [Fatherland Front] so shall the Communist delegates to the National Congress be the most numerous."[73]

Barnes left little doubt as to the purpose of his lengthy reports on prospects for upcoming elections: the State Department should consider invocation of the Yalta pledges if prospects for a future free Bulgarian government were not to be precluded. In case Washington had overlooked the tone and thrust of this message, five days later Barnes cautioned that the proximity of the Fatherland Front Congress and continued reports of a common list for upcoming elections meant that "if there is to be any prior consultation between the three principal Allies with respect to elections in Bulgaria, immediate action to this end is indicated." The next day, Barnes offered a personal interpretation of the reason why the Bulgarian Communists had achieved such successes to date, suggesting that a refusal by Washington and London to act more decisively would continue this discouraging trend: "The fact that this minority party is able to wield such influence may be attributed to four primary factors: the astuteness and ruthlessness of the communist leaders, the lack of leadership and arms (repeat, arms) on the part of the Agrarian party, frequent intervention by Soviet authorities . . . and the apparent reluctance of the United States and Great Britain to make their influence felt."[74] As Barnes had predicted, the Communist-dominated Fatherland Front Congress gave approval in the second week of March to a single list of candidates. Further details were promised in an electoral law soon to be published.[75]

The seriousness with which the Communists pursued their campaign for unity on the basis of their own platform became even more evident with the approval by the congress of a new law designated as in "Defense of People's Power."[76] Under its provisions, severe penalties were prescribed for all individuals or groups convicted of disrupting the power of the Fatherland Front or challenging its policies. Section 1, perhaps the most threatening to the Communist opposition, asserted: "Whoever within the state or in a foreign country forms or leads an organization with a fascist ideology which aims at the overthrow, subversion, or weakening of the power of the Fatherland Front, is punished by imprisonment up to life in solitary confinement, or by death. Members of such organizations are punished with solitary confinement for five years." Somewhat less drastic penalties were provided for spreading false rumors designed to subvert the Bulgarian military and for employees and employers who failed to meet assigned quotas. On March 12, the Fatherland Front Congress confirmed the seriousness with which the new law would be applied, issuing a public manifesto with the key paragraph: "Anyone who attempts to hinder the Fatherland Front, to conspire against it, will be destroyed without quarter. Such is the burning expressed will of the First National Congress of the Fatherland Front Committees."[77] To prevent any enemies of the Front from breaching this carefully designed network of prohibitions, the congress resolved that any delegate elected in the forthcoming balloting might be recalled if he transgressed the common Fatherland Front platform.[78]

Barnes's deep concern over the diminishing prospects for free Bulgarian elections was forcibly expressed to his British colleague, Houstoun-Boswall, to whom he stressed the applicability of the Yalta decisions to the situation at hand. As a result, Houston-Boswall informed the British Foreign Office: "From this [Barnes's discussion about Yalta] His Majesty's Government would appear to enjoy the right to express themselves in the subject of Bulgarian elections. Now that elections are being discussed in the press, I would suggest an opportunity to be taken by the U.K. to issue more or less simultaneously with the U.S., a statement to the effect that His Majesty's Government took a keen interest in proposals for Bulgaria to hold a general election, and that they would watch the manner in which the elections were conducted . . . as it would be the first election to be held in a former satellite country." On March 11, this cable and others received from the British diplomats in Sofia reflecting the common concern over the impending elections were forwarded to the State Department accompanied by a statement of British policy. Viewing Houstoun-Boswall's call for a common U.S.-U.K. statement on the importance of the coming elections as unlikely to elicit sympathy from the Soviet government, the British note concluded that a crisis was indeed at hand.[79]

The strident warnings from Barnes and expressions of British concern reached a State Department already deeply involved in averting similar Communist machinations in Bulgaria's northern neighbor, Rumania. A February crisis in Bucharest attending the formation of the pro-Soviet Groza cabinet through direct intervention by Soviet representatives had given rise to America's first use of the powers implied in the Yalta declaration. On March 14, Ambassador Harriman informed Foreign Minister Molotov that "it is the view of my Government that the consultations looking to the formulation of policies and procedure to be employed in implementing the Crimean decisions with respect to Rumania might well take place in the first instance in Moscow, between you, the British Ambassador and myself." Once such consultation was completed, Harriman continued, a tripartite committee might be established in the Rumanian capital to guarantee that the existing problems engendered by formation of the Groza government were resolved consistent with the Yalta agreement.[80] Three days later, a near record given the usually extended periods between American requests and Soviet responses, Molotov rejected the American proposal. The crisis in Rumania, he argued, had passed, making any intervention unnecessary. More important, the American proposal, if implemented, would subvert the existing Allied Control Commission in Bucharest, "emasculating the role of the Chairman."[81] In an interpretation previously unmentioned by Moscow, Molotov boldly asserted that the Soviet-dominated control commissions operating in Eastern Europe held responsibility for implementing the Yalta pledges.

The Soviet suggestion that consultation as provided for at Yalta was being met through the functioning of the Allied Control Commission in Bucharest was immediately rejected by the State Department.[82] Yet the initial U.S. demands were not pressed. Rumania was clearly under Soviet control with the State Department earlier having recognized a sharp distinction between U.S. interests in that state and her southern neighbor.[83] As Roosevelt informed Churchill in mid-March, "Rumania is not a good place for a test case." Of equal importance, sensitive negotiations on the future of Poland were then in progress, making an incident over Rumania especially distasteful.[84]

The disconcerting outcome of America's first use of provisions contained in the Yalta agreement prompted a new awareness within the State Department of the problems soon to be faced in Eastern Europe. Charles Bohlen informed Secretary of State Stettinius: "We are, however, more interested in getting Soviet agreement to apply in the future the principles of the Yalta Declaration than in insisting on a review of the Soviet action of last February or on a drastic reorganization of the Rumanian Government."[85] The pleas by Maynard Barnes for guidance and perhaps for intervention, coming as they did on the heels of the Rumanian crisis, galvanized the department to act so that formation of a second nonrepresentative East European government might be averted. Bulgaria now promised to be the first state in which general elections might be held; their form and procedure would demonstrate the degree of commitment extended by the three Allies to the Yalta agreement. Benefiting from procedural mistakes made in the Rumania debacle, the State Department rephrased its demand for consultation so as to avoid the anticipated objection that such Yalta provisions already operated in the Bulgarian control commission. The time and the opportunity had arrived for direct American intervention.

On March 29, Harriman was instructed to invoke the Yalta agreement to prevent an undemocratic election in Bulgaria: "We agree with Barnes that the operation of democratic processes in Bulgaria and the principles of representative government will meet a major test in the forthcoming elections. Our concern with this question now passes beyond the historic interest of America in the progress of the Bulgarian people and our rights and obligations under the armistice, and becomes a responsibility which this Government together with the Soviet Union and Great Britain has publicly proclaimed in the Crimean Declaration." Drawing Harriman's attention to abiding U.S. objections to the presentation of a common electoral list by the Fatherland Front and stressing the need for safeguards to protect the sanctity of a free ballot, Harriman was told, "Please inform the Soviet Government that our information regarding Bulgarian electoral plans contains clear indications that the Bulgarians are not able without assistance to hold 'free elections' by which governments can be established which will be 'responsive to the will of the people.'" Harriman was to invoke the Yalta provisions for joint consultation by suggesting "that in order to ensure the application of these policies and procedures a committee be formed in Sofia, independent of the ACC . . . for the purpose of advising the Bulgarian Government in electoral matters and reporting to the three Governments on all developments. . . . Alternatively, we would be willing to participate in a special tripartite commission to be sent into the country for this purpose."[86] The purpose of these commissions would be to ensure the conducting of free elections. The State Department immediately informed the British Embassy of its instructions to Harriman. By early April, the British ambassador in Moscow had been told to support the American initiative.[87]

In sharp contrast to the spring Rumanian crisis, the American intervention in Bulgaria was an unqualified success. On April 11, Foreign Minister Molotov responded to Ambassador Harriman's note by suggesting that concerns for possible three-power supervision in Bulgaria were premature, "especially as, according to its [the Soviet Government's] information, there is no intention to carry on elections in the near future."[88] This transparent falsehood revealed the magnitude of the American victory. Early elections had been accepted by the December 1944 Central Committee Plenum, with spring 1945 the date selected.[89] Since then, Communist Interior Minister Anton Yugov, Foreign Minister Stainov, and Petkov had stated that immediate elections were being planned. Upon hearing of Molotov's response, a delighted Barnes informed Stettinius, "Petkov also gave the lie to Molotov's statement . . . that 'there is no intention to carry on elections in Bulgaria in the near future.' He pointed to the fact known to everyone in Bulgaria that the Communists are pressing hard to dominate the Agrarians in the Fatherland Front or to pulverize them with a view to forcing immediate elections that will give them domination of Parliament."[90] Clearly, a precedent had been set. American reliance upon the Yalta declaration had produced the first concrete results.

If the State Department could take pride in the postponement of the Bulgarian elections, the tone and the content of Molotov's reply suggested that disputes lay just ahead. Drawing attention to the future, when the issue of elections would again arise, Molotov warned that further American intervention would be opposed: "Should the Bulgarian Government have in mind, however, to conduct parliamentary elections, then, in that case according to Soviet opinion, there would be no need for foreign interference in the holding of such elections just as there was no need for such intervention in the recent Finnish elections." Interestingly, Molotov's reply, in sharp distinction to his notes dealing with the earlier Rumanian crisis, presented no specific objection to American suggestions for formation of a tripartite commission that would advise the Bulgarian government and report on the conducting of elections.[91] Only the need for such action, not its legitimacy, was placed in question. Encouraged by this development, Bohlen advised Stettinius that such provisions of the Yalta agreement should again be invoked if the specter of unfair elections arose in the future:

> We suggest that Mr. Molotov be informed that we are glad to learn that there is no intention of holding elections in Bulgaria in the near future and are gratified by the implication in his message that the Finnish precedent will be followed in Bulgaria. Information has reached us . . . to the effect that it is planned to have a single "Fatherland Front" electoral list. . . . Should this be the case . . . we feel that we should again press our request for consultation. Since such action is not only permissible but becomes an obligation under the Yalta Declaration on Liberated Europe, we are unable to comprehend why the invocation of the Declaration should be cause for misunderstanding. The American people fully expect that the Declaration will be given reality in the treatment of liberated and ex-enemy peoples.[92]

The decision to postpone the Bulgarian elections in response to the concerted American and British pressure gave a new sense of urgency to the Bulgarian Communist efforts to silence all dissenting voices within the domestic political spectrum. Throughout April, messages flowed into Sofia from the local communities of the Fatherland Front reporting the purge of Gemetoists from local organizations and detailing measures taken to preserve unity." On April 27, the National Committee of the Front met to appraise the campaign, with Communist Politbureau member Dimitur Ganev warning that the removal of Gemeto from public life had done little to end manifestations of his anti-Front attitude. Six days later, a declaration of the Front dispatched to all local committees again condemned all who might oppose the common position of the Front, insisting upon their removal from local committees. Such individuals, the declaration charged, "express their evil views in (a) efforts to conduct defeatist work via the slogan 'Peace, Bread and Freedom,' (b) the undermining of the strength of the Fatherland Front and mass organizations, and by actions against the unity of the unions, womens groups, etc., (c) by efforts to sabotage governmental economic programs through sabotage of requisition and quotas, the loan of freedom, demagogic slogans for higher farm prices, propaganda against the trade agreement of March 14 with the USSR, (d) by underground work and propaganda against the Government's foreign and domestic policy."[93] Certainly this expansive definition of "opponents" served notice that anyone who might question the broad policies of the Front would be liable to punishment either by exclusion from local organizations or by prosecution under the recent law, the Defense of People's Power. General Biriuzov and his deputies in the Allied Control Commission directly intervened, informing the Agrarians that there should be no dispute over existing Communist domination of national and local administrative organs.[94] In May, Petkov told the American military mission that terror was now being employed against his Agrarian party and that many leading members, including the doctors attending Gemeto, were under arrest.[95]

In the face of this concerted Communist drive for "purity," both the Agrarians and members of Zveno stiffened their own resistance. In early April, a conference of Agrarian youth resolved to seek parity for their parent party within the existing administrative organs and militia and to form an independent Agrarian trade union. The same month, the Agrarians in the Stara Zagora District voted "to seek from the other parties of the FF and especially from the RP (k) [Workers Party, Communist] to cease actions, deeds and articles which leave the impression that they are the ruling party in the administration of the FF and others are without significance in our state."[96] Petkov, when told by Communist Regent Pavlov that he should publicly condemn Gemeto, responded that he would do so only if he emphasized

Gemeto's abiding belief in the principles of Anglo-Saxon democracy, a condition Pavlov immediately rejected.[97] In late April, Zvenoist Minister of Foreign Affairs Petko Stainov lashed out at Communist efforts to gain full control of the Fatherland Front through domination of the local committees. Appearing before a congress of Zveno youth, Stainov boldly argued: "If there are still individuals in the villages who continue to threaten diligent Zvenoists, who block their admission to FF Committees, who seek to embroil them and force their doors at night and intern them, then it may be said that these people, irrespective of their party affiliation, are not true supporters of the FF but are saboteurs."[98] Faced by such concerted resistance at the provincial, district, and local levels, the Communists and their supporters resolved upon a direct assault against the most prominent leaders of the larger Agrarian party.

Throughout the month of April, special meetings of the "Friends of the Agrarians" were held during which the separatist position of Petkov and Gemeto was reviled. In tandem with such rallies, the Communist units at the local levels convoked joint assemblies with willing Agrarians designed to recruit compliant members for local Fatherland Front committees. By May the enrollment patterns for committees in the Varna District revealed near parity between Communists and Agrarians, an indication of the success achieved in diluting rural support for the Petkov-Gemeto opposition. The final stage in this concerted effort to undermine the Agrarian dissenters came in an appeal by certain "leftist" Agrarians on May 5, calling for an immediate conference to "free the [Agrarian] Union from the empty line into which Gemeto and his friends have brought it."[99] Petkov, who had been informed four days earlier by Politbureau member Traicho Kostov that a conference of the Agrarians was needed in which the "left-wing" would rule, refused to participate, a refusal seconded by the other three Agrarian ministers in the Fatherland Front coalition.[100] As Petkov subsequently informed Barnes, security at the May 8–9 conference was so strict that many of the regional Agrarians who consented to the meeting were refused entry.[101] Nevertheless, the goal of discrediting Petkov and his allies was achieved. The conference stigmatized the followers of Gemeto as "a new attempt from the side of hostile fascist, pro-fascist and reactionary elements to destroy the unity of workers and peasants." In a state where the recent law for Defense of People's Power prescribed death for such crimes, the implications of this charge were evident to all. The demand for independent peasant power and for equality of representation for Communists and Agrarians in administrative organs and in the militia was rejected as an insult to Fatherland Front unity. Speaker after speaker emphasized that the most active members of the Front were Communists, and the conference promptly resolved "to break uncompromisingly with those hostile groups whose ideas and political motives lead to an open struggle with the Communists, [who] are leading the BZNS into fratricidal conflict."[102] All followers of "Gemetoism" were to be expelled from the party, Front, and administrative positions. As if oblivious to Molotov's recent denials, the conference resolved to conduct early elections, using the disputed single electoral slate.[103] Upon conclusion, a joint meeting of the Communist Politbureau and the newly elected Agrarian Standing Committee voted full approval of the conference resolutions and called for a final struggle with "rightest" opinions remaining in the Agrarian party. Members of local Agrarian groups were to verify their political attitudes immediately.[104]

As a final enticement to Nikola Petkov, the May conference reconfirmed his appointment as general secretary of the party despite his absence from the meetings. Shortly thereafter, Communist Minister of Interior Yugov officially ruled that henceforth all assets of the Agrarian party, its headquarters, and newspaper now belonged to the newly elected leadership. The protests of Petkov and his three Agrarian cabinet colleagues were to no avail. Refusing to compromise his position, Petkov established a new headquarters in his own home and began plans to rally his supporters.[105] As Petkov informed Barnes in mid-May, the old Agrarian leadership had decided the time was ripe to take a firm stand against the Communist intrigues. Barnes informed Stettinius, "In other words, the incipient crisis of the past months has now reached the point where the Prime Minister and/or the Russians must act."[106] Anticipation of continued American support in line with the protests that postponed the spring elections certainly figured in this bold decision. According to Bulgarian sources, in mid-May Barnes invited both Petkov and the leader of the Bulgarian Democratic party, Stoicho Moshanov, to his villa for a strategy meeting. Although Petkov was unable to attend, Barnes told Moshanov that the new Truman administration had established a series of conditions for eventual recognition of the Bulgarian government centering upon fulfillment of the Yalta agreement. As Bulgarian historian Mito Isusov readily concluded, the content of Barnes's message undoubtedly was communicated to Petkov as well.[107]

If the Communist strategy of isolating Petkov from his followers was limited to political tactics, the goal of removing Gemeto from all areas of influence involved his physical elimination. In late April, the Fatherland Front government issued instructions to remove Gemeto from his home in preference to a labor camp so as "to deprive him of the possibility of continuing his defeatist wartime activities."[108] The order, however, was temporarily stayed, awaiting Gemeto's recovery from an illness; a twenty-four-hour guard was assigned to watch his residence. In late May, friends informed Gemeto that his arrest was hours away. At 4:00 A.M. on May 24, Gemeto appeared at Barnes's villa asking for refuge. For tbe next four months, while awaiting the success of American efforts to fly him from Bulgaria, Gemeto remained within Barnes's home. In this period Barnes, already well acquainted with the intrigues and plans spawned by the Communists and Fatherland Front, received an in-depth report on all aspects of contemporary Bulgarian politics.[109] Given the restrictions still impeding the collection of information by the American military mission, Gemeto's information and insights undoubtedly formed an important part of America's growing knowledge of Bulgaria's likely future.

The first months of 1945 witnessed a revival of American involvement in Bulgaria both because information about domestic political activitiy was now adequate for the formation of specific directives and because of the approaching end of the war. Having temporarily acquiesced in the Soviet domination of the Allied Control Commission on military grounds, the State Department refused to maintain silence when confronted with events that threatened to create a postwar Bulgaria totally at odds with past American planning. The threatened demise of the non-Communist opposition, which would have removed all possibility of Bulgaria's democratic future, prompted an invoking of the Yalta accord so as to block patently unfair elections. It had not been for such charades that America had expended men and treasure in the European conflict, and notice was so served. The success of this initiative and the evident feisty resistance of the Agrarian and Zveno parties to Communist machinations revealed that America had local allies in the drive to direct Bulgaria's future onto a more democratic course despite pressure from the Soviets and their domestic supporters. The end of the war in Europe removed the self-imposed prohibition on equal American participation in the control commission, and Washington now made plans to reassert the earlier demands for a determining role in guiding the course of Bulgaria's political evolution. With the spring elections temporarily postponed, reform of the control commission in conjunction with augmented opportunity for the American mission to play a more decisive role in the future became the State Department's central objective.

5 The Campaign for Tripartite Administration

The political disputes that surfaced in the spring of 1945 both in Rumania and Bulgaria brought into sharp relief the disadvantages under which the U.S. military missions in the Balkans continued to operate. The earlier distinctions drawn by the State Department as to differing degrees of American interest in the future of these states began to wane in the face of a perceived common threat posed by Soviet and domestic Communist activities that followed a disturbingly similar pattern. During the Rumanian crisis in March, the Soviet refusal to consider formation of a tripartite commission for fear of undermining the Rumanian Allied Control Commission reemphasized the crucial role such institutions were designed to fulfill. The same month, Major-General Crane cabled from Sofia that Nikola Petkov and the Agrarian agricultural minister, Asen Pavlov, foresaw the possibility of free elections in Bulgaria only in conjunction with a reformed Allied Control Commission in which the Western role would be greatly augmented. "The Agrarians, who claim to be in the majority, want elections to be held under the protection of the ACC (Allied) rather than ACC (Soviet) representatives."[1]

A more balanced directorship within the control commission, however, was but one of the requirements for deeper American involvement in Bulgaria's troubled evolution from defeated enemy to sovereign state. The U.S. mission also was charged with supervising Bulgaria's fulfillment of the October 1944 armistice terms. By the spring of 1945, both the USSR and Great Britain tendered suggestions that recognition of the existing Bulgarian government might soon be forthcoming.[2] Since such recognition would imply acceptance of Bulgaria's compliance with the armistice terms, it became increasingly imperative for the American representatives to become involved in the control commission's monitoring of such deeds. In April 1945, General Crane sent a formal request to Soviet ACC Chairman Biriuzov asking for a plenary session of the commission—the first since the previous December. Biriuzov politely replied that it was not possible to convoke such a meeting in the "nearest future."[3]

In addition to its assigned functions under the armistice, the American mission was the main source of intelligence both about local Communist efforts to thwart free political expression among domestic political groups and the civil and military activities of the occupying Soviet forces. By the spring of 1945, uncertainty in Washington about Soviet intentions in the postwar world made the full use of such listening posts imperative, especially because Soviet forces in Bulgaria posed a potential threat to Western interests in Greece and Turkey. Expansion of the military mission's activities promised great benefits in all areas of concern and an end to the humiliating restrictions under which the mission had functioned in the initial period of its existence.

The U.S. military mission officially had begun its activities shortly after the arrival in mid-November 1944 of four officers and seven enlisted men in Sofia. A portable radio at first provided access to the military intelligence network in Bari, Italy, with scheduled times for transmissions. On November 26, Major-General Crane, head of the mission, arrived in the Bulgarian capital; an additional contingent of officers and men did not arrive until a month later because of continuing disagreements with Soviet authorities about the arrival and departures of U.S. planes. By then, a permanent radio connection had been established with Allied Forces Headquarters in Caserta. In the subsequent months, the U.S. mission grew, although always under the watchful eyes of the Soviets, who arbitrarily insisted on a top limit of fifty. As the official military historian of the mission aptly noted: "What difference a few dozen American soldiers more or less made in Bulgaria when the whole country was swarming with Russians, no one ever discovered but the fuss made by the Soviet command suggested that this was a matter of vital importance."[4] Although General Crane vigorously protested that as an Ally, America alone ought to decide the size of its complement, in fact he stuck close to the magic number. Records reveal that in late March 1945, the coordinator of War Department libraries in Washington assigned books to the mission in Bulgaria for Crane, fourteen other officers, and thirty-one enlisted men. Three months later, the total number of officers and men stood at exactly fifty.[5] Members of the mission were housed primarily in the American College near Simeonovo, about six miles southeast of the capital, although some officers maintained private quarters in the city.[6]

The mission was carefully divided in sections consistent with its official purpose of supervising fulfillment of the armistice terms and with its specific and sporadic intelligence assignments, the two activities being so closely intertwined that interference with one naturally hindered the other. The most important unit was the Ground Section headed by Lieutenant Colonel John Bakeless. Bakeless, fifty years old in 1944, held a Ph.D. from Harvard, was fluent in French and German with some knowledge of Russian, and had been involved in Bulgarian affairs for several years, having served in the office of the U.S. military attaché in Ankara.[7] His section's primary function was to obtain intelligence, a task complicated by the absence of enlisted personnel trained for such duty and by the presence of but one enlisted clerk. Intelligence requests arrived on an ad hoc basis directly from the War Department without passing through the hands of Bakeless's superior, General Crane. One of the section's first assignments was to prepare orders of battle for both the Soviet and Bulgarian military, documents which Crane required in his capacity as superviser of armistice compliance, but also of great interest in Washington.[8]

Besides orders of battle, the Ground Section acted upon requests from Washington to examine the capabilities and disposition of Bulgarian and Soviet intelligence and counterintelligence units, followed the underground activities of known fascists and Communists, analyzed the police and militia organizations of the Fatherland Front government, and researched subjects of interest in the areas of economics, politics, sociology, and geography. By the spring of 1946, the section had submitted 815 written reports to Washington in addition to cables, photographs of military interests, maps, and local Bulgarian and Soviet publications. It maintained an extensive "Who's Who" card index of important local personages, submitted regularly to G-2 in the War Department. A translation department within the section, employing up to eight translators in the spring of 1945, provided information to the other sections of the U.S. mission. Bulgarian letters destined for Western Europe and America were accepted by mission personnel, although the use of army postal facilities for civilian purposes was forbidden by ACC rules. From such letters, the Ground Section gathered information on conditions in Bulgarian concentration camps, the identities of black market dealers, and the identity of a currency smuggling group with representatives in Athens, Sofia, and New York. With the outbreak of civil war in Greece, this section expanded its investigation of intelligence and currency networks connecting Sofia and Macedonia. The Yugoslav mission in Sofia was closely watched.[9]

To fulfill its numerous assignments, the Ground Section relied mainly upon its own members' observations. It kept no paid agents among the Bulgarian populace, although information received from disgruntled Bulgarian intelligence officers and even from members of the Bulgarian Foreign Office was gladly evaluated. For constructing and updating orders of battle, the Ground Section maintained close ties with the British military mission and with the Greek attaché in Sofia.[10]

Such connections, however, could not replace the need for direct observation, and the restrictions upon U.S. movements within Bulgaria quickly became a major source of U.S.-Soviet friction. Increased freedom of movement would improve and facilitate the gathering of intelligence data, but demands to inspect the various areas of Bulgaria were fully consistent with U.S. responsibilities to supervise compliance with the armistice. These two tasks were impossible to separate, both supporting the American mission's increasingly vocal requests as Bulgaria prepared for elections in the spring of 1945.

The mission Ground Section was complemented by an Air Section formed shortly after Crane's arrival in Sofia. This unit was initially foreseen as a liasion with the corresponding Soviet Air Section within the guidelines of the control commission. The refusal of the Soviets to arrange regular ACC plenary meetings, much less sessions of the various military sections, quickly converted the Air Section into an intelligence department. Orders of battle were constructed for both the Soviet and Bulgarian air forces. The latter combat arm was deemed of special importance because it was known that the most anti-Communist officers in the Bulgarian military were located in this service branch. When possible, Air Section members made trips about Bulgaria to inspect airdromes and verify rumors of force movements. Frequent meetings with the British and Turkish attachés were of great assistance because representatives of the Air Section were not invited to confer with their Soviet counterparts until September 1945. At this meeting, information about the strength of the Bulgarian Air Force was provided, and a new era of cooperation appeared to be on the horizon. But after the second meeting with the Soviet Air Section, it was concluded that little additional information would be gained and that what had been provided was of doubtful validity. A Naval Section created in December 1944 under the direction of Lieutenant Commander Willis Hazleton was also ignored by the corresponding Soviet Naval Section, not holding its first meeting until the fall of 1945. Thereafter, regular meetings were held and information exchanged. In addition to conferring with its Soviet and British colleagues, the Naval Section provided intelligence information, studied Bulgarian naval affairs, the conditions of Bulgarian ports, and the problems of river navigation. Although an impressive number of joint U.S.-Soviet Naval Section meetings were held after the fall of 1945, the quality of East-West interaction left much to be desired. As might be expected, relations between the American and British naval sections were considered excellent. The severe restrictions placed upon travel enhanced the importance of these intra-Allied connections.[11]

If the Ground, Naval, and Air sections followed strict military discipline, fulfilling their divergent tasks as best they could, such could not be said of the Economic Section, which remained disorganized throughout much of its existence. The official history of the mission sadly noted that not a single assigned officer worked within this section through the entire period from the fall of 1944 to the spring of 1946, and little continuity was evident in matters pursued. No formal directives were issued to guide the section, although in February 1946 the commanding officer, Major H. P. Woodward, stated that his responsibilities were to assemble and coordinate available data relating to the Bulgarian economic capacity, production, and resources; make analyses as required for advising the commanding officer of the mission on Bulgarian economic matters including fulfillment of reparations and other claims; and provide an agency for collection and integration of Bulgarian economic information. Little progress was apparent in assembling information on the domestic economy until the spring of 1945, when a set of topical files was activated and data collected. Even then, the primary source for information was published statistics, newspaper clippings, and limited field observations.[12]

A partial explanation of the erratic work of this section lies with its goal of investigating the sporadic requests for information on behalf of Americans with claims to Bulgarian property or reparations. In March 1945, a list of propertyholders was drawn up by the Bulgarian government and forwarded to the section. The unwillingness of the Soviet authorities in the ACC to discuss such cases before the resolution of more "pressing" issues hindered prompt verification of the claims, and not until March 1946 was a tripartite subcommittee established within the ACC to screen all claims.[13]

It appears that the American personnel assigned to the mission, regardless of their specific duties, arrived with expectations of warm greetings from the local populace and open, friendly relations with their Soviet allies. Several of the officers had served in Bulgaria before the war and had friends in the capital. A number of officers and men were of Slavic ancestry. But in a short time, their optimistic expectations universally gave way to a more skeptical and cynical appraisal. As the history of the mission stated in 1946: "It is hard to think of anything that either the Russians or the Bulgarians failed to do to change the friendly or at least neutral attitude with which the Americans arrived. Constant espionage, so clumsily conducted as to be entertainingly obvious, open and covert hostility, wire tapping, sabotage, actual violence and the threat of violence, evasion, procrastination, delay, incompetence and insolence soon changed the initial attitude of the Americans to amusement, contempt and a certain mild dislike."[14]

It quickly became obvious to all concerned that the two major functions of the mission—participation in the ACC to include meetings between the Allied sections so as to verify armistice compliance and gathering information—would be rebuffed whenever and wherever the Soviets and their domestic allies desired. Given the grudging American commitment to abide by the disputed terms of Article 18 of the armistice until the conclusion of the conflict against Germany, General Crane could do little except to increase his complaints in the frequent dispatches routed to the War Department. As the Bulgarians began to prepare for the first postarmistice elections in the spring of 1945, Crane's frustrations and his expressed complaints dramatically increased.

Restrictions upon American participation in monitoring the armistice were not the only major problems facing the U.S. mission. As early as November 1944, the Soviets forbade U.S. personnel to land planes in Sofia without advance notice to Moscow; the official reason given was the absence of adequate radio facilities in Bulgaria. Planes allowed to land after the lengthy exchange of information between the Bulgarian and Soviet capitals were required to become airborne again within two hours. All cargo arriving in Sofia had to be described in detail, and all manifests were checked for correct weights. In case of discrepancy, the entire shipment was held under guard awaiting investigation. Such restrictions impinged upon the American mission's functions. An example was the detention in February 1945 of a shipment of radio supplies, which included much-needed teletype equipment. As late as November 1945, the Soviets still insisted that the Americans could land no more than five planes a month, thus forcing long delays in rotating U.S. personnel in and out of Bulgaria.[15]

The limitations placed upon the mission and the virtual absence of ACC meetings during the initial twelve months of his duty gave General Crane little choice but to focus his efforts upon intelligence matters.[16] Undoubtedly aware of this sole American option, the Soviets took pains to confine mission members to narrowly defined areas of Sofia and the American College at Simeonovo. If they requested travel, a Soviet officer would be assigned as liaison but only after significant delay. In April 1945, General Crane was informed that henceforth liasion officers would be available only for him and his representative, a further restriction upon mission travel. By then, travel outside the Sofia perimeter was not only exceptional but dangerous. Lieutenant Colonel Bakeless, having received the required permit to travel and flying the American flag, was held at gunpoint twice during an inspection tour verifying armistice compliance.[17]

Such incidents eventually led Crane to tramsmit some of his most discouraged comments to Washington. He cabled just before his own departure from Bulgaria in the spring of 1946: "Restrictions put on our movement in Bulgaria had been unreasonable and dictatorial, and have made us and America [the] laughing stock not only of Russians but of Bulgarians and of many other nationalities that are here. Remark is frequently made to effect that it was thought that we and not [the] Bulgarians are Allies of Russians. For first time in my life I have had to hang my head with shame that my country should permit such treatment of her representatives." [18] This blot on the honor of America as a victorious Ally was but one reason for Crane's frequent ire about the unjustified restrictions on his mission. Equally important were his fears that without increased U.S. participation in the evolution of peacetime Bulgaria, both within and without the ACC, the Communist domination would lead to the emergence of a pro-Soviet satellite. As he informed the War Department in 1945, elections held while America's participation in armistice supervision was restricted would produce candidates that might as well be picked by Stalin personally: "The Communist Party, backed by the Red Army is in complete control here. Every move the Bulgarian Government makes is directed by a Russian." The only way to ensure freedom of choice in upcoming elections, Crane cautioned, was to insist upon "(1) Full participation in ACC with no restrictions by Russians as to number of our Mission, (2) free entry and exit for planes, (3) full freedom of movement in Bulgaria, (4) announcement that elections cannot be held until the three countries can all assure themselves that conditions are such as to permit free elections." [19]

To place the grievances of General Crane in greater perspective and to provide fuller justification for his obvious discouragement, it is helpful to examine the personalities and activities of his Soviet ACC counterparts. As one might imagine, their accounts of the Soviet mission's experience in Bulgaria offer a radically different point of view both as to goals and problems of enforcing the Bulgarian armistice. The Soviet chairman of both the Soviet mission and the Allied Control Commission was technically General Tolbukhin, but General Biriuzov was assigned by Tolbukhin to function as his replacement. In day-to-day matters, however, it was not with Biriuzov that the Americans most frequently bumped heads but with his deputy, General A. I. Cherepanov, or with Biriuzov's chief of staff, General A. I. Suchkov. These latter two officers in conjunction with the former Soviet ambassador to Bulgaria, A. A. Lavrishchev, supervised the regular activities of the 270-man Soviet mission, which included 4 generals, 1 rear admiral, and more than 100 officers. [20]

General Cherepanov, like his superior, Biriuzov, made a career of the military, having taken his first command in early 1918 against Germany in northwestern Russia.[21] In the interwar period, Cherepanov performed both military and diplomatic tasks and was assigned to China in the 1920s. In the fall of 1944, Cherepanov was recalled from the front and informed that his next assignment would be in Sofia. He was given extensive briefings in the Soviet Foreign Ministry about problems he might encounter; the section headed by Deputy Foreign Minister Vyshensky led these discussions. According to Cherepanov's memoirs, suspicion of Western intentions was an integral part of his conversations. Cherepanov's last session with Vyshensky, however, was subdued. Handing him his final orders, Vyshensky paternally cautioned the general that his new duties would demand new methods and tactics: "You are passing from one front to another, the diplomatic. On this front you will need to fight not with weapons but with a coffee cup in your hand."[22] The next day, Cherepanov left for Bucharest to confer with the Soviet chairman of the Rumanian ACC on its operations and problems—a route General Suchkov would soon travel, accounting in part for the similarity of eventual American complaints about Soviet operations in the two Balkan ACCs.

Unlike General Crane, General Cherepanov's experiences in Bulgaria were friendly and productive from the moment of his arrival. His first session with a representative of Prime Minister Georgiev's staff produced an emotional reunion when Cherepanov discovered his contact to be an old comrade-in-arms, a Bulgarian Communist with whom he had worked in China two decades before. Observing the joyous meeting, General Biriuzov remarked that it symbolized the opening of a new era of diplomatic goodwill: "We now fought not only for Slavic blood but also for Slavic ideas." The high point of Cherepanov's first month in Sofia was the gala celebration staged by the Bulgarian Communists on the anniversary of the Soviet 1917 Revolution at which the "legendary Sonia" (Tsola Dragoicheva, leading Politburo member and chairperson of the National Committee of the Fatherland Front) spoke. "Our brothers," she said, "Bulgarians of the older generation express their unlimited love and gratitude to the Russian people."[23]

In such a hospitable atmosphere, Cherepanov experienced none of the problems that confronted Crane and his staff when dealing with armistice verification. Through regular meetings with local Communist leaders such as Traicho Kostov, Dimitur Ganev, and Regent Todor Pavlov, privileged information on the course of Bulgaria's evolution was immediately at hand. "Thanks to their help, we were promptly [made] aware of the most minute details on the questions with which we dealt," he later wrote.[24]

Cherepanov's regular contact with the Fatherland Front government was a special commissariat formed within the Foreign Ministry with the expressed purpose of complying with ACC demands.[25] General Biriuzov's letter of November 29, 1944, permitted only Soviet officials to communicate with this and other Bulgarian departments, ensuring a total monopoly of control of which Cherepanov made extensive use.[26] Thus between formal and informal ties, Cherepanov and his subordinates were assured of deep involvement in every important aspect of Bulgaria's present and future at a time when their Western Allies were directing their energies at lifting the humiliating restrictions that limited even requests to survey the Bulgarian landscape.

General-Major A. I. Suchkov, Biriuzov's chief of staff, arrived in Bulgaria from a tour as deputy chief of staff of the First Ukranian Front. He, too, was initially briefed in Moscow, presumably by Vyshensky's section of the Foreign Ministry, and dispatched for a period of on-the-job training with the Soviet staff of the Rumanian control commission. Upon arriving in Sofia, Suchkov was assigned direct supervision over the various sections of the Soviet Military mission: military, naval, aviation, economic, administrative, military transport, signal, transportation, security, and administrative-economic. The inability of General Biriuzov to separate the roles of chairman of the ACC and commander of Soviet forces in Bulgaria complicated Suchkov's duties. For Suchkov, as for Cherepanov, no important distinctions were drawn between the task of enforcing the armistice and assisting the socialist future of Bulgaria. He commented: "The fundamental tasks of the ACC were naturally the questions connected with ensuring from the Bulgarian government the conditions of the armistice, with rendering aid to the Bulgarian people to establish a new democratic path of development, . . . the active participation of the Bulgarian army in the war against fascist Germany, liquidation of all remnants of the fascist regime, affirmation of the new popular democratic order." In accord with efforts to diminish and eventually end bourgeois influence in Bulgaria, Suchkov supervised his mission's Economic Section, which "participated most actively in the first complete economic reorganization led by the Bulgarian people and their avant-garde, the Communist party." Unlike the disorganized American Economic Section, its Soviet counterpart consisted of individuals selected for their expertise in various areas of economic theory and practice. Lieutenant Colonel Remennikov had been trained in industrial planning, Colonel Ilvovsky in finance, and Lieutenant Colonel Beglovin in agricultural planning.[27] With direct Soviet advice and assistance, the Bulgarian government passed its first law on agricultural cooperatives in the spring of 1945, and more than one hundred "labor-collectives" were founded by year's end. Thirty-six thousand farm machines, ranging from tractors to horse-drawn plows, were supplied by the Soviet Union.[28] This goal of enhancing the prospects for Bulgaria's socialist future was pursued by the Military Section, which also was under Suchkov's supervision. As a recent Soviet study concluded: "Great significance accrued, during the fall of 1944 in Bulgaria, to the activity of the committee of the Bulgarian Communist party [which] with the help of the Soviet army political organizers [undertook] the ideological-political education of the Bulgarian population. Direct contact was established between the organs of the new power and Soviet co-workers for the solution of a series of questions concerning ideological work."[29]

When the normal routine of guiding Bulgaria's political and economic evolution into safe harbors required exceptional measures, General Biriuzov was available for direct intervention. As mentioned above, it was Biriuzov who, at Cherepanov's request, informed Bulgarian Prime Minister Georgiev that Order Number 4, which undermined the growing Communist control of the army, must be immediately canceled. And it was Biriuzov who "suggested" that Gemeto resign his post in the Agrarian party—an intervention into domestic politics repeated in the spring of 1945. Thus between regular duties and specific cases of crisis management, the Soviet mission to the ACC maintained tight control over Bulgaria's present and future.

As might be expected, Western efforts to break this monopoly of supervision and surveillance led to numerous disputes and lingering hatred between the Americans and key Soviet personnel. Surprisingly, General Crane made the best impression despite his constant calls for ACC reforms and for ending restrictions on travel. As General Biriuzov later recalled: "Crane was a man not seized by passions, having pulled duty in the Pentagon. Often he told me of his long friendship with Franklin Roosevelt, but he also enjoyed rural themes. A hereditary farmer of good spirit, to a degree phlegmatic, John Crane dreamed not so much of a military or diplomatic career as about a good yield of milk or a high price for wheat. In his pocket there were always crumpled photos, and he enjoyed showing them to whomever he spoke. Portraits of the general's family were interspersed with snapshots of breeding cattle, horses and pigs. John Crane, to the degree possible, attempted to fulfill on time the armistice [tasks] which did not elicit any sympathy in him."[30] To General Cherepanov, Crane appeared as reasonable and proper, "without emotion as if unwilling to defend his point of view."[31]

Crane's British counterpart, Major-General W. H. Oxley, was perceived in a much more evil light by the ever-suspicious Russians. "General Oxley, tall and lean, was a professional spy. In the past, he had commanded British intelligence services in the Balkans and had gained notoriety in his career. He was most interested in the districts where our army was quartered and the location of our airfields. He often tried to enter these districts under the ploy of 'hunting.' " At times, Oxley left Sofia without the required permission or escort on such "hunting excursions" and would often "stumble" upon Soviet military posts.[32] A similar view of Oxley as the "lover-of-the-hunt" is given by General Suchkov.[33]

The restrictions the Soviets placed on Oxley and his fellow British "hunters" reflected an important contest between the British military mission and the Soviet-dominated ACC. The proximity of Bulgaria to Greece prompted the British to increase their surveillance of both Soviet and Bulgarian forces, and their mission numbered 160 members—more than three times the size of the Americas.[34] Activities by this mission were naturally viewed with jaundiced eyes by Soviet officers, and various direct and indirect measures were taken to abort British intelligence operations, including cuts in food allotments.[35] London, in turn, made repeated protests to Moscow, seeking removal of Soviet restrictions on mission movements. Having forsworn direct participation in the control commission during the October 1944 Moscow Conference so as to ensure Soviet "benign neglect" for British activities in Greece, the Foreign Office focused its attention on improving British travel rights and the autonomy of the British mission.

In early December 1944, Anthony Eden informed Foreign Minister Molotov of British complaints. Molotov's reply was deemed unsatisfactory, although the issue was not pressed because of the delicate negotiations then in progress dealing with the Allied Control Commission for Hungary.[36] In late January, after the Hungarian armistice was signed, British Ambassador Sir A. Clark Kerr approached Molotov to request that rights just granted Western delegates in Budapest be extended to Sofia.[37] This effort fo find a parallel between Bulgaria and Hungary, however, drew an immediate rebuff from Molotov, who cynically replied that Britain had already received her "twenty percent" share of influence in Bulgaria and somewhat more influence than she deserved in Hungary.[38] In late February, Clark Kerr drew upon a new analogy in his continuing efforts to free his country's representatives from Soviet restrictions. Avoiding the case of Hungary, the British ambassador requested that British representatives in Bulgaria be given the same facilities and rights of movement accorded the Soviet representatives in Italy. As Kerr pointed out, Soviet officers in

Italy could travel without the presence of Western liasion and were issued travel permits by their own commanding officers—Western permission being needed only for journeys made in British or American transport vehicles.[39] This demarche, too, brought no success, and Kerr concluded that it would be useless for Britain to argue further over Bulgaria or Rumania. The Russians, he advised his Foreign Office, would show greater respect if issues of genuine British concern over such areas as Greece and Turkey remained the focus of future East-West discussions.[40]

During this period, when the British tried without success to revise the rules governing the activities of the Western missions in the Balkans, the American State Department remained silent, refusing to seek piecemeal revisions while the war against Germany was in progress. The identical notes delivered in protest of Article 18 of the Bulgarian armistice to both Britain and the USSR clearly spelled out the American intention to live with the existing restrictions until the German conflict terminated. Thereafter, the entire issue would be open for comprehensive discussion and change. As Acting Secretary of State Joseph Grew informed Harriman, "We have been aware that in the first period [from the armistice until defeat of Germany] certain military operations were based on Bulgarian territory and that direct military responsibility in Bulgaria lay with the Soviet High Command. This Government accordingly was willing *temporarily* to subordinate its own interests and responsibilities in Bulgaria to the common interest and responsibility in the successful prosecution of Allied military operations since military considerations were regarded as overriding."[41] By the spring of 1945, having been rebuffed in their own attempts at reform, the British, too, decided that an eventual full review of ACC rules offered the best hopes of satisfying their objectives. In mid-March, the American representatives in Sofia were advised that a British proposal to this effect had just been delivered to the State Department. Including demands for full Western participation in ACC meetings, direct access to Bulgarian governmental authorities, and a more equitable sharing of occupation responsibilities, the British proposal so closely matched long-range American plans for revision that the earlier emphasis upon freeing up travel was omitted.[42] In their response, Crane and Barnes, while accepting the British points as given, suggested that freedom of travel and unrestricted movement in and out of Bulgaria for Western personnel be added.[43]

The death of President Roosevelt in mid-April and the inevitable policy review that shortly followed the inauguration of the new chief of state advanced by several weeks the long-planned American reappraisal of its Bulgarian and Balkan policies. The forthright stance taken by the new president augured well for policy revisions that would incorporate "hard-line" suggestions which many of State Department's East European diplomats had long proposed. In a discussion with Harriman, attended by Stettinius, Grew, and Bohlen, President Truman asserted that "he was not in any sense afraid of the Russians and that he intended to be firm but fair since in his opinion the Soviet Union needed us more than we needed them." He would "make no concessions from American principles or traditions for the fact of winning their favor."[44] When, shortly thereafter, Truman upbraided visiting Foreign Minister Molotov over Soviet policy in Poland, American diplomats sensed that a new era had dawned. As Soviet specialist Loy Henderson remarked, "Departmental morale began to soar."[45] It was into this revitalized atmosphere that General Crane and his Rumanian counterpart, General Cortlandt Van Rensselaer Schuyler, returned in late April to discuss possible changes in America's Balkan policy.

Taking advantage of the policy review, Maynard Barnes drafted a lengthy memorandum detailing conditions in Bulgaria and suggesting alternative solutions. To ensure a hearing, Barnes addressed his missive to his old friend, H. Freeman ("Doc") Matthews, director of the Office of European Affairs, and sent it along with General Crane. Consistent with his straightforward, even abrupt demeanor, Barnes asserted that the situation in contemporary Bulgaria bore a striking and ominous resemblance to the atmosphere in Russia during the November 1917 Revolution. Restrictions still in force prevented the Western missions from arresting this fateful historic progression.[46]

Such practices and others, spelled out in detail in Barnes's seven-page memo, required, in the author's view, prompt and extensive change. Combining the various recommendations which he and Crane had forwarded to Washington at frequent intervals in the past, Barnes presented a five-point program for guaranteeing the proper functions of the ACC in the future:

1. American and British representatives to take their places as full members of the Commission with the right to be present at all meetings and to participate fully in the handling of all questions before the Commission. They should have the right to direct access to the Bulgarian authorities.

2. Decisions issued in the name and authority of the Allied Control Commission should be unanimous. . . .

3. The degree to which the United States and United Kingdom representatives shall participate in the administrative and execu-

tive work of the Commission is a matter for determination on the spot. However, they must certainly have the right to membership in any sub-committee or executive organ dealing with United States and United Kingdom rights and property.

4. Unrestricted movement in and out of Bulgaria of United States and United Kingdom aircraft required by representatives for communication and transportation.

5. Unrestricted movement of necessary personnel into and out of Bulgaria and freedom of movement within Bulgaria.

And yet Barnes, a veteran of numerous discussions and disputes with the Soviets, knew there was no guarantee that Moscow would consent to even a few of these needed changes.[47]

While Barnes's conclusion appeared to plumb the depth of despair, General Crane's recommendations were only slightly less pessimistic. In a letter to the Joint Chiefs sent while Crane was in Washington for the policy review, the general listed three possible courses of action now that the war against Germany was drawing to a close. America might leave responsibility for the future of Bulgaria entirely to the Soviets, accepting the inferior status currently accorded the U.S. representatives. Or America might withdraw from the ACC, announcing that henceforth armistice supervision lay solely with the Soviets. The preferred solution, however, was a lifting of restrictions limiting America's participation in the ACC.[48]

As expected, the policy review to which Generals Crane and Schuyler were invited focused on ways to revise Soviet domination of the Balkan control commissions. As Acting Secretary of State Grew informed President Truman, "For both representatives and in both countries [Bulgaria and Rumania] the problem is essentially the same; namely, the difficulty of maintaining the position of this Government in an area where the Soviet Government considers its interests paramount." By now, nearly eighteen months after drafting of the initial OSS plan for Bulgaria, and aware that a common pattern of Soviet restrictions had been imposed upon America's Balkan representatives, Grew was less inclined to draw sharp distinctions concerning America's interests in each Balkan state than his predecessors. Although he was willing to "concede that Soviet interests in Rumania and Bulgaria are more direct than ours," Grew insisted that in both nations America ought to "take a strong stand vis-a-vis the Soviet Government in support of the principles of joint Allied action in the political sphere and non-exclusion in the economic sphere."[49] Perhaps because of Grew's strong commitment to the Yalta declaration, Crane in his meeting with Truman omitted the negative option of withdrawing representation from the Bulgarian ACC. When Truman asked if any benefits might accrue from following such a course, Grew immediately responded that ACC reform was the best solution.[50] The following day, in a memorandum to the president, Crane confirmed his and Grew's position on reform: "The Allied Control Commission, Bulgaria, is completely dominated by the USSR. Russia, through the medium of the Allied Control Commission, is proceeding to impose a Communist-dominated government on Bulgaria despite the fact that this type government is not desired by the overwhelming majority of the population." The time had come, Crane concluded, to end this appalling situation: "U.S. must insist all restrictions on movements be withdrawn immediately," he wrote, and later "It is suggested that no time could be more propitious than the present for such action on the part of the United States for, as indicated by Article 18 of the Armistice terms, more truely tripartite action on the part of the Control Commission was contemplated during the period following cessation of hostilities with Germany."[51]

The warm response Crane's suggestions met in Washington and his ability to state his case before the highest reaches of government, including even the president, rekindled a fighting spirit which clearly had flagged during the depressing days of the previous spring. Upon his return to Sofia, Crane determined to take matters into his own hands without further sanction from Washington. On May 18, he informed the War Department that he soon would meet with Chairman Biriuzov to demand immediate reform of the ACC consistent with provisions under Article 18 of the Bulgarian armistice.[52]

Although Crane's proposals were fully consistent with the developing consensus in both the State and War departments, his point of initial attack, Bulgaria, had been rejected by Washington in favor of Hungary. As General Joseph McNarney, commander of the Mediterranean theater of operations, commented when forwarding Crane's message to Washington: "I concur in principle with Crane's 1682 but believe similar requests should be made simultaneously with respect to Rumania and Hungary, preferably through our Ambassador in Moscow."[53] The importance of the issue prompted an immediate reply from Chief of Staff Marshall which confirmed that the subject of the Balkan ACCs was under intense study and that "these matters must be handled on governmental level. State, at present drafting message to Soviets which will be presented by Harriman in Moscow. Consequently you should not follow course proposed pending further instructions. It now appears first stand will be taken in Hungary as statutes there give best case on which to establish precedent for presentation of Bulgarian and Rumanian case."[54] Although Crane bowed to military discipline, accepting Marshall's explanation, he could not forego a further message stressing the unique American situation in Bulgaria as justification for his initiative.[55] This was to be but the first example of an American representative in Sofia maintaining that policy initiatives should arise from the Balkan capital and that the situation in Bulgaria constituted the crucial test of future U.S.-Soviet relations.

The selection of Hungary rather than Bulgaria for the initial demand for revision of the control commission stemmed from the State Department's judgment that the relevant clauses in this armistice were much clearer. In late January 1945, both the State Department and the British Foreign Office informed Foreign Minister Molotov that provisions just accepted to guide the ACC in Budapest would require significant change upon termination of hostilities in Europe.[56] As written, the clause in question acknowledged a clear distinction between the first and second periods of ACC rule while granting the Western representatives the right of travel and determination of mission size in both periods.[57] In contrast, the signing of the Bulgarian armistice the preceding fall had been the occasion of disagreements, with the British refusing to acknowledge the propriety of the identical notes handed both the Soviet and British governments giving Washington the right of revision once the war with Germany ended. Hungary offered the best opportunity to initiate a revision and to set a precedent that might then be extended to Bulgaria and Rumania, and in late May, just ten days after Crane had suggested he take the initiative in Sofia, Ambassador Harriman was instructed to raise the issue of Hungary in Moscow. Discussion of changes in the Hungarian ACC, Harriman was told, should revolve about the following points:

(1) The ACC, the functions of which should remain limited to the enforcement of the terms of the Armistice, should operate henceforth under standing instructions of the three Allied Governments, whose principal representative in the ACC would have equal status, although the Soviet representative would be Chairman.

(2) The ACC decisions should have the concurrence of all three principal representatives who would refer to their respective Governments for instructions on important questions of policy.

(3) All three Allied Governments should have the right to be represented on the sections and subsections of the ACC but need not be represented in equal number.

Specific reference to demands for freedom of travel and the size of the mission was deemed unnecessary because "these grounds for complaint will of course disappear if the ACC operates henceforth as a tripartite body."[58] On June 8, Harriman was instructed to request similar discussions concerning proposed revisions of the Rumanian ACC and, four days later, the Bulgarian.[59]

From the perspective of Crane and Barnes in Sofia, State Department action came just in the nick of time. On June 6, the first units of the reformed Bulgarian army returned from the war against Germany—a potential prerequisite for the holding of elections. The next day, the Bulgarian press published the long-awaited electoral decree, and although it failed to order the feared single list of candidates, it did include provisions for such a list at the discretion of the participating parties. On June 11, Barnes advised the State Department that elections were likely by the end of August. Five days later, continuing his messages of alarm, Barnes cautioned that not even the tripartite commission foreseen in notes sent to Moscow the preceding spring would ensure democratic balloting; consultation among the Allies was the sole recourse.[60]

Stress upon the impending and unfair elections was but one means Barnes used to make his government aware of problems in Bulgaria. Seeking to place Bulgaria within the larger perspective of U.S. policy, Barnes, on the eve of the Potsdam Conference, advised his superiors that seven months in Sofia had given him special insight into Russia's aims in the Balkans, which included "use of Bulgaria as a stepping stone to seizure and retention of control of the Dardanelles and. . . . Use of Bulgarian [sic] and Yugo[slavia] to assure access to the Med[iterranean]." This alarming message was shortly followed by another reporting rumors of an impending Soviet military thrust through Bulgaria against the Turkish Straits.[61] Crane also maintained pressure on both the War Department and the new secretary of state, James Byrnes, by reporting that two months after conclusion of hostilities against Germany, the ACC had not met—a clear violation of the armistice agreement. "Can't we talk a little tough to the Russians in Moscow, and avoid being kicked in the face every day?" he asked.[62]

On July 11, the long-awaited Soviet response was released directly to General Crane in Sofia, one full day before a similar release in Budapest. The note acknowledged that changes in the operating rules of the Bulgarian ACC indeed were in order given the resolution of the German war. Henceforth, the representatives of the Western powers would have the right to free travel about Bulgaria after the ACC had been informed of time and route. The size of each mission would be the sole responsibility of the West, and rules restricting the entry and dispatch of mail would be reformed.[63]

The sharp eye of Barnes quickly caught a major discrepancy in these new provisions. Although the initial three clauses of the reform provisions promised regular meetings of both the ACC and its individual sections, resolution of disagreements still lay with the Soviet directors. As provided in the draft handed Crane, the chairman or deputy chairman, both of whom remained members of the Soviet mission, were bound only to "consult" with their Western colleagues before issuing directives binding on the Bulgarian government. Western participation in the ACC sections was considered "general consultations."[64] Barnes quickly informed Washington: " 'Consultation' as provided in numbered paragraphs 1, 2, and 3 of the Soviet statement of procedure could in my opinion only make our representation and that of the British on the Allied Control Commission even more effective as a tool of Russian policy than has been the case hitherto. If we accept the procedure outlined, the Russians will be able to contend with better face than ever that directives of the Commission are Allied in character." Much more than a mere promise of "consultation" was required, Barnes thought, to justify removal of the issue of ACC reform from the agenda of the impending Potsdam Conference.[65] Since the Soviet response to America's demand for ACC revision in Hungary was judged unclear, and no response had come for Rumania, Secretary of State Byrnes resolved to raise the entire issue at the three-power meeting in the German capital.[66] On July 31, at the eleventh plenary meeting, Byrnes introduced his own proposal for ACC reforms while merely acknowledging receipt of the earlier Soviet drafts.[67] When Molotov quickly pointed out that a Soviet proposal to accept the statutes of change suggested for the Hungarian ACC had already received American approval, Byrnes rejoined that such was only in principle; the bargaining would continue.[68]

Byrnes's tactics in dealing with Molotov about the preferred rules for guiding the ACCs in Eastern Europe revealed a subtlety and a patience much at odds with the brash approach of his subordinates in Sofia. Eschewing for the moment the issue of "consultation" which Barnes saw as the most threatening term in the Soviet proposal, Byrnes concentrated his attention upon demands for "regular and frequent" ACC meetings in each country. In reply to Molotov's rebuttal that the Soviet guidelines suggested meetings every ten days, Byrnes insisted that the crucial issue was Soviet acknowledgment of the actual need for frequent meetings—the philosophical bases on which meetings every ten days or perhaps even more often could be justified and demanded. Having made the point for the record, Byrnes received agreement from both the British and Soviet foreign ministers that the substance of the Soviet proposal for Hungary be extended to Bulgaria and Rumania. Then, despite Molotov's evident confusion, Byrnes suggested that the

Soviet draft be sent to a committee for final editing, the supposed object being to omit a portion of the American counterdraft, confirm three paragraphs in the Soviet draft, and produce a final product suitable for the three East European ACCs.[69] But when the final protocol of the Potsdam Conference was released, it became apparent that much more important concessions had been gained in the "editing" process than might have been expected. The Hungarian draft revision as submitted by the USSR on July 12 was the basis of the final agreement for all three East European states but in a changed manner. No longer would "directives of the ACC on questions of principle be issued . . . by the President of the Allied Control Commission after coordinating these directives with the English and American representatives."[70] Nor would the chairman have only to "consult" with his colleagues as provided in the Bulgarian draft revisions that were presented to Barnes. Rather, "directives of the ACC on questions of principle will be issued . . . by the President of the Allied Control Commission *after agreement* on these directives with the English and American representatives."[71] Such a shift of wording in one stroke transformed the initial Soviet proposal for Hungary, now to be extended to all three ACCs, from its original pro-Soviet biases into a rule providing equal tripartite control of ACC undertakings. Sections 3, 4, and 5 of the final draft confirmed the already promised rights of travel and autonomy. At the end of August, the Soviet authorities transmitted the new rules for the Bulgarian ACC to Sofia, remaining true to the wording adopted at Potsdam. Regular meetings at least three times a month were promised, frequent interaction among the members of the various sections envisaged, and all directives of the ACC on matters of substance would be directed to Bulgarian authorities only "after agreement has been reached" with the Western representatives. An extensive list of rights and privileges granted to the Western delegates was included.[72] At first glance, Crane and Barnes could only have concluded that a new era of Allied cooperation was dawning. Time was to prove such conclusions unfounded.

Fortunately for the historian, a complete set of transcripts, Soviet and Western, exist for the twenty-seven plenary sessions of the ACC spanning the period from September 1945 until the final meeting of January 23, 1947.[73] Western transcripts for special sessions called ad hoc to deal with such issues as the elections of 1945 and 1946 also survive. The chairman for these sessions usually was General Biriuzov or his deputy, General Cherepanov, although Soviet Chief of Staff General Suchkov directed sessions in the absence of his superiors. The Soviet contingent to meetings usually consisted of from five to seven individuals, normally selected from the Soviet section whose proposals were on the day's agenda. Several interpreters and stenographers rounded out the Soviet component. The British mission was represented by General Oxley, accompanied by three or four of his section heads as well as a stenographer and translator. The British provided the transcripts for the American delegation, which was led by Major-General Crane or his designated assistant, Colonel James de B. Walback, from September 1945 to March 1946, when Crane was replaced as head of the mission by Major General W. M. Robertson. Because of the independent position of Maynard Barnes as U.S. political representative to Bulgaria, the Soviets did not permit him to attend ACC meetings. Only in the tumultuous days of the fall 1945 postponement of the scheduled Bulgarian elections was Barnes invited to participate in the debates, an invitation he accepted with relish. Several section heads usually rounded out the American delegation at ACC meetings, in addition to a translator.

The purpose of the Allied Control Commission, Bulgaria, as provided in the much-disputed Article 18 of the 1944 armistice, was supervision of Bulgarian compliance with the additional armistice terms, and the majority of meetings followed a Soviet agenda listing the armistice clauses to be examined on a given day. Since Article 3 provided for freedom of movement for Allied forces, and several others dealt with the autonomy of each mission, earlier quarrels over freedom of travel and size of missions were rephrased after September 1945 in terms of the relevant clauses when necessary. The normal procedure was for the various sections responsible for examining Bulgarian fulfillment of the armistice to meet several days before a plenary ACC meeting to discuss the information available. According to the American history of the U.S. mission, "In most instances the Soviets were reported cordial and friendly at the meetings although the specialists frequently complained that they either could not receive the answers to questions asked, or met with unwarranted evasion or delay."[74] The same Soviet refusal to allow their Western colleagues too deep an involvement in the process of armistice supervision characterized the plenary sessions of the ACC. In November 1945, General Crane complained to presiding Chairman Cherepanov that to date the Soviets had merely read statements of purported Bulgarian compliance with specified provisions without previously forwarding the necessary information or documents. Such materials, Crane argued, ought to be dispatched to the Western missions well in advance of meetings to allow time for translation, study, and preparation of possible rebuttals. Cherepanov, rejecting Crane's proposal, weakly argued that time constraints made advance notification impossible.[75] This pattern of Soviet caution and, at times, confrontation, can be illustrated by reference to some of the more important topics discussed in the ACC transcripts.

In the period following the Potsdam Conference, the Western representatives sought to gain Soviet permission for the unrestricted importation of books, journals, and other objects of culture consistent with provisions in Article 8 of the armistice, which stated: "The publication, introduction and distribution in Bulgaria of periodical, or nonperiodical literature, the presentation of theatrical performances or films . . . will take place in agreement with the Allied (Soviet) High Command."[76] During the eighteen months following revision of the ACC rules, the Soviets took every opportunity available to frustrate importation of even the most innocuous Western materials. As early as the ACC session of September 25, 1945, the Soviet representative, M. I. Levitshkin, stated for the record that importation, distribution, and sales of English literature did not fall under the provisions of the armistice but were a matter for discussion between Western representatives and the proper members of the Bulgarian Ministry of Trade. Apparently still unfamiliar with the Soviet techniques, General Oxley inquired whether Levitshkin's statement ought to be interpreted to mean that the ACC held no objections to the sale of English-language novels, journals, and the like, responsibility resting with the Bulgarians. Such, Cherepanov rejoined, was not precisely the situation. While the Bulgarians should determine desired quantities, the ACC would still have to approve the general transaction. In short order, Oxley realized that an agreement had been reached beforehand between the Russians and their Bulgarian comrades aimed at furthering the persistent Bulgarian effort to reestablish normal trade relations with the West. Biriuzov revealed a detailed understanding of current British-Bulgarian discussions toward this end, including the proposed price London might pay for rose oil. The meeting closed with Biriuzov reconfirming that entry of Western literature must first be decided between Sofia and the West and then approved by the ACC.[77]

The next plaintiff regarding cultural issues was General Crane. Having discovered from Bulgarian sources that all Western films would be withdrawn from local theaters as of October 25, Crane demanded an immediate explanation. General Cherepanov, presiding for General Biriuzov, curtly explained that such prohibitions were covered under Article 8, and suggested that fuller information must await the return of his superior.[78] When Biriuzov rejoined the ACC meetings in late November, little additional information was provided except a statement that exhibition of films could take place only with the prior agreement of the Allied (Soviet) High Command.[79] Only at the following meeting did this pointed reference to the High Command become intelligible. Once again Levitshkin took the floor, explaining that under the relevant armistice provisions, the Bulgarian Ministry of Propaganda was entrusted with restricting all cultural forms with fascist tendencies. Importation of films, he continued, required approval not from the ACC but from the Soviet High Command, and such permission had not been sought. Up until October, Levitshkin noted, the Soviet representatives had not realized that the Bulgarians had failed to request such permission, and, having realized the true state of affairs, the Bulgarians had been told to withdraw all films imported without the required approval. For the first time in the history of the Allied Control Commission, the Soviet representatives argued that a clause in the armistice had not been faithfully honored by their Bulgarian friends. In the future, Levitshkin concluded, the Western Allies might import films as they wished, provided that sanction was first sought from the Soviet High Command. In short, the situation had been reversed, with the negotiations with the Bulgarian government no longer the initial or key step in importation of cultural objects. A "catch 22" situation was apparent.

The confusion within the Western representation to this ACC meeting is evident from the surviving transcript. Crane responded that he failed to understand Levitshkin's interpretation of the word "agreement" within Article 8 since the American head of mission had agreed to nothing, having simply been informed that the films in question were being withdrawn by order of the Allied (Soviet) High Command. In response, Levitshkin made the Soviet position clear. Under the cited clause, no provision existed requiring anyone to agree with the Soviet position. Rather, the "agreement" of the Allied (Soviet) High Command was required for certain activities such as the showing of Western films. In other words, the sole function of the tripartite ACC was to forward requests to General Biriuzov in his alternate capacity as head of the Soviet command and await his decision. When the British representative inquired whether past permits authorizing Western cultural imports signed by Cherepanov or Suchkov remained valid, Cherepanov responded that henceforth such permits would require High Command validation.[80]

The months that followed failed to bring any improvement in this issue, which pitted two wartime Allies against a third, and restrictions soon were extended to the right of foreign correspondents to tour Bulgaria. In July 1946, both the American and British delegations presented formal protests from their respective governments but to no avail.[81] By the fall of 1946, Soviet censorship was extended to forbid publication in local newspapers of official letters exchanged between Secretary of State Byrnes and the Bulgarian prime minister despite their routine release to the press in the West. Letters sent by Maynard Barnes to local Bulgarian papers detailing American policy were also censored by an order from Biriuzov, a blatant demonstration of inequality among the three delegations.[82] At the second to last ACC meeting, in the fall of 1946, the problem of Soviet censorship again burst forth because four thousand copies of the American magazine *Life* had been confiscated. In a shift of position, Cherepanov argued that responsibility lay with the Bulgarian Ministry of Propaganda, which perhaps had concluded no market existed for this publication. When pressed by the American representative, however, Cherepanov restated the earlier position that all such imports required approval of the Soviet High Command. When asked who had in fact forbidden the sale, Cherepanov abruptly ended the meeting.[83]

The protracted dispute over the rights of two of the "victors" to import cultural items into a defeated state demonstrated in stark fashion the growing unity between the Soviet mission and the former enemy government. As a recent Soviet history aptly notes: "Soviet officers frequently stood on the side of their Bulgarian friends during disagreements with the representatives of the other states in the Allied Control Commission (English and America) and helped in deciding a series of questions in the interest of the Bulgarian side."[84] To the consternation of both Crane and Oxley, the Soviets often argued that the sovereignty of the Bulgarian government should not be limited by either its past surrender or the signing of the armistice. In July 1946, presiding ACC Chairman Suchkov startled the Western representatives by stating that Bulgaria had not surrendered unconditionally; the armistice terms constituted the conditions of capitulation. Therefore, no demands not specified in the armistice could be presented to Sofia.[85] This same subtle distinction was offered by the Soviets to limit Bulgaria's responsibility in providing reparations to Greece. In response to a sizable Greek request supported by the Americans and British, the Soviets invited the Bulgarian foreign minister to the ACC meeting for rebuttal. Bulgaria, he affirmed, was bound only by the armistice clauses and not by the protocol because it had been appended only after the armistice had been signed by the Bulgarian delegation in Moscow. Once again the question was whether Bulgaria had capitulated unconditionally, an issue never resolved to Western satisfaction and one that permitted the Soviets great latitude in dealing with the local government.[86] General Crane prophetically concluded, "One man with a small suitcase will be able to carry away all reparations the Greeks will get."[87] Such support for Bulgarian sovereignty allowed the Soviets to resist Western claims for reparation and restitution of Western property and hindered a solution to the fate and future of the Bulgarian royal family.[88] In each debate, the Soviets and their Bulgarian clients were ranged against the former Western Allies.

If questions about Bulgaria's sovereignty constituted a most important substantive issue of disagreement, continuing restrictions placed upon the Western missions were the most emotional. Under Article 3 of the armistice, "The Government of Bulgaria will afford to Soviet and other Allied forces freedom of movement over Bulgarian territory in any direction if, in the opinion of the Allied (Soviet) High Command, the military situation so requires, the Government of Bulgaria giving to such movements every assistance."[89] Although Soviet restrictions on travel in the first year of the ACC had caused great protest, it was assumed that revisions adopted at Potsdam would swiftly end the Western frustrations. Such was not to be. In late September 1945, agreement was reached whereby the Western representatives would notify Biriuzov of planned journeys; objections were to be filed by the Soviets within three hours. Permits were not to be required for travel. But despite scrupulous adherence to the rules, General Oxley informed an ACC session in early October 1945 that his men had been halted on the outskirts of Sofia. General Crane reported to the same meetings that his representative had also been detained by Soviet guards, who demanded permits despite clear understanding that they were not required. Crane and Oxley demanded to know whether the past agreements covering travel negotiated both in Sofia and at Potsdam be honored. In the future, they concluded, neither Western mission would apply for a permit.[90]

Cherepanov, presiding for Biriuzov, replied that despite the agreements at Potsdam, permission would indeed be required for travel to regions in which Soviet troops were stationed.[91] When the Western representatives raised the issue anew at subsequent sessions, Cherepanov responded that only General Biriuzov could modify the regulations.[92] As a further violation of the Potsdam agreements, Cherepanov announced in the summer of 1946 that the rations heretofore provided the Western missions were "excessive" and that henceforth no supplies would be allocated for the American political representative or his staff. Bulgarian employees of the American and British missions were to receive smaller quantities of food as well.[93] Since the providing of food and other supplies was an obligation assumed by Bulgaria under Article 15 of the armistice, Cherepanov demonstrated once again his willinghess to interpret the provisions to the benefit of Bulgaria.

In the spring of 1946, Major-General Crane completed his Bulgarian tour of duty, leaving for hospitalization in Naples for an unspecified illness. His last message to the Joint Chiefs offered a useful summary of persistent East-West problems since conclusion of the Potsdam Conference, as well as a personal statement of frustration. Ever since arriving in Sofia, Crane asserted, his mission had been in a "most humiliating position. . . . Restrictions put on our movement in Bulgaria had been unreasonable and dictatorial and have made us and America laughing stock." Hopes that the Potsdam Conference would alleviate these restrictions had not borne fruit in spite of specific agreements: "Mr. Truman and Mr. Stalin agreed in Potsdam that we should have right 'to be allowed free movement in the country with condition that ACC be previously informed of time and march route of trips.' This appears clear and definite but interpretation put on it by Russians is entirely different. We must give written notification as required, then we must wait until they tell us that we can go. This may take from 2 hours to 2 weeks. But also we have been notified that Russians here reserve to themselves right to deny us entry into any place where there are Russian troops and there are Russian troops almost everywhere." To add potential injury to insult, Crane continued, the Bulgarian militia—a force representing a defeated enemy—watched every American movement, frequently threatening Bulgarian employees of the mission and repeating that "their accounts will be settled when Americans leave." Orders issued in the name of the supposedly tripartite ACC still remained unknown to the Americans, and Soviet permission was required before planes carrying needed materials to the mission could land. If such restrictions and humiliations continued, Crane finally concluded, "our representation on ACC should be withdrawn."[94]

Following sixteen months of ceaseless frustration, Crane's despairing conclusions appear reasonable. Despite a concerted, often creative American effort to guarantee truly tripartite administration of the Bulgarian armistice, few tangible gains were apparent by the time of Crane's dpatein he early spring of 1946. The failure to ensure the active participation of American representatives stationed in Sofia meant that policies aimed at promoting the emergence of a democratic Bulgaria would proceed through direct interaction among American and Soviet diplomats at the highest levels. And by the spring of 1946, the State Department already had expended considerable effort in pressuring both Moscow and Sofia for needed reforms as the price of Bulgaria's eventual reentry into the peaceful postwar family of nations. A policy of nonrecognition in conjunction with directives forbidding the reestablishment of all financial transactions between Bulgaria and the West was deemed the preferred course of confirming the State Department's abiding concern for Bulgaria's future. It is to this policy, which accompanied demands for control commission reforms, that we must now turn. As with the directives aimed at tripartite administration, this policy, too, emerged from the extensive reviews of America's approach to East-West relations that characterized the initial months of the new Truman administration.

6 Planning for Postwar Bulgaria

No one who has inhabited the offices of the State or Defense departments during periods of change from one presidential administration to another ever forgets the creative confusion that overwhelms the everyday routine of business, confusion whose plasticity makes most difficult the historian's efforts to impose form or coherence. Individuals once assumed to be placid and uncaring suddenly write daily memorandums to section heads, revealing whirlpools of personal and professional discontent where before indifference seemed to reign. Previous supporters of existing policy directives and their underlying assumptions take on a conservative posture, awaiting emergence of a new consensus they can join. And if such are the broad parameters of a normal shift from one presidency to another, the uncertainties, competition, and newly expressed opinions that accompanied Harry S. Truman's elevation to Chief Executive contained several unique elements. The unknown proclivities of a man little schooled in the intrigues and intricacies of foreign policy presented a promising opportunity for diplomats long frustrated by Roosevelt's insistence that foreign policy be tightly controlled by the president's office. Truman's willingness to rely upon State Department advice because, as he admitted, "he was not up on all the details of foreign affairs," led a joyful Soviet specialist at State to remark that, unlike Roosevelt, the new president "was playing the game according to the rules."[1]

The international scene contained new and unknown elements as well. By mid-April it was clear that victory over Germany was rapidly approaching, and the past reticence to challenge questionable Soviet behavior for fear of undermining the European alliance became increasingly difficult to justify. Even the long-assumed requirement for Soviet assistance in the continuing war against Japan became subject to close scrutiny in the new administration as analysts reexamined the room for diplomatic maneuver vis-à-vis Moscow. In early May, Acting Secretary of State Joseph Grew requested the War and Navy departments to assess whether "the entry of the Soviet Union into the Pacific War at the earliest possible moment [is] of such vital interest to the United States as to preclude any attempts by the United States

Government to obtain Soviet agreement to certain desirable political objectives in the Far East prior to such entry."[2]

It is clear in retrospect that the new president, though feeling bound by the general commitments of his predecessor, focused a suspicious eye upon the Soviets from his first days in office. It would not be he who would break faith with Roosevelt's "grand design" but rather the Russians through noncompliance with existing pledges and agreements. And by the time of Foreign Minister Molotov's visit to Washington in late April, such noncompliance was evident. As Truman informed Secretary of War Stimson, "Our agreements with the Soviet Union so far had been a one-way street and that could not continue; it was now or never." When Stimson raised the issue of Soviet support for the soon-to-be-opened United Nations, Truman pointedly refuted past policy of overlooking Soviet transgressions for the sake of the new institution. Acknowledging that American support for the United Nations remained firm, Truman bluntly stated that "if the Russians did not wish to join us, they could go to hell."[3] By the end of April, the president was informed by his advisers that the Soviet Union had unilaterally established a provisional government in Austria in which "Moscow-trained Communists seemed to hold the key positions of Minister of Interior and Minister of Education and Religion." In Yugoslavia, Acting Secretary Grew reported, armed forces loyal to the Communist Tito were confronting Allied troops in the disputed region about Trieste.[4] In early May, Grew, along with Generals Schuyler and Crane, told the president of Soviet activities in the Balkans. As Truman later recalled, "In Rumania, General Schuyler informed me the Russians were running the Allied Control Commission without consulting the British and American members. The government was a minority government dominated by the Communists which . . . represented less than ten percent of the Rumanian population. . . . In Bulgaria, General Crane reported the situation was as bad."[5]

Both the content and the style of the numerous discussions regarding East-West problems in the initial months of the Truman administration logically led to the conclusion that the USSR must be restrained in areas where agreements were being violated. In distinction to earlier the American practice of withholding specific protests until outstanding negotiations had been resolved—the hesitancy to demand reorganization of the Rumanian government before resolution of the status of Poland being a prime example—Truman soon came to view Soviet behavior as of whole cloth. When the American political representative to Poland, Bliss Lane, suggested to Truman in early June that "our attitude toward Soviet Russia in connection with the Polish issue should be integrated with the many other issues in Central Europe, particularly the Soviet blackout in the Balkan states and the status of Central Europe. The President said that he had precisely the same opinion and that this would be the fundamental subject which he intended to discuss at the Big Three Meeting." That same month, the "commonality" of Moscow's expansive and undemocratic policies from Poland to the Balkans received further confirmation in a Soviet demand that a new Russian-Turkish treaty be negotiated.[6]

In these crucial first months of the new administration, Acting Secretary of State Grew bore the main burden of advising the president on international affairs. Although Truman also sought advice from his old friend and future secretary of state, James Byrnes, especially on U.S. commitments at Yalta—Byrnes having made a copy of the more important Yalta sessions—[7] Grew led the parade of East European diplomats to the White House. And if Harry Truman's attitude toward the USSR perceptibly hardened in this period, much of the responsibility must be accorded to Grew. Throughout the initial months of the Truman presidency, Grew stood duty for Secretary of State Stettinius, who was occupied with the opening session of the United Nations in San Francisco.[8] A veteran of more than forty years of diplomatic service, Grew had a sense of historical pattern that by May 1945 had produced the conclusion that war with the USSR was inevitable. As Grew wrote in a memorandum read to Ambassador Harriman and Charles Bohlen and subsequently locked in his personal files: "Future war with Soviet Russia is as certain as anything in this world can be. It may come within a very few years. We shall therefore do well to keep up our fighting strength and to do everything in our power to strengthen our relations with the free world. Already Russia is showing us—in Poland, Rumania, Bulgaria, Hungary, Austria, Czechoslovakia and Yugoslavia—the future world pattern that she visualizes and will aim to create. With her certain stranglehold on these countries, Russia's power will steadily increase and she will in the not distant future be in a favorable position to expand her control step-by-step through Europe."[9] Here lay the underpinnings for the belief that Soviet policy must be perceived as part of a greater whole regardless of whether the Soviet challenge came in Poland or Bulgaria.

The growing consensus that Soviet activities in Eastern Europe threatened both past East-West agreements and the stability of the postwar world erased once and for all earlier distinctions about the degree of American interest in the various Balkan states. Henceforth violations of past agreements concerning Rumania would be treated with the same concern as similar deeds in Bulgaria because the entire framework of U.S.-Soviet relations was equally jeopardized in both cases. In May and June, the White House and State Department drafted a common program designed to promote Soviet compliance with the relevant Yalta provisions foreseeing the emergence of democratic governments in the Balkans. As the *Briefing Book* prepared for the Potsdam Conference unambiguously defined the situation: "Information received from our representatives in Rumania and Bulgaria indicates that the Soviet authorities and the local Communist parties are actively engaged in establishing regimes based on the one-party or 'one-front' system, thus excluding from political life all democratic elements which do not subordinate themselves." The recommended solution was a U.S. demand for government reorganizations consistent with the letter and spirit of the Yalta Declaration on Liberated Europe. Pending such changes, America would refuse diplomatic recognition to the offending states and would postpone indefinitely the conclusion of peace treaties. The signatories of the Yalta agreement, plus France, ought to "consult" in an attempt to determine how the existing unrepresentative governments might be aided in complying with these demands.[10]

Since the proposed "consultation" on government reorganization could succeed only with Soviet cooperation, an unlikely prospect since Moscow was perceived as a main cause of Bulgarian intransigence, the significance of the U.S. proposal must be sought in its other provisions. The pointed refusal to recognize an unreconstituted Bulgarian government or to sign a peace bore the main thrust of the U.S. plan. In early June, Truman informed Stalin through Harriman that nonrecognition of the undemocratic regimes in Sofia and Bucharest was a mainstay of his emerging East European policy, a position warmly supported by Maynard Barnes.[11] British backing for this approach was sought in the weeks preceding the Potsdam Conference and was grudgingly extended after a series of cables between Washington and the Foreign Office.[12] Britain would support America at Potsdam, the British first secretary in Washington confided to a member of the State Department. But if the Soviets refused to acknowledge the propriety of withholding recognition, Britain might feel free to advance its own plans for early recognition and conclusion of peace agreements.[13]

At first glance, reliance upon an apparently passive policy of nonrecognition in the face of an active Bulgarian and Soviet offensive to promote left-wing control in Sofia strikes the contemporary researcher as a weak reed upon which to pin U.S. hopes for major government reorganization. But such a conclusion would overlook both the problems and possibilities of the postwar world. Until recognition and the subsequent peace treaties were granted the former Nazi satellites, these countries would remain outside the normal economic and political intercourse of nations, denied participation in formulating the rules and organizations that would eventually constrict or facilitate national development. Refusal of recognition meant that the trade embargoes invoked during the war would continue to wreak havoc with domestic plans for economic recovery. Nonrecognized regimes would be denied an official role in future peace conferences with the major Axis states, severely limiting any claims regarding border modifications or reparations. For Bulgaria, this might mean that Greek claims for territorial change in the disputed areas of Macedonia would find favor among the Western Allies without a corresponding Bulgarian rebuttal. The longer nonrecognition was in effect, the more probable the unfavorable results of the Western numerical majority at upcoming peace conferences on behalf of international claims contrary to Bulgaria's interest. In the interim, Bulgaria would remain under an oppressive and humiliating occupation whose costs she bore and which even before Potsdam threatened to bankrupt the fragile economy. In May 1945, the Bulgarian finance minister, Petko Stoyanov, remarked that the cost of maintaining Soviet forces of occupation and the Soviet-directed Bulgarian army had reached 3.5 billion leva per month and that "these expenditures would have a disastrous effect on the Bulgarian economy if they continued indefinitely beyond cessation of hostilities in Europe."[14] In a plaintive appeal for recognition, Bulgarian Foreign Minister Stainov also stressed the hardships nonrecognition engendered: "Bulgaria is taken up with the process of healing up her wounds from the criminal policy of the past pro-German Government and from the consequences of the war. . . . It follows and will continue to follow this road, in spite of the economic and other hardships which inevitably surge in similar turns of politics like the one which Bulgaria had just made. . . . It is hoped that the efforts of the Bulgarian nation . . . to overcome these handicaps might be understood and appreciated properly by the Allies."[15]

Documents which have become available in the past two decades reveal that by the advent of the Truman administration, the Bulgarians had begun a determined effort to break free of their economic and international isolation. As would be expected, the Soviet Union was the first power approached. In early January 1945, the Bulgarian political representative in Moscow, Dimitur Georgi Mikhalchev, requested Soviet Deputy Foreign Minister Vyshensky to plead his nation's case for recognition as a co-belligerent, a crucial first step toward full recognition. Vyshensky promised to present this plea to his government for consideration. When no response was forthcoming, Bulgarian Foreign Minister Stainov renewed the request by a personal letter to General Biriuzov with a copy to Mikhalchev in Moscow. Four days later, Mikhalchev was instructed by Stainov to gain Soviet support for an invitation to Bulgaria for the upcoming opening of the United Nations. With unusual frankness, the Soviet government informed the Bulgarians that the problem of Bulgaria's reentry into normal international activity arose from the negative feelings of Moscow's Western allies. It would be difficult to receive such an invitation for Bulgaria because detailed rules had been established as to which nations might attend, two categories of states being eligible for invitations. "You are neither one nor the other," the Soviet response concluded.[16]

The fundamental economic problem attending Bulgaria's continued status as an unrecognized nation and the cause of her ceaseless search for reintegration within the accepted international community are best revealed in an appeal by Stainov to Biriuzov sent in the spring of 1945. As the Bulgarian foreign minister confidentially wrote:

> You know well the difficulties which the Bulgarian economy must surmount. These difficulties arose as a consequence of the damage carried to us prior to September 9, 1944, and in connection with the impossibility of restoring Bulgaria's trade.
>
> In this regard, a serious hindrance is the fact that Bulgaria continues to be on the blacklist of the United Kingdom and the United States, the result of which is that the neutral governments continue to withhold reestablishment of economic relations with us.
>
> Thus, on April 6, [1945], the trade attachés of Great Britain and the United States of America in Switzerland officially informed the Bulgarian mission that they continued to regard Bulgaria as an enemy state . . . and that as a result, they will block conclusion of any trade arrangement and the transfer of monetary sums between Bulgaria and neutral states, and they consider Bulgarian goods and monetary investments in these states sequestered.
>
> Communicating this information, I have the honor to request you, Mr. General-Colonel, considering the difficult economic position of the state, to put forward measures to the governments of the United Kingdom and United States for lifting the restrictions placed upon Bulgaria so as to give her the possibility of reestablishing her trade both with the Allied governments and with the neutrals.[17]

The lifting of such restrictions remained tied to the future recognition of the Bulgarian regime.

The American decision to continue withholding recognition pending democratic reorganization in Sofia was fully supported by U.S. diplomats on the spot. When Acting Secretary of State Grew requested Barnes and Crane to respond to a British suggestion on behalf of early recognition, a lengthy rebuttal quickly returned from Sofia. Bulgarian Foreign Minister Stainov's direct appeal for recognition at Potsdam was greeted by Barnes with the same negative advice. This appeal ought to be considered, Barnes cabled, only as a means for extracting truly democratic reforms. And yet, while supporting the department's position, Barnes and Crane argued that stronger and more direct methods ought to be employed if reorganization was to be assured. Ever since the postponement of the spring elections, America's representatives in Sofia had pushed for greater U.S. involvement, viewing Bulgaria as a central test of U.S.-Soviet postwar relations. As Barnes informed Grew: "If we are in a poker game of world affairs, and I assume we are, then we should play the game to the best of our ability. I believe that we have more chips than anyone at the table. Circumstances in this area suggest that we should play our cards close to the chest but that when we do have a good hand, we should not fail to make a bet."[18] As time would show, the scenario of a card game would become apt as Bulgaria once again prepared for national elections.

In the two months preceding the Potsdam Conference, the political disputes within and without the Fatherland Front intensified, confirming Barnes's conviction that free elections remained impossible. The Standing Committee of the Bulgarian Agrarian Union, which had been elected at the pro-Communist May conference, examined ways to handle the refusal of Nikola Petkov to accept the purge of his followers. On June 12, Petkov was declared "removed" as general secretary of the party and was replaced with the more docile Alexander Obbov.[19] By now, the other members of the Fatherland Front who were unwilling blindly to follow the Communist lead had been forced out of their respective parties. The Bulgarian socialist party had initially been purged in January, but a further exclusion came in the early summer following the unsuccessful efforts of Kosta Lulchev, Grigor Cheshmedzhiev, who served as minister of social welfare in the Bulgarian cabinet, and several others to convene a Socialist party congress. Individual members of the National Union-Zveno were singled out for Communist criticism for their alleged insufficient fervor on behalf of the continuing campaign against Gemetoism within local

Fatherland Front committees.[20] By now, the government had acquired tight control over the supply of newsprint in an effort to restrict dissemination of dissenting views.[21]

In mid-June, amid the intensifying domestic political struggle, the Bulgarian government announced that national elections would be held on August 26. In an immediate report to Washington, Barnes noted that although the government had yet to state provisions of the expected electoral law, it was likely to include use of a single electoral list for all participating parties. Elections held in this fashion, Barnes continued, would make a mockery of pledges to conduct open and democratic balloting: "With Burov, Mushanov and the important Agrarian leader Gichev locked up in prison and with Dimitrov [Gemeto] in refuge, the great bulk of such truly democratic elements as do exist in the country will be deprived of any effective leadership and of any means of expression during the electoral campaign." Given prospects for a bogus Communist victory, the mere refusal to extend recognition to the Sofia regime struck Barnes as inappropriate. Little short of direct intervention by the three Yalta powers could guarantee the possibility of free elections. Not only was General Crane in full sympathy with this position, Barnes concluded, but so were the heads of the British mission.[22]

While awaiting a response from Washington, Nikola Petkov, certainly aware of Barnes's efforts on his behalf, took steps to bring the incipient electoral crisis to a head. Specifically excluded from participation in the proposed electoral list by the rump Standing Committee led by Obbov on June 29, and informed that he must resign his position as an Agrarian cabinet minister, Petkov resolved to confront his challengers.[23] With the Potsdam Conference scheduled to open ten days hence, Petkov issued a circular letter to local chairman of the Agrarian Union. Denouncing the May 8–9 party conference as "pernicious" and as a blatant attempt to divide the party, Petkov lashed out at the Communists for interfering in Agrarian internal matters, which "is not useful for the good relations between the two organizations or for the unity of the FF which is so necessary for the future of Bulgaria. . . . Feeling that they could not master the organization spiritually, the Comrades who took only the premises thought they could master it by force." Although such action had failed to destroy the Agrarian party, Petkov noted, urgent steps were now needed to restore unity and purpose and to ensure "really free legislative elections." All regional, county, and local Agrarian leaders appointed before the disruptive and illegal May conference were ordered to remain at their posts. Meetings between Agrarians and Communists should be convened at which "the unfortunate attempt made by some . . . comrades on May 8 and 9 of the current year to split the Union" would be explained. Expulsion of loyal Agrarians by the Obbov faction was not to be recognized, and candidates for the upcoming elections were to be selected only from the most "worthy" of the Agrarian ranks. Future reports of local Agrarian activities were henceforth to be forwarded to Petkov alone, the circular concluded. Petkov signed the document as secretary of the Agrarian party and minister without portfolio. Six additional signatures followed, including that of Asen Pavlov, minister of agriculture.[24]

Petkov's bold circular, complete with the signature of key Agrarian leaders, sent amid rumors that at least two non-Agrarian ministers had offered full support, created an immediate political crisis. Realizing that the expulsion of Petkov and his followers would be viewed unfavorably by the heads of state due shortly to assemble at Potsdam, the Bulgarian Communists opted to open discussions with the growing opposition.[25] On July 12, Anton Yugov, Politburo member and Communist minister of interior, proposed to Petkov that a compromise be struck between the rival wings of the Agrarian movement. Both the Petkov and Obbov Agrarians would advance candidates for a common electoral list, with resolution of conflicting nominations to rest with a special commission composed of representatives of both factions in strengths reflecting relative support as indicated by recent district meetings of the party. Additional representatives to the proposed commission would be appointed by the Communists. No controversial issues would be raised by either political faction until after the election, and the Agrarian ministers loyal to Petkov would remain as members of the cabinet.[26] Well aware that reference to recent party meetings indicated Yugov's true intention of supporting the Obbov faction, Petkov countered that both selection and confirmation of candidates be made by a commission composed of three representatives from each of the two rival Agrarian executive committees without participation of additional Communist appointees. Resolution of difficulties would be by Agrarian district committees "in all cases where these meetings were regular." The two executive committees must be represented in all matters dealing with the elections, and publication rights for the traditional Agrarian paper, *Zemedelsko zname,* would be returned to Petkov.[27] As might have been predicted, the talks quickly broke down, and the expulsion of the Agrarian ministers appeared but a matter of days.

By mid-July, the fast-moving Bulgarian events prompted Barnes to request additional guidance from Washington. He informed Grew, "In the absence of info from Dept., I, of course, have no way of knowing whether Bulgarian election situation will be deeply probed at meeting of Big Three." Might the president's recent telegram to Stalin explaining why America would not recognize the undemocratic Balkan governments and a recent article in the department's *Current Foreign Relations* be used to acquaint the Bulgarian opposition with the American position?[28] But with the Potsdam Conference just beginning, and uncertain of the Soviet response to U.S. plans calling for immediate consultation on the offending Balkan governments, Grew decided to advise caution: "Meanwhile, pending outcome considerations at that meeting, we think it inadvisable for you to give expression to our position in conversations with Bulgarian political and Govt leaders."[29]

Barnes could appreciate the caution shown by his superiors, given the delicate negotiations in process at Potsdam, but the depth of the crisis in Sofia prompted him to advise Washington that decisive action was imperative. On July 23, Barnes cabled that the time was ripe "to demand postponement of elections and amendment of the electoral law." Possessed of information that the struggle between Petkov and the Communists would shortly result in the expulsion of the former from the government and that such action would weaken America's future ability to enforce any demand for free elections, Barnes continued to plead for direct action. Two days later, the expected confrontation occurred when Petkov and two ranking Agrarian leaders appealed directly for Allied supervision of the impending election. Thereafter, Petkov and his followers left the cabinet, convincing a saddened Barnes that a unique opportunity to influence the course of Bulgaria's future development had been lost. He now informed Grew, "I feel very strongly that time has come when Dept must tell me what if anything, the US Govt [is] really prepared to do about local political and election situation. If for some reason we can not make a stand . . . I believe that I and the local leaders who have been resisting the Communists should be told the facts"[30] That same day, having received Barnes's message, Acting Secretary of State Grew convened an urgent session of the Secretary's Staff Committee to discuss the Bulgarian situation, sending an immediate cable to Byrnes at Potsdam requesting guidance at its conclusion.[31] Unknown to the diplomats in Sofia, the issue of free elections in the Balkans had already been forcefully prepared for the Potsdam Conference by the new American secretary of state, James Byrnes.

Byrnes, who received his appointment on the eve of Potsdam, brought a wealth of government service to his new office rarely equaled in the annals of State Department history. Having served in both the House of Representatives and the Senate, Byrnes had resigned an appointment to the Supreme Court in 1942 to accept a crucial position in Roosevelt's executive branch. Roosevelt took Byrnes to Yalta, sending him back to Washington during the closing days of the conference to alert an anxious American public about the agreements reached. Upon Roosevelt's death, Byrnes became an intimate adviser to the new president, and was designated as secretary of state a week before the departure for Potsdam.[32] Right up to the opening session of this conference, Byrnes immersed himself in the extensive State Department studies and recommendations, determined to avoid charges of unpreparedness such as had greeted Roosevelt's return from Yalta. Byrnes later recalled: "We worked hard on board the *Augusta*. Memoranda had been prepared in the State Department to cover every subject which conceivably could arise at the Conference. Every morning throughout the trip, Ben Cohen, H. Freeman (Doc) Matthews and Charles E. (Chip) Bohlen would meet with me in my cabin to consider these papers."[33]

The papers dealing with the Balkans reiterated the department's view that nonrecognition be maintained until a significant reorganization of the governments in question had been completed. It advised that "the three Allied Governments agree in principle to the reorganization of the present governments in Rumania and Bulgaria, and should it become necessary, in Hungary." The Big Three ought to engage in tripartite consultation as foreseen at Yalta so as "to work out any procedures as may be necessary . . . to include representation of all significant democratic elements with a view to the early holding of free and unfettered elections." Although anticipating that such tripartite discussions would determine the ground rules for future elections in the area, the State Department recommendations did not specify the procedure desired.

Study of these recommendations by both Truman and Byrnes facilitated the emergence of a combined strategy designed to reverse as much as possible the apparent Soviet efforts to gain control of important sections of Eastern Europe.[34] And yet this new determination did not necessarily imply that a perfect coincidence in strategy and tactics existed between the American delegation at Potsdam and the political representatives stationed in the East European capitals.[35] To Byrnes, the potential effectiveness of the Yalta agreement assumed a continuing unity of purpose among the three Allied governments and a willingness to work jointly to remove obstacles to the peaceful reconstruction of Europe.[36] Responsibility for what issues would be presented to the Soviets and the manner of their discussion was reserved for the highest officials of government, whose task of conducting overall foreign policy transcended the needs and goals of subordinates assigned to specific problem areas. Equally important, Byrnes and Truman realized that a framework of U.S.-Soviet cooperation was required within which problem solving for particular issues could take place without disrupting the bonds of friendship painstakingly established between East and West during the most destructive war in history. From the first meeting at Potsdam, the American leaders attempted to harmonize the requirements for an effective framework of conflict resolution with their desire to implement the Yalta agreement.

On July 17, at the initial plenary meeting of the Potsdam Conference, President Truman presented his administration's position on recent events in the former German satellites of Eastern Europe, reading a carefully prepared document entitled "Implementation of the Yalta Declaration on Liberated Europe." Although this document generally followed the earlier recommendations of the State Department, certain important changes were soon apparent. Whereas the earlier drafts had proposed that the three powers "agree in principle" to reorganization in Bulgaria and Rumania, Truman asserted that "the three Allied Governments should agree on the necessity of the immediate reorganization of the present governments in Rumania and Bulgaria." Whereas the State Department had recommended that provisions ought to *"be made"* for tripartite consultation, Truman now demanded "that there be *immediate consultation* to work out any procedures which may be necessary for the reorganization of these governments."[37] In short, Truman sought to avoid the rancorous disputes that had characterized efforts to invoke the right of consultation the preceding spring and to convert Potsdam into the forum for such consultations. Pending acceptance of the American request and the subsequent demanded reorganization, recognition and the conclusion of peace agreements with the states in question would be indefinitely postponed with all the harmful consequences entailed. Since Byrnes and Truman proposed to handle the drafting of peace treaties at a series of foreign ministers' conferences following Potsdam, pressure for "consultation," if ineffectual now, could be maintained at the highest level for the foreseeable future. This policy would permit the State Department to adopt a consistent course, avoiding the difficulties and recriminations that invariably greeted attempts to raise general issues on a country-by-country basis. Most important, pressure for democratic reorganization could be expected from the governments in question once America's resolve to exclude them from the political and financial benefits of normal international intercourse was understood.

If the general principles of consultation and reorganization were clearly understood by the American delegation, the means by which they might best be effected soon evoked significant disagreement from the Soviet representatives. Even though Truman and Byrnes wished to avoid direct U.S. participation in future Balkan elections, the secretary of state informed Molotov that America would consider a supervisory role if necessary to ensure compliance with the Yalta agreement.[38] When Molotov objected to such interference, a compromise was struck whereby a written Soviet pledge to allow Western journalists to report the political progress of the states was accepted.[39] Although this Soviet pledge fell short of guaranteeing the propriety of future elections, it did provide further proof that American recognition would not pro forma follow without substantial evidence that future balloting was in accord with Western demands. Molotov's pledge to allow entry of foreign journalists and the Soviet approval of the reorganization of the East European Allied control commissions were the maximum concession Moscow was willing to make.

In subsequent discussions the Soviets demanded that conditions in Italy and Greece be investigated, a sign that little progress could be expected. Aware that the Balkans, however important, were but one point on a busy agenda and convinced that only a continuation of East-West harmony could provide the framework required for eventual reconciliation, Byrnes and Truman wisely moved on to other problems. Notice had been served that the situation in the Balkans would remain unacceptable until measures consistent with the Yalta agreement were undertaken. The final protocol reiterated that each of the three Allied governments would exercise its own judgment as to recognition of the former German satellites and that peace agreements would be drafted at an upcoming meeting of the foreign ministers.[40] Consultation would continue at this next session, and America could withhold recognition until a satisfactory situation was reached. Far from disappointment, the American delegation expressed resolve when it returned to the United States. As President Truman announced to the American people: "At Yalta it was agreed, you will recall, that the three governments would assume a common responsibility in helping to reestablish in the liberated and satellite nations of Europe Governments broadly representative of democratic elements in the population. That responsibility shall stand. . . . These nations are not to be spheres of any one power."[41] Even the skeptical American representatives in Sofia concluded that a new day had dawned in East-West relations. "No one could be more delighted with or convinced by such evidence of power of US as the President's radio speech on the Berlin Conference than General Crane and myself," Barnes cabled. And yet

despite Barnes's joy at America's new resolve, important tactical differences remained between Washington and its representatives in
Sofia.[42]

For Maynard Barnes, the prospect of elections in Bulgaria was
much more threatening than for his superiors in Washington. The
publication of the feared "single list" in late July effectively excluded
the participation of the pro-American opposition, and the short time
allotted for filing individual candidacies precluded Petkov and his
followers from mounting a meaningful national campaign. By now,
Barnes was deeply involved in opposition politics because of his close
contacts with the non-Communist regent, Ganev, and with Petkov. At
a "clandestine" meeting in late July, Barnes found Petkov fearful that
if no direct Western action were forthcoming, some members of the
opposition might reconsider their position. Efforts to register an alternative electoral slate, he informed Barnes, had been blocked, sometimes through the use of violence. Recent charges of fascism against
the opposition augured ill for even a semblance of free elections.[43]
Ganev seconded Petkov's position, suggesting to Barnes that given the
deepening Bulgarian crisis, indication of direct American support for
tripartite supervision of the elections would have a most beneficial
effect.[44]

Direct American intervention, however, was sharply at odds with
the strategy approved by Secretary Byrnes at Potsdam. Pressure for
democratic reorganization, Byrnes maintained, should arise from the
non-Communist members of the governments concerned in response to
certain knowledge that without significant change, recognition would
be postponed indefinitely. As Byrnes cabled the American political
representative in Hungary, where elections also were in preparation,
"Dept does not feel that ACC which is charged only with the execution
of Armistice terms should intervene at this time either collectively or
through individual members."[45] If requested by the Hungarian government or in the event that it became blatantly obvious that free elections
would not occur, consultation would be initiated by Washington, the
upcoming London Foreign Ministers' Conference being only a month
in the future. This approach to the issue of elections would avoid the
uncoordinated and ineffectual protests characteristic of the preceding
spring, retaining control tightly in the department's own hands. In the
interim, American representatives in Eastern Europe would focus their
efforts on convincing regimes to which they were accredited of the
seriousness of America's nonrecognition stance. Washington, in turn,
would supply its representatives with ample material indicating its
continued dissatisfaction. Similar pressure would be exerted by the

British government, which, on August 9, informed Washington of its intentions to express public objection to the recently published Bulgarian electoral law.[46] Byrnes then requested Barnes to deliver a stiff note to the Bulgarian regime confirming America's objections in the coming election.

> The US Govt is desirous of recognizing and of establishing diplomatic relations with a Bulgarian government which will be adequately representative of all democratic opinion in that country as soon as conditions in Bulgaria give evidence that the free expression of political views and the free exercise of political rights are sufficiently safeguarded. However we cannot overlook the preponderance of current evidence that a minority element in power in the country is at present endeavoring by the use of force and intimidation to prevent the effective participation in the scheduled elections of a large democratic section of the electorate. In the absence of full and unhampered participation in the election . . . a situation would seem likely to result so as to preclude the formation of a fully democratic government.[47]

That same day, Byrnes forwarded the relevant portions of Truman's recent radio address which affirmed America's continued commitment to the democratic evolution of the former Axis satellites.[48] Barnes immediately took these documents to the Bulgarian Council of Ministers.[49]

On August 14, following delivery of Byrnes's messages to the Sofia cabinet, the Bulgarian situation took a sudden turn which threatened to undermine Byrnes's carefully thought-out strategy. On that day the four remaining opposition ministers—Petkov having been excluded from government some two weeks before—informed the prime minister that barring the postponement of the elections and the restoration of full civil liberties in Bulgaria, they would resign forthwith from the cabinet.[50] Whether this action was solely the result of Byrnes's messages or reflected further clandestine interaction between Barnes and the Bulgarian opposition remains unclear. Recent Bulgarian studies suggest that Barnes, in his transmission of Byrnes's cables, embellished his instructions and requested a postponement of the elections, a charge that received partial support in the puzzling comment by the British permanent secretary, Sir Orme Sargent, to U.S. Ambassador John Winant several days later in which Sargent noted that his government wished it had had advance warning of recent statements made to the Bulgarians.[51] No evidence, however, exists either in the published records or the U.S. archives to substantiate a charge of personal indiscretion, and Bulgarian authorities, if they possess such documentation, have yet to reveal it.

The resignation of the opposition ministers and the announcement that the elections would proceed as scheduled brought into question the efficacy of Byrnes's hopes that nonrecognition would induce non-Communist members of the various East European coalition governments to petition for reorganization. With the opposition having left the Bulgarian cabinet, and in the face of the Soviet decision to extend diplomatic recognition to Bulgaria on August 14, prospects for moderation by the remaining ministers seemed slight. The position of the rump cabinet was clearly indicated in the welcoming response sent by Prime Minister Georgiev upon announcement of Soviet recognition: "In this act of the Soviet government, the Bulgarian people see once again recognition . . . of their efforts in the struggle against nazism and acknowledgment once more of activities to establish a democratic order in the state since September 9."[52] It was now evident to Barnes that the democratic future of Bulgaria was intrinsically tied to events in Bulgaria regardless of any plans for consultation at the future London Conference. As he informed Byrnes the day after the Soviet recognition, "Whatever the Dept may decide in the circumstances to do, the fact remains that views expressed by US Govt . . . have brought true state of affairs in Bulgaria into the open."[53]

The rapidly developing Bulgarian situation ought to have prompted an immediate policy review in Washington. Remaining records of the Secretary of State's Staff Committee, however, show that no discussions of the Bulgarian situation were held between August 8 and October 9, 1945, a reflection perhaps of Secretary Brynes's full concentration on the agenda of the soon to convene London Conference.[54] Without review, tbe State Department continued to follow established policy, informing Barnes that "in the opinion of the United States Government, the effective participation of all important democratic elements in the forthcoming elections is essential to facilitating the conclusion of a peace treaty with a recognized democratic government. The will of the majority of the people can be determined only if all the people are able to vote free from fear and intimidation."[55] This message was forwarded at once by Barnes to the Bulgarian prime minister in an effort to buttress already substantial Western pressure for a voluntary postponement; Barnes dispatched a copy to the chairman of the ACC despite expressed directives that the duties of such commissions were restricted to fulfillment of the respective armistices.[56] By now the confusion between the American and British positions as expressed by Sargent had been overcome, and on August 21, Houstoun-Boswall

presented identical protest notes to the prime minister, foreign minister, leaders of the opposition, and General Biriuzov in which Britain
noted that the upcoming elections would not satisfy Western demands
for a more democratic procedure. "I am accordingly instructed to
inform you," the British note concluded, "that His Majesty's Government will be unable to recognize as democratic or representative any
Bulgarian Government as a result of elections held under these conditions."[57] The next day, the British protest was released publicly in
London, giving rise to the conclusion in Sofia that at least a tacit
agreement had been reached by the two Western powers to forestall the
pending elections.[58] On August 23, Barnes cabled the State Department that Generals Crane and Oxley would meet that evening with
General Biriuzov to discuss what steps the control commission might
take to resolve the electoral crisis.[59]

In the absence of specific instructions from their respective governments asking for postponement, yet certain that such a delay was the
sole means to resolve the current impasse, Crane and Oxley resolved to
follow a strategy reminiscent of Barnes's earlier depiction of U.S.
policy in Bulgaria as a poker game with the West advised to play its
cards "close to the chest." At 6:00 P.M. on August 22, Crane and
Oxley informed Biriuzov that they had come to see him as a result of
the notes recently passed by their respective governments to the Bulgarians. An immediate conference of control commission representatives and members of the Bulgarian cabinet and of the opposition was
requested so that discussion might ensue to determine a "future procedure that will be acceptable to all." The visibly shaken Biriuzov
quickly inquired as to the precise nature of the Western demands.
What, he rejoined, was the meaning of "future procedure"? Was the
future of the elections at issue or future relations with the Bulgarian
government in general? When Crane, acting as spokesman, confirmed
the former interpretation, Biriuzov responded that nothing within the
armistice provisions covered this issue. While acknowledging that the
Bulgarian government was bound to obey any command the control
commission might give—a not inconsiderable concession in view of
recent Soviet efforts to establish the sovereignty of the Sofia regime—
Biriuzov restated his uncertainty about the exact purpose of this visit.
To his ire, Crane blandly responded that he wished not to discuss
matters of substance but only to arrange the meeting. An official
response from Biriuzov was requested for the following day. Once
more, Biriuzov pointed out that such a meeting was not covered by the
armistice provisions and that he would require advice from Moscow
before acting further. What, he asked, ought he to tell his superiors

since neither Crane nor Oxley had formulated a specific question? "What did they want him to say? What did they object to—the present government or the coming elections, or what?" Again in a subdued fashion, Crane indicated that the attitude of the American and British governments had been expressed clearly in the recent exchange of messages, copies of which Biriuzov possessed. In plainest terms, no government elected under the existing conditions would be recognized by the West, and no future peace treaty would be signed. By now, Biriuzov's anger and frustration had reached its limit. Pointing out the window at a crowd of Bulgarians assembling for a preelection rally, Biriuzov retorted, "Are these people going to an electoral meeting being driven at the point of bayonet, or are they going of their own free will?" When Crane and Oxley, true to their agreed-upon deportment, refused to discuss the matter further, Biriuzov, "who was almost in a *frenzy* got up to signify the end of the interview."[60]

Since specific instructions requesting postponement of the elections were yet to be received from Washington, the bold strategy advanced by Barnes, Crane, and their British colleagues appeared in jeopardy and might have floundered had not aid arrived from a most unexpected source: the Bulgarian cabinet. At about the same moment as the blustering confrontation between Biriuzov, Crane, and Oxley, the Bulgarian foreign minister, Petko Stainov, was finishing a news conference before local correspondents of the foreign press. As anticipated, the issue of the elections was raised. Stainov's reply, however, caught the reporters by surprise. Confirming that his government had indeed received notes from Washington and London expressing deep displeasure with the situation to date and commenting upon the lack of specific demands from the Western capitals, Stainov took America and Britain to task for not directly approaching the Allied Control Commission: "Our juridical position under the armistice terms is such that the demands can be directed towards us only by or through the ACC. Messrs Houstoun-Boswall and Barnes cannot make demands on us except through the ACC which until now they have not done. ACC which alone can make demands has not done anything until now. . . . If by midnight on Saturday August 25 there is no order from the Foreign Ministers of the three Great Powers submitted to us through the ACC the elections will be held as scheduled." Here at long last was the wedge Barnes could use to compel Biriuzov and the commission to consider Western demands for postponement without allowing recourse to the standard canard of Bulgarian sovereignty. That evening, Barnes informed Secretary Byrnes of this new development, following with a second cable the next morning telling Byrnes that Crane and

Oxley had just sent identical letters to Biriuzov specifically requesting postponement.[61] Convinced that Washington was following the Bulgarian situation closely in the final hours before the election, Barnes must have assumed that his superiors would countermand his actions at once if they appeared at odds with department policy. That same day, Barnes sent a note to Stainov acquainting him with the new American "demand" and enclosing copies of the requests given Biriuzov by Crane and Oxley.[62]

For contemporary historians, a question remains as to whether Stainov, in providing a new option for Western action, acted in concert with Barnes or merely spoke without sufficient forethought. Modern Bulgarian historians tend to accept the latter explanation. Petur Ostoich states that "in these difficult circumstances, the imperialists used a response of Petko Stainov at a press conference of foreign journalists concerning the rights of the ACC."[63] On August 27, three days after the announcement that the elections had been postponed, the Central Committee of the Bulgarian Communist party discussed the issue of Stainov's complicity, resolving that the party would take no action against him that might lead to a conflict with the Zveno party to which Stainov belonged.[64] Stainov remained in the cabinet until the following spring. And yet the sheer coincidence of events suggests that Stainov was, at least, acting so as to provide a final opportunity for postponement. A standard Bulgarian history of the Zveno party notes that "rightest" elements began to agitate within the party during the summer of 1945 and that an August 30 declaration of the Zveno Central Committee included unacceptable criticism of both the Fatherland Front and the Communist party.[65] More suggestive is an unpublished cable from Barnes dealing with the spring 1945 elections in Bulgaria. On April 11, Barnes cabled Stettinius that Stainov had informed the Americans that although he was in no position singlehandedly to oppose efforts by the Communists to hold early elections, he nevertheless was doing all he could to facilitate efforts by others to gain a delay.[66] Perhaps this desire once again to postpone elections in which the Communists possessed unparalleled advantages led to Stainov's announcement. In any event, a crack had been opened in the solid Soviet–Fatherland Front defenses, and the Western representatives decided to exploit their advantage carefully. Aware that only three days remained, and yet uncertain of their respective governments' precise position, Crane and Oxley continued the tactic of a "grand bluff."

At 10:00 P.M. Crane and Oxley returned to meet with Biriuzov to discuss the identical letters sent that morning asking for postponement.

Rebuking the Western representatives for casting doubt on the honor of the ACC through Barnes's direct approach to Stainov that morning, Biriuzov suggested that discussion proceed. Now it was the turn of Crane and Oxley to show concern. Lacking specific instructions, the two generals attempted to continue the stall of the preceding day. It was not possible to mediate the issue now, Biriuzov was told, pending an invitation to government and opposition delegates as mentioned in the earlier meeting. Raising the stakes, Oxley and Crane, having noted that as mere soldiers they were unfit to discuss issues of high policy, suggested that their respective political advisers be called to the future meeting. When Biriuzov unexpectedly agreed, Crane realized he had overplayed his hand. Barnes's whereabouts were unknown to him, Crane replied, and Oxley argued that formulation of the precise Western objections to the elections would require time. Might Biriuzov not simply postpone the elections while the Western political representatives were located and position papers prepared? But Biriuzov, sensing confusion, had decided to call. Given the brief period between the present meeting and the elections, Biriuzov argued, he could not take personal responsibility for such a serious decision unless his Western colleagues were prepared to state their exact positions. When Crane and Oxley suggested that they might be able to bring their counterparts to the table by the following evening, Biriuzov curtly noted that this would be too late. The generals finally decided to adjourn, reconvening an hour later accompanied by their political advisers. It was now or never.[67]

The new turn of events signaled by Biriuzov's ultimatum compelled Barnes to assume full responsibility for acting without specific instructions from his superiors. That very day, Barnes had cabled an update on the rapidly changing situation to Washington, relating that Western efforts to secure postponement had reached a crucial stage and suggesting that "if Dept makes very strong representation immediately Moscow, there is possibility Aug 26 elections may be postponed."[68] Crane and Oxley's efforts to stall for time had been designed to win a pause until instructions might arrive. That tactic had failed. At midnight, as scheduled, a grand session of the ACC convened with each military representative flanked by his corresponding political adviser. The transcript of the meeting, which continued until dawn the next morning, reflects the often vitriolic debate. Despite earlier pleas that time was needed before the Western position could be clearly presented, General Crane immediately offered an extensive series of demands whose fulfillment might eventually allow Western recognition of any future Bulgarian regime. Postponement of the August 26 elections was the first point, followed by insistence that a new Agrarian party congress be held to overturn the bogus assembly of May 8–9, that the same be held for the Socialist party, and all parties be free to select whether to run candidates on a separate or common list, and that freedom of speech, press, and assembly be implemented in addition to secret balloting. While such changes were in progress, the Bulgarian government should be reorganized to create a temporary cabinet charged with the sole duty of conducting free elections, with the Bulgarian regency empowered to issue decrees in the interim. Opposition members ejected from the Fatherland Front in past months were to be reinstated.[69]

As Crane read off each point, Biriuzov offered his objections, which were met in turn by immediate Western rejoinders. By now the discussion were no longer polite, with the deeper feelings of hostility among the representatives coming to the fore. Refuting Biriuzov's assertion that Petkov's replacement in the Fatherland Front, Obbov, was a true man of the people, Barnes bitterly responded that "Obbov was a man who has been paid by almost every European government, a man who sold the Salt Concession to the Fascists and lived on it ever since." Recounting the undemocratic nature of the existing Bulgarian electoral code, Barnes blurted out that "if he were to examine the law word for word, he would *vomit*."[70] In his rebuttal, the Soviet political representative, Kirsanov, argued that Petkov's July call for tripartite supervision of the Bulgarian elections had been perceived by more solid citizens as treason. By the wee hours of the morning, no resolution of the now hardened positions seemed possible, and Biriuzov concluded the session by stating that he would not comply with the Western request for postponement without authorization from Moscow. When Barnes asked whether such authorization could be expected before election day, now two days off, Biriuzov answered that he did not know.

At 11:00 that night, Biriuzov opened a new meeting of the military and political representatives called at short notice. He began by reading a note just received from the Bulgarian government accepting the Western request for postponement. This compliance was presented by Biriuzov as a sincere indication of the cabinet's persistent effort to improve relations with the Allies in the interest of removing impediments to Bulgaria's reentry into normal international life. Biriuzov then announced that "the ACC considering the wishes of the Bulgarian government will postpone the elections which were scheduled for 26 August until a later date. The ACC considers that it can satisfy the demands of the Bulgarian government."[71] At the session's completion, an excited Barnes hastened to cable the news to Washington. For the second time in six months, Western objections to undemocratic elections in Eastern Europe had received satisfaction. So great was Barnes's joy that his midnight telegram to Byrnes suggested that Biriuzov, his nemesis of a scant day before, ought to be the beneficiary of an American award for his "honest and statesmanlike move."[72]

Documents that might establish the precise series of events and orders leading to Biriuzov's decision for postponement undoubtedly lie buried in the archives of Moscow and Sofia. Biriuzov told his Western counterparts that postponement came at the request and initiative of the Bulgarian government, a position fully supported by his chief assistant, A. I. Cherepanov, in his memoirs.[73] Although such an assertion certainly advanced the outstanding Bulgarian claim to increased sovereignty, logic compels one to approach it with caution, given the stakes involved and the precedent set. Certainly an issue of such importance would have been referred to the highest reaches of the Soviet government before decision, and suspicion remains that Biriuzov's direction came not from Sofia but from Moscow. In an article written in the 1970s, the well-known British political and military analyst Malcolm Mackintosh credited the initiative for postponement directly to Stalin. According to Mackintosh, who served as a member of the British mission in Bulgaria during 1945 and was present at the sessions, the phone rang in the General Biriuzov's anteroom at 1:40 the morning of the lengthy and acrimonious discussions among the military and political representatives. A Soviet major who answered stood stagestruck with the phone by his ear, and Biriuzov, believing his subordinate had suddenly fallen ill, seized the phone himself. Coming to immediate attention, Biriuzov listened for five minutes in silence to a voice which Mackintosh claims was audible across the room. Then he said, "Yes, Comrade Stalin," hung up, and returned to the group to inform the delegates that the elections would be postponed. The Bulgarian prime minister was sent for and the polling booths closed.[74] Although this explanation would provide many of the missing details, it must, unfortunately, be dismissed as unlikely. The transcripts of the ACC sessions in question reveal that but one meeting, that of August 23–24, lasted through the night and that at its termination the three powers were as far apart as ever. The decision to postpone was taken two days before the elections, on the evening of August 24; Barnes's excited cable was sent that same midnight. Mackintosh states that the phone call from Stalin arrived on the morning of the election, two days later. Surely such a dramatic conclusion to a tense situation would have been mentioned by the American political representative as well.

The revelation that the Bulgarian elections would be postponed inspired a flurry of diplomatic messages, some laudatory and some not. On August 25, Secretary Byrnes informed Barnes that a congratulatory statement directed to the Bulgarian and Soviet governments had been released that day: "It is especially gratifying to me that the representatives in Sofia of the Soviet Union, British and United States Governments were unanimously in accord with the decision of the Bulgarian Government. This is a striking demonstration of the unity of purpose of the three nations to work together to assist the liberated peoples of Europe in the establishment of democratic government of their own choice." That same evening, a second message from Byrnes instructed Barnes to convey America's appreciation directly to the Bulgarian government.[75] The Soviet Union also expressed approval, with Vyshensky telling the Bulgarian ambassador in Moscow that "having postponed the elections, the Bulgarian government proved its desire to cooperate with the Allies. . . . The English and Americans no longer will have a basis to speak about the absence of democracy in Bulgaria. Likewise, the external position of Bulgaria during this time has noticeably strengthened."[76] London also congratulated the Bulgarian government.[77]

The private cables, however, spoke a different story. On August 24, not yet having received news of the postponement, Byrnes took Barnes to task for suggesting departmental intervention in Moscow on behalf of the Crane-Barnes proposal. It would even be a mistake, Byrnes cautioned, to press the issue before the control commission in Bulgaria: "Instructions contained in Deptel [departmental telegram] 249 Aug 11 authorized you to inform the members of Bulgarian Government of our attitude toward situation existing in Bulgaria but before taking further steps Dept should have been consulted. The views . . . did not contemplate our making specific request for postponement of elections, and Dept has consistently felt the formation of a representative democratic Government in Bulgaria is matter for Bulgarians to undertake and in absence of pertinent provisions in armistice not for consideration by ACC."[78]

Barnes, in an immediate explanation dispatched the following day, argued that his activities were inspired by the "logic" if not the exact content of recent departmental instructions, but there could be little doubt that the overall State Department guidelines established by Byrnes for treating with Eastern Europe had indeed been violated.[79] Barnes's August 23 appeal for representation in Moscow took no note of Byrnes's decision to use the upcoming Foreign Ministers' Conference as the primary avenue for discussions of Yalta violations, an approach designed to impart maximum coordination in America's future disputes with the USSR. Equally important, Byrnes had made amply clear his belief that the respective East European control commissions were not authorized by the terms of the armistice to consider issues exceeding armistice provisions.[80] Had the initiative authored by Barnes and Crane produced stalemate instead of success, there appears little question but that a review of their fitness to remain in Sofia would have been ordered by Washington. Such action now would reveal significant differences within the American diplomatic community at a time when America's prestige in Bulgaria had reached a new height. The exact meaning of this Soviet concession would perhaps be made clear at the London Foreign Ministers' Conference due to open in the following two weeks. Pending further investigation and discussions in London, Barnes was instructed that Washington must be consulted before any further proposals were made to the Bulgarian government and even before Barnes considered any suggestions advanced by the Soviet and/or British representatives which might "lead to commitments in behalf of this Govt."[81] Sufficiently chastised, Crane, in early September, requested departmental guidance as to whether any new demands would be presented in Sofia once the Bulgarians had rescheduled the election.[82] By then, Barnes had left Sofia for London so as to impress his opinions on the arriving secretary of state.

Any suspicions that Byrnes's response to the demarche of Barnes and Crane represented a weakening of Washington's commitment to the Yalta agreement or that a retreat from the confrontation of Potsdam was being prepared for the London Conference was quickly put to rest by departmental action concerning a similar political crisis in Rumania. There the American representatives were informed that in conversations with the Rumanian opposition within the Groza government, "you may let it be known in general terms that this Govt hopes to see established in Rumania, through the efforts of the Rumanians themselves, and if necessary with the assistance of the three Allied Govts as provided in the Crimean Declaration on Liberated Europe, a more representative regime."[83] The next day, upon receipt of the American message, the Rumanian king precipitated a cabinet crisis in which, following discussions with the non-Communist members of his cabinet, Groza's resignation was demanded.[84] One day later, the State Department informed both the British and the Soviets that it was prepared to invoke the right of consultation as provided at Yalta.[85]

In retrospect, it is clear that the Rumanian situation provided a paradigm of Byrnes's strategy designed to achieve democratic reforms in Eastern Europe. Although the "prompting" arose in Washington, the decision to call for a reorganized cabinet lay with the king and the non-Communist government officials. Unfortunately, no such opportunities existed in Bulgaria because of the opposition's resignation from the government. In Sofia, Barnes and Crane had substituted an appeal to the control commission for the more ideal protest from within the government. Because a determined Soviet objection to such a tactic could be expected, Washington stood little chance of effecting a long-range solution. Aware that Soviet willingness to resolve the impasse in Eastern Europe would be lessened if intrigues between local American representatives and the Rumanian and Bulgarian opposition were blatant, Byrnes took pains to warn his subordinates to avoid intensifying the domestic crises. He swiftly cabled Bucharest following the king's action: "We hope no action will be taken which might seem to give ground for Soviet suspicion that crisis was brought about by 'Anglo-American intervention.' Contact with Rumanian political leaders should be avoided at present stage." By early September this cautious but determined strategy bore fruit when Soviet Foreign Minister Molotov consented to consultation in Rumania. One caveat in Molotov's message, however, threatened to undercut Byrnes's plan: Molotov insisted that "this consultation shall take place at some time after the completion of the work of the upcoming session of the Council of Foreign Ministers in London." Byrnes cabled his ambassador in London that Molotov's request would not be honored: "Since it is intended that the preparation of a peace treaty with Rumania be discussed at the London meeting, the Govt with which the peace treaty can be concluded should naturally be the subject of the discussion as well; the US Govt proposes to raise this question.[86] Consultation over the future of Bulgaria and Hungary naturally would be included as well. As planned at Potsdam, the issues of diplomatic recognition and peace treaty negotiations would provide the forum for insisting upon democratic reforms in all three East European states.

To the contemporary student of the Cold War, it is apparent that the London Conference was both the zenith and the nadir of America's effort to resist Soviet domination in the Balkans. Thereafter, other crucial issues of East-West relations involving such overriding problems as the future of Germany and Japan would occupy the central position in declining relations with the USSR. Although Byrnes was still willing to acknowledge the evident Soviet desire to see governments friendly to the West in Eastern Europe, he perceived no contradiction in demanding democratic reorganization in Rumania and Bulgaria before these states were readmitted into the family of postwar nations. Refusing to believe that Moscow might fear free elections in these countries despite some evidence to the contrary, Byrnes refused to modify his chosen approach.[87] Not until the London Conference had reached an impasse did Byrnes acknowledge the depth of the problem, believing "the chief cause of our difficulties appeared to be our failure to agree on the recognition of Rumania and Bulgaria."[88]

The deadlock over a mutually acceptable arrangement for Rumania and Bulgaria emerged at the second session of the conference, when Soviet Foreign Minister Molotov tabled identical draft treaties for the states in question based only upon acceptance of the existing armistice provisions.[89] This draft produced an immediate objection from the American delegation, which noted that acceptance of such conditions "would have the effect of confirming the present situation under which these countries are under effective Soviet domination and would mean abandonment of the opportunity for establishing democratic governments in these countries."[90] The American drafts next submitted were prefaced by a clear warning that neither diplomatic recognition nor agreement upon a peace treaty would occur without fundamental political reorganization: "This suggested directive is submitted by the United States Delegation with the understanding that the United States will not negotiate a treaty of peace with Bulgaria until there has been established a government broadly representative of all democratic elements in the population and pledged to the earliest possible establishment through free elections of a government responsive to the will of the people, which can be recognized by the United States." An identical statement was presented concerning Rumania.[91] When Molotov rejoined that such a written preface "was in effect a challenge directed against the Soviet Union" and demanded that Byrnes downgrade his objection to an informal, oral statement, the American secretary of state refused.[92] Despite a number of private meetings, the clear divergence of views remained. The same lack of success greeted Western insistence that the foreign ministers "consult" in an attempt to resolve the Rumania crisis.[93]

Once it was clear that there would be no agreement on the Balkans, Molotov took steps to bring the conference to a close. In a private meeting with Byrnes, the Soviet foreign minister insisted that the conference be reorganized because of an error in procedure that violated the mandate of the Potsdam Conference. The French and Chinese representatives, Molotov charged, were illegally participating in discussions of peace treaties with the former Axis satellites although China had not been at war with any of the states in question and France had been at war with only Germany and Italy. Although Byrnes took pains to refute Molotov's contention and a letter was dispatched directly to Stalin under President Truman's signature, the Soviets remained unmoved.[94] On October 2, 1945, the London Conference adjourned, the first time a meeting of the wartime Allies at the highest level had ended without sufficient agreement to permit even the semblance of a final protocol. The concluding communiqué simply noted that "the Council of Foreign Ministers met twice today, Mr. Molotov presiding in the morning and Dr. Wang in the afternoon. At the second meeting the Council decided to terminate its present session."[95] No provisions were mentioned for a future conference despite continuation of the Rumanian deadlock in Bucharest and an announcement in Sofia that the postponed elections had been rescheduled for November.

In retrospect, the contemporary analyst of postwar East-West relations is justified in concluding that the abortive London Conference signaled a turning point in the Soviet Union's policy toward Bulgaria. In the initial months following the Soviet occupation, Moscow had subordinated long-range political objectives to the more pressing military needs that still united the Allies, as shown by the postponement of the spring 1945 elections. With the conclusion of the European war, both the opportunities and potential problems attending the war in the Far East prompted Moscow to retain sufficient flexibility to allow a second postponement while awaiting a detailed review of American policy at the London Conference. But when at this meeting America insisted upon maintaining claims to influence the evolution of Balkan states under Soviet occupation while denying corresponding Soviet demands to affect developments in areas under American occupation such as Japan, Moscow apparently concluded the time had come to assert full dominance in Rumania and Bulgaria. Belatedly, even Secretary Byrnes realized the full connection between the two opposite parts of the globe. In his memoirs he wrote, "Ambassador Harriman, who was present at London, agreed with me that the Balkan issue was the crucial one. Now, we suddenly realized we had been wrong. The remarkable performance that had led to the breakdown of the London Conference had been stimulated by the Russians' belief that they were not being consulted adequately by our officials in Japan."[96]

The resignation in the summer of the Agrarian and Socialist members from the Sofia cabinet suggested that Washington's intransigence was more than matched by the Bulgarian opposition and that little gain might be expected from future tolerance of either domestic or foreign criticism of Soviet policy in Bulgaria. The immediate vehicle for a dramatic reassertion of Soviet control was the election, now rescheduled for November. As usual, the Bulgarian Communist party already had taken steps to prepare for a resounding if fraudulent result even as the Soviet foreign minister explored possibilities of a new American concession at the London Conference. Curiously, many more months and one more East-West conference at the highest level were to pass before Secretary of State Byrnes acknowledged that American plans for an independent and democratic Bulgaria no longer possessed reasonable prospects for success. Denied the advantage of hindsight and hopeful that pledges for free elections in Hungary would set a precedent for a democratic government America could recognize, Byrnes stubbornly refused to abandon Bulgaria after the London Conference, opting instead to introduce a new flexibility in his negotiating position in preparation for the upcoming Moscow Conference. Undoubtedly Byrnes would have subscribed to the views of H. Stuart Hughes, who occupied the position of director of the State Department's Division of Research for Europe in 1946: "I did not think that the future had been foreclosed. The range of choice might be narrowing, but alternative paths still lay open."[97]

7 The Search for Compromise

While the Allied foreign ministers gathered in London to debate the future of the former Axis satellites, the Bulgarian Communists were taking steps to ensure that the recent election postponement would not rebound to their disadvantage. On August 27, the party's Central Committee approved the postponement and, three days later, resolved to admit into the reorganized Fatherland Front all groups sincerely in support of its programs who "stand on the position of defense of Bulgaria's independence from foreign interference." A proposal to allow separate lists for the individual Front parties was rejected, and the following day all Agrarians who had suggested such separate lists before the postponed elections were dismissed from the Obbov-dominated Bulgarian Agrarian National Union. Joint sessions between Communists and Obbov Agrarians quickly became the order of the day throughout Bulgaria in an effort to explain future plans of the Fatherland Front. In the first week of September, the Front announced that new elections would be held shortly in conformity with revisions of the electoral code designed to guarantee all nonfascist groups the right to form political parties with their own press organs. A central commission was to be created with sections posted in each electoral district to observe democratic procedures. In midmonth, the Bulgarian regents issued a decree establishing November 18 as the new election day and announced minor changes in the code easing the guidelines for allowing opposition candidates to file separately from the common list.[1]

The Communists and Obbov Agrarians were not the only political groups active in the weeks immediately following the postponed elections. Throughout September, Petkov and his followers energetically organized their supporters in each electoral district, with significant results. In the Pleven district, membership in the BZNS-NP (Bulgarian Agrarian National Union—Nikola Petkov) reached 7,724 with more than 3,000 enrolled in the youth section. In the Varna district, 3,536 members were listed. By the end of September, conferences of Petkov's party had been held in Plovdiv, Ruse, Vidin, Sofia, and other key cities.[2] By now, the opposition movement included important sections of the Socialist, Radical, and Democratic parties as well.

Although Zveno officially remained within the Fatherland Front, its newspaper, *Izgrev,* in the words of a contemporary Bulgarian historian, "listed almost the entire oppositional demand in the areas of politics and economics."[3]

The growing strength of the opposition assembled about Petkov made the Communists more receptive to reaching an agreement before the new elections; an initiative emerged from the Communist Politburo to open direct discussion with the Agrarian leaders. On September 12, the Standing Committee of Petkov's BZNS-NP dispatched a letter to the Bulgarian cabinet demanding further changes in the electoral law. A second message sent shortly thereafter insisted that the traditional Agrarian newspaper, *Zemedelsko zname,* be returned to the Petkov party.[4] The following day Petkov, whose ties with the American mission had by now greatly expanded, related that the Communists had promised him the foreign ministry in return for his support in the upcoming elections. Having told the Communists that political liberties in Bulgaria were in perpetual question as long as a Communist held the position of minister of interior, Petkov told the Americans that he would meet soon with Vasil Kolarov, an old Communist leader who had just returned from Moscow after a twenty-year exile in the USSR. Four days later, Milton Rewinkel, who was Barnes's substitute while the latter was in London, cabled the State Department that the Petkov-Kolarov meeting had ended in failure. Petkov had offered a ten-point demand as a precondition for the return of the Agrarians and Socialists to the cabinet. Included in his harsh requirements were the transfer of the prime minister to the Agrarians and the removal of the Communist minister of interior. The Communists would have to acknowledge their mistaken interference into the affairs of other Front and non-Front parties, and the Agrarian and Socialist newspapers would be returned forthwith. Freedom of press, person, and property would be restored by the new cabinet at once.[5]

As the preelection political struggle in Bulgaria intensified, the State Department attempted to tailor its advice to the changing situation. In late August, the British had informed Washington that the British representative would shortly raise the issue of modifying the electoral code within the control commission. Acting Secretary of State Dean Acheson instructed Rewinkel to support this position but emphasized that reorganization of the existing cabinet offered the best hope for future free elections, a position fully consistent with that of Petkov and his followers.[6] Throughout the month of September, Petkov maintained pressure on the Communists for government reorganization, informing Barnes in early October that revision of the election code was no longer a crucial issue. Citing a lengthy memorandum which Barnes had drafted for the London Conference suggesting major changes as a prerequisite for free elections, Petkov told Barnes that the opposition was now willing to participate in elections if the Communist minister of interior were replaced and the national militia reorganized and brought under control.[7] Hints that the opposition would not contest the election on separate lists if the demands for reorganization of the cabinet to include the admission of opposition representatives were met filled the editorial sections of Petkov's newspaper.[8]

By mid-October, two possible future courses appeared open to the Bulgarian Communists if they wished the opposition and its Western supporters to approve the upcoming elections. Reorganization of the cabinet with important slots reserved for Petkov and his followers might allow a common list and near universal popular support. Lesser concessions, the replacement of the minister of interior and a curbing of the militia, would permit the parties outside the Fatherland Front to contest the elections as a loyal opposition. But the Communists and the Sofia regime selected neither option. No further talks were scheduled with the opposition, and reports continued to speak of growing militia assaults directed against Petkov and his followers.[9]

Aware that the just-concluded London Conference had failed to demonstrate any new American flexibility in the face of growing Soviet and Communist dominance in Bulgaria, the Fatherland Front opened a massive electoral campaign on October 15, holding more than three thousand public meetings in the various districts. Thousands of pro-government committees were formed and dispatched to the provinces, and nearly two thousand "work-cultural brigades" enrolling seventy-five thousand began to instruct the peasantry on the political issues at stake. In early November, the aged leader of the Bulgarian Communist party, Georgi Dimitrov, returned to Sofia to take personal charge. His return lent both symbolic and substantive assistance to the Communist bid for total domination. While Dimitrov had resided in Moscow, excesses displayed by his comrades in Sofia could plausibly be denied if they threatened to interfere with more general Soviet interests that might require some residue of East-West cooperation. But with his return, any failure by the domestic Communists to complete their conquest of power could be viewed only as abject failure for one of Stalin's closest confidants. Dimitrov, who had gained an enviable reputation as the man who defied Hitler at the famous Leipzig trial, could be expected to do no less when faced with Western and local efforts to retard implementation of ideals to which he had devoted a lifetime. By now, Soviet policy toward Bulgaria had evolved to the point that Dimitrov's advice in Moscow was no longer required. And if any doubt existed about Soviet willingness to grant concessions to the opposition, Dimitrov's comments in Sofia in November quickly put them to rest: "It is clear that behind the opposition parties stand Bulgarian reactionaries who strive to restore the past." In the face of such intransigence and aware that free elections remained beyond reach, Petkov and the opposition concluded that their best hope lay in a boycott of the elections in combination with appeals to the regency and the Western powers for government reorganization before any balloting took place. The regents were informed that the existing cabinet must be dissolved if foreign interference in the elections was to be avoided and free elections guaranteed.[10] Approaches to the West took the normal course of petitions to Barnes and to Mark Ethridge, who arrived in Sofia as the personal representative of Secretary Byrnes consistent with Molotov's pledge at Potsdam to permit the entry of foreign journalists to observe conditions in Bulgaria.

In an article written six years after the events in question, Ethridge explained his three-week tour of Bulgaria as the direct result of Molotov's frequent complaints "that Secretary Byrnes was poorly informed regarding conditions in Bulgaria and Rumania."[11] The purpose of the visit of this respected editor of the *Louisville Courier Journal* was to refute suggestions that the U.S. political representatives on the spot had misled the secretary and would serve to place the Balkan situation in proper perspective. Yet as archival materials testify, Byrnes also planned to use Etbridge's findings in a future face-to-face meeting with Soviet leaders. The diary of Byrnes's aide, Walter Brown, reveals that even before the adjournment of the abortive London Conference, Byrnes had resolved to bring America's objections to Soviet rule in the Balkans directly to Stalin's attention.[12] Ever since the special visit of Harry Hopkins to Moscow in the early days of the Truman administration, Byrnes had harbored the opinion that Foreign Minister Molotov frequently acted to confuse the Soviet dictator on crucial points of dispute among the Allies, a suspicion reinforced by Molotov's unexpected behavior in London. Ethridge's report would thus provide an "independent" assessment for a future meeting in the Soviet capital.[13]

During his first week in Bulgaria, Ethridge conducted extensive discussions with "Bulgarian people of all political complexions and all social strata, including leaders of Gov't, the opposition and independent organizations to the number of approximately one hundred." Given the proximity of the November elections, it was natural that

Ethridge's activities moved beyond mere reporting, assuming a judg-mental form within the parameters of the Yalta agreement. Ethridge informed the secretary: "It became apparent to me and was confirmed even by members of the Gov't including the Prime Minister . . . that the Gov't as presently constituted is not representative in the sense of the Yalta Declaration and that large democratic elements are excluded. It is also apparent to me . . . that under the circumstances there can be no free elections."[14]

Ethridge, although naturally reluctant to exceed his modest assign-ment of reporting, broached the possibility of a visit to Moscow during a face-to-face meeting with General Biriuzov, a suggestion quickly seconded by Barnes. Two days later, the State Department eagerly accepted this proposal.[15] Ambassador Harriman was informed that a frank discussion between Ethridge and Soviet leaders might aid in overcoming disagreements about Bulgaria's future, especially since Ethridge's observations would give further credence to America's motives in refusing to recognize any Bulgarian government proceeding from unfree elections. For Byrnes, this semiofficial exchange of views would test the waters for subsequent discussions planned between the American and Soviet foreign ministers. Ethridge was instructed to seek out Molotov's opinion on possible resolution of the present impasse and, in the event of an unsatisfactory response, to announce that gov-ernment reorganization in Sofia was necessary before American recog-nition would be considered. In the interim, Bulgaria might be advised by the three Yalta powers that the November elections be postponed.[16] On November 11, one day before leaving for Moscow, Ethridge in-formed Prime Minister Georgiev that the existing Bulgarian govern-ment was unrepresentative within the terms of the Yalta agreement and that holding of the planned elections would provide no solution: "I then informed him of my instructions to press at Moscow for postpone-ment of elections and added that if no agreement could be reached on that point, our Gov't would probably stipulate reconstruction of Cabi-net and holding of new elections as prerequisite to recognition."[17] If Georgiev and his fellow Zveno ministers acknowledged the propriety of the American position, perhaps internal pressure from the non-Communist members of the cabinet would be added to the U.S. de-mand for reorganization, a scenario fully consistent with Byrnes's hope that nonrecognition would inspire a reform attitude from within the cabinet.

Two days later, Ethridge was ushered into the Soviet Foreign Minis-try, being greeted not by Molotov as expected but by Deputy Foreign Minister Vyshensky. To Ethridge's assertion that the upcoming elections would not produce a government America could recognize, Vyshensky responded that politics in Bulgaria differed little from those in other countries and that the Soviets believed the existing Bulgarian government was sincerely attempting to restore democracy. Harriman reported: "As regards the allegation of Soviet interference in Bulgarian affairs, he replied categorically that no such interference had taken place." When asked whether the Soviet government would be receptive to suggestions that as a Yalta signatory Moscow should request the Bulgarian government to postpone the scheduled elections, Vyshensky retorted that such an action would constitute "unjustifiable intervention in Bulgarian affairs." Perceiving a gleam of hope in Vyshensky's acknowledgment that a request for advice on postponement from the Bulgarian government itself would be treated more seriously, Ethridge concluded that the sole remaining hope lay in Sofia and not Moscow.[18] That same day, Barnes informed the State Department that rumors of growing unrest within Georgiev's Zveno party in the face of the upcoming elections were rampant and that the senior Bulgarian regent, Ganev, was willing to offer his own resignation so as to precipitate a government crisis that might postpone the balloting. Having received reports that even some of the Obbov Agrarians were debating withdrawal from the Fatherland Front, Byrnes decided to appeal once more to the Georgiev cabinet.[19] Barnes was instructed to deliver a three-paragraph message stressing America's belief that the elections would be undemocratic and reconfirming Washington's refusal to establish diplomatic relations with any resulting government.[20] In view of Vyshensky's refusal to associate the Soviet government with any initiative by the Yalta powers, a specific request for postponement was deemed inadvisable. The following day the Bulgarian foreign minister acknowledged receipt of the message but stated that the election would proceed on schedule.[21] A copy of Byrnes's message delivered by Harriman to Vyshensky received the same negative response.[22] On November 18, as planned, Bulgarians went to the polls.

The announced results of the balloting reported that of about 4.5 million eligible voters, slightly more than 3.85 million participated in the elections—a difference of just under 650,000. Among the ballots cast, however, 45,000 had been either left blank or defaced with slogans. Although these "official" results suggest that about 20 percent of the electorate had heeded the opposition call for boycott, the end result was the same. As expected, the Bulgarian Communists and their Agrarian allies dominated the newly elected assembly, gaining 190 of the 270 seats available.[23] The Fatherland Front and its Soviet backers still held the future of Bulgaria tightly in their hands. Shortly after publication of the final tally, the opposition issued a scathing ten-point denunciation, emphasizing the atmosphere of sheer terror created by the Communists and the militia during the campaign. Threats of physical violence had been ever-present, with the slogan "Death to the opposition" appearing on numerous placards and posters. Even with the balloting completed, blacklists were being invoked, denying employment to those who refused to cast a vote.[24] With the impasse between government and opposition now as firm as ever, the possibility of a reconciliation remained remote. Any last hope for a democratic Bulgaria now awaited action by the Yalta powers, and the soon-to-convene Moscow Foreign Ministers' Conference became the central forum for further discussion.

In a diary entry of mid-December 1945, George Kennan charged that Secretary Byrnes arrived in the Soviet capital that month unconcerned about the fate of smaller nations under Russian occupation. His only goal, Kennan concluded, "is to achieve some sort of an agreement, he doesn't care what. The realities behind this agreement, since they concern only such people as Koreans, Rumanians, and Iranians, about whom he knows nothing, do not concern him. He wants an agreement for its political effect at home."[25] If such indeed was Byrnes's true purpose, it stands in sharp contrast both with the carefully prepared position papers brought to the Moscow Conference covering the Balkan dilemma and with the tenacity the secretary exhibited in his dealings during the conference with his Soviet counterpart, Molotov. What Kennan mistook for indifference may well have been a vague sense of hope, a belief that direct access to Stalin might clear the way for an acceptable solution. In an effort to demonstrate that America was not pursuing an anti-Soviet policy in Eastern Europe as Molotov frequently charged, Byrnes had approved recognition of the Hungarian government two months earlier upon receiving assurances that free elections there would shortly follow. In early November, the Hungarian voters had returned a non-Communist, Smallholder majority, producing a multiparty coalition government in which the Smallholders held the positions of prime minister and president, with the secretary-general of the Communist party, Matthias Rakosi, being appointed as vice-premier. Such a compromise seemed a good precedent for similar reconciliations in Bulgaria and Rumania. And the negotiations in Moscow to resolve the deadlock as to which nations might be invited to a future peace conference dealing with the fate of Bulgaria, Rumania, and the other former satellite states gave credence to Byrnes's optimism. Initially rebuffed by Molotov on the U.S. choices for such a conference, Byrnes wisely bided his time until meeting directly with Stalin. At the conclusion of this meeting between Byrnes and the Soviet leader in which the former emphasized his belief that no major issues would remain unresolved if both sides bargained in good faith, Stalin informed Molotov that Byrnes's list of nations to be invited to the future peace conference had his approval.[26]

The American proposals detailing the conditions that might permit recognition of Bulgaria and Rumania met the usual abrupt rejection from the tireless Soviet foreign minister. According to Byrnes's position paper, the three signatories of the Yalta agreement were obliged to inform Bulgaria that government reorganization was needed, so as to include representatives of all parties participating in the Fatherland Front as of September 9, 1944. This reformed cabinet, in turn, would pledge to hold free elections for a new National Assembly within six months, and the legislative power of the existing assembly would be restricted in the interim.[27] In Rumania, the Yalta signatories should send a joint answer to King Michael's appeal of the past August, advising that representatives of the two major opposition parties be admitted to the Groza cabinet and that a pledge be given to hold free elections within a specific time interval.[28] Once these conditions were met, the United States would extend recognition to both states. After a series of fruitless debates with Molotov, Byrnes again sought an audience with the Soviet dictator.

In a wide-ranging discussion with Stalin on December 23, Byrnes reiterated America's abiding support for the Yalta declaration, "which provided for joint efforts to establish temporary governments broadly representative of the people." Pointing out that conditions in Finland, Hungary, Austria, and Yugoslavia had allowed Washington to extend recognition—evidence that American policy in Eastern Europe was free from any anti-Soviet bias—Byrnes raised the problem of the two remaining Balkan states in which the Soviets possessed armies of occupation. Might the Generalissimo offer help in this matter?[29]

Stalin's response suggested that a compromise might indeed be possible. Although refusing to demand new elections in Sofia, which, Stalin argued, would be perceived as intolerable outside interference, he consented to "advise" the Bulgarians to include some members of the "loyal opposition" in the new cabinet. In the case of Rumania, where elections were still pending, Stalin suggested that it might be possible to meet Byrnes's proposal for a fuller reorganization of the existing government. He agreed that a commission composed of Vyshensky, Harriman, and a British representative be dispatched to Bucharest to supervise the entry of two additional ministers representative of the Rumanian opposition. The precise wording of the agreement on Bulgaria and Rumania would be left to the foreign ministers and their deputies to be completed before adjournment of the Moscow Conference.[30] Subsequent discussions with Molotov were stormy and unsettling, but a final agreement was reached. With regard to Bulgaria, the concluding communiqué stated that the three powers had agreed that the Soviet government would tender "friendly advice" to Sofia that two representatives from other democratic groups be admitted into the Bulgarian cabinet, representatives who "(a) are truly representative of the groups of the parties which are not participating in the government, and (b) are really suitable and will work loyally with the government." At Byrnes's insistence, the wording had been meaningfully changed from Stalin's initial suggestion that only the "loyal opposition" be considered for entry. American and British recognition of the reorganized cabinet in Sofia would follow only if Washington and London were "convinced that this friendly advice has been accepted by the Bulgarian Government and the said additional representatives have been included in its body."[31] The West would retain its original position if the additional representatives were not judged truly representative."

The agreement dealing with Rumania also followed the broad outline sketched by Stalin. The three governments promised to advise King Michael that one member from the National Peasant party and one from the Liberal party should be admitted into the cabinet, and a special commission composed of Vyshensky, Harriman, and the British ambassador to Moscow, A. Clark Kerr would leave for Bucharest to work out details with the king. This agreement, however, allowed less flexibility than its Bulgarian counterpart. Representatives were to be individuals who "are suitable and will work loyally with the government." Eventual recognition would depend less upon the satisfaction of each Yalta power that a real change had occurred than upon the formalities of reorganization: "As soon as these tasks are accomplished and the required assurances have been received, the Government of Rumania . . . will be recognized by The Government of the United States and the Government of the United Kingdom."[32] Yet despite the potential shortcomings in the wording of the Rumanian accord, the communiqué and the compromises it represented offered the first hope since the Potsdam Conference that a new spirit of reconciliation had replaced Soviet intransigence. It was to the spirit as much as to the letter of the communiqué that Byrnes and his advisers pinned their hopes for the future. Perhaps this new mood of guarded optimism was best captured by Byrnes himself: "No one who had shared my experience at Potsdam, London and Moscow doubted that there were still many trying days ahead. But we did face the new year of 1946 with greater hope as a result of the Moscow Conference. Perhaps the rest of the world did too. I hoped so."[33]

The speed with which the Bulgarian cabinet responded to the Soviet "advice" to broaden the existing government lent immediate support to Byrnes's qualified optimism. On December 28, the crucial sections of the Moscow communiqué were published in the main Bulgarian Communist daily, *Rabotnichesko delo,* and in the first days of the new year, the government began talks with the opposition. On January 3, Nikola Petkov informed Barnes that although prospects for a rapid resolution of outstanding disputes were dim, there was cause for hope with regard to future prospects for democracy in Bulgaria. The opposition remained united, he stated, in its insistence that the Ministry of Interior be relinquished by the Communists, that the recently elected assembly be dismissed, and that free elections be conducted using separate electoral lists.[34] Without such concessions, the opposition would stay outside the cabinet, in the hope of producing a new crisis within the context of the Moscow agreement. According to an article published in early January in *Rabotnichesko delo,* the opposition prerequisites for cabinet entry were augmented to include a Communist pledge to forego the Ministry of Justice.[35]

In view of the obvious deadlock, Petkov's belief in Bulgaria's democratic future strikes the contemporary reader as misguided. In fact, it arose from Petkov's awareness of very real political strains within the Fatherland Front produced by the November elections and centered within the National Union-Zveno, the party to which the prime minister, war minister, and foreign minister belonged. In the final months of 1945, the Central Committee of Zveno created a special committee to gather information on "arbitrary, illegal and irresponsible activities" within Bulgaria, and dissatisfied members began an exodus from the party. Despite Communist efforts to regain support by expanding the number of administrative positions assigned Zveno members, the leadership of the party argued for a greater political role within the Fatherland Front. In January 1946, the Zveno paper, *Izgrev,* appealed for a general amnesty and the reestablishment of religious teaching in schools and barracks. By now, the more conservative members of Zveno were mounting a campaign to convince Bulgarians that a program combining the ideals of patriotism and religion held the best hope for the nation's future because such a program avoided the "idealism" of Adam Smith and the "doctrinaire utopianism" of Karl Marx. According to a recent Bulgarian analysis of Zveno at this stage in its postwar evolution, "In almost every Zveno organization there was an active left group, but almost everywhere these groups were a minority."[36] Throughout the spring of 1946, high-placed Zveno officials secretly pressured Barnes to stand firm against Communist efforts to convert Bulgaria into a red satrapy.[37]

The first indication that the Sofia cabinet's willingness to engage in sincere discussions with the opposition was rapidly coming into conflict with Communist and Soviet policy came in an official announcement over Radio Sofia on January 6. All discussions for "completing" the government would have to be based exclusively on the letter of the Moscow agreement, and "those who are to nominate the opposition representatives to participate in the government must be in agreement with the home and foreign policy of the Fatherland Front government."[38] The next day, Prime Minister Georgiev and Foreign Minister Stainov—the two most prominent Zveno leaders—in the company of the trusted Communist minister of interior, Anton Yugov, arrived unexpectedly in Moscow. As Stainov cabled his anxious colleagues in the Bulgarian Foreign Ministry on the second day of his visit, Molotov and Stalin "explained that the friendly advice in the name of the three foreign ministers via the Soviet representative *has a limited objective [e imal ogranichena zadacha]*: to counsel the Bulgarian government to include in its ranks . . . two representatives . . . under condition that they are found to be suitable and will work loyally with the Bulgarian government. After receiving this explanation of the objective, the delegation recommends to our colleagues in the [Bulgarian] Council of Ministers to remain within these parameters in the event they meet once more with representatives of the opposition." No discussion of the recent elections, possible changes in the existing assembly, or the conduct of Bulgaria's domestic and foreign policy was to be allowed. To ensure that the Bulgarian cabinet would not deviate from the narrow Soviet interpretation of the Moscow agreement, Deputy Foreign Minister Vyshensky was ordered by Stalin to proceed to Sofia. As Stainov reported, "His arrival is connected with the task of turning the attention of the opposition to what is reported above."[39]

On January 9, with the Bulgarian delegation still in Moscow, Vyshensky touched down in the Bulgarian capital, immediately arranging discussions with both the Bulgarian cabinet and the opposition, including Petkov and the Social Democrat leader, Kosta Lulchev. As might have been predicted given Vyshensky's prime task of stiffening the position of the cabinet without the interference of Georgiev and Stainov, an impasse quickly ensued. As Foreign Minister Stainov confided to Barnes, Stalin was upset that "the Bulgarian Government seemed to have gotten into deeper water than was intended by the

Moscow Accord." Thus Vyshensky was not in Sofia to act as "broker between Government and opposition, nor as he [Stainov] again put it later in talk 'to mix up batter in Bulgarian political kitchen composed of opposition and FF ingredients.' "[40] Bowing to this direct pressure from Moscow, the Bulgarian cabinet broke off all talks with the opposition on January 12, the day Vyshensky left Sofia, his work completed.[41] The next day, the official Soviet news agency, TASS, announced the failure of Vyshensky's mission, placing blame upon the opposition while lauding efforts by the Bulgarian government to achieve a solution to existing problems: "However, the representatives of the [opposition] groups, Mr. N. Petkov and Mr. Lulchev declined the [Government's] suggestions, having raised in this connection conditions for participation in the government which fundamentally contradict the Moscow meeting of the three ministers." Vyshensky had used his presence in Sofia to advance prospects for satisfying the Moscow accord, TASS concluded, but Petkov and Lulchev had torpedoed his efforts, refusing to affirm their loyalty to the government and insisting upon their "absurd conditions."[42] Soviet readers could have little doubt as to whom the Soviets believed was at fault.

The extremely rapid pace of diplomatic activity concerning Bulgaria in the initial two weeks of the new year caught Secretary Byrnes and his advisers somewhat unprepared. An inquiry to Kennan in Moscow as to the reasons behind the surprise visit of Georgiev and Stainov of January 7 produced the response that information on the secret Soviet-Bulgarian talks was difficult to come by. Not one to overlook an opportunity to advance his own speculations when hard information was lacking, Kennan informed Byrnes that the Soviet Union remained adamant that Bulgaria be a "security sphere" of Russia; such security was ensured through domination in Sofia of elements "in disciplinary subordination to Moscow." Reference to the Russian heavy hand upon Bulgaria also formed the basis of Barnes's account of why the Moscow accord appeared in trouble and why Moscow was attempting to fix blame solely upon the opposition: "I believe any such contention to be without solid foundation, in fact that just the contrary is the case—that developments here as they have been currently reported by this Mission since November 1944 conclusively prove that responsibility [for the] unsatisfactory situation that now exists rests solely on Russia and Russia-abetted Bulgarian Communists." For Barnes, who, like Kennan, had held little hope that the Moscow agreement would resolve longstanding difficulties in Bulgaria, the best course of U.S. action was a stubborn resistance to clear Soviet designs upon the entire Balkan penninsula: "Russia is determined to fashion a South Slav Union dominated by it and to be used by it to emasculate Turkey and Greece and to place Russia squarely on the eastern Mediterranean and Adriatic."[43]

The bleak responses from Kennan and Barnes arrived at a State Department already under heavy attack for "concessions" at the Moscow Conference. In early January, Truman had read the final Ethridge report, concluding much as had the diplomats abroad that "Russia intends an invasion of Turkey and the seizure of the Black Sea Straits to the Mediterranean."[44] Presidential adviser Admiral Leahy had informed both Byrnes and Truman of his own deep reservations about Moscow's provisions for Bulgaria and Rumania, the congressional Republicans were demanding a firmer stance toward the Soviets.[45] And yet to Byrnes, the assembled evidence appeared inconclusive to warrant the conclusion that Moscow had rejected all efforts at compromise in preference for a policy of naked imperialism. A report produced by the State Department's Research and Analysis Division at the close of 1945 cautioned that "it could not be conclusively determined that the Soviet Union had charted a fixed course of military and ideological expansion."[46] More important, East-West negotiations on the reorganization of the Rumanian government were proceeding toward a successful conclusion. Remaining problems in Bucharest appeared to be based upon objections from within the Groza cabinet, with the Soviet representative on the three-man commission appointed at the Moscow Conference showing a willingness to accommodate his Western colleagues.[47]

In mid-January, the Rumanian cabinet had been enlarged as planned through the admission of two opposition representatives, and a pledge of free elections to be held in the "shortest possible time" had been extracted.[48] Although some difficulties remained, Byrnes concluded that Vyshensky had fulfilled his responsibilities. As the memorandum following January talks between Byrnes and Vyshensky noted, "The Secretary replied that he felt the [Rumanian] Commission had made an honest and genuine attempt to carry out the Moscow decision and that the U.S. Government was now considering the results and would communicate its decision promptly."[49] True to the pledge of "promptness," the State Department in mid-February announced that recognition was being extended to the reorganized Rumanian government.[50] Thus only Bulgaria remained unrecognized, elevating that state once more to the unique position it had held in America's policy during the final years of the war. And once again Soviet intentions toward the Balkans would be gauged, in part, by Moscow's willingness to accommodate American interests in this southernmost Slavic state.

On the last day of January, Secretary Byrnes sent a long and thoughtful message to his personal friend and State Department counselor, Benjamin Cohen, who was attending the initial session of the United Nations General Assembly in London. Reflecting upon reports that Vyshensky had recently informed the British that his abortive efforts in Sofia had fulfilled Russia's responsibility for implementation of the Moscow agreement, Byrnes insisted that America was not disposed to pressure the Bulgarian opposition to jettison its political principles in order to enter a reorganized Bulgarian cabinet. Recalling that the Bulgarian Constitution of 1879 provided that the National Assembly might call for elections during its normal term of office, Byrnes suggested that Cohen approach Vyshensky to ask that such a request be made to Sofia in the name of the three powers. Washington would promise to extend recognition once elections were called and assurances of full civil liberties given.[51]

Barnes, too, was informed that America would not pressure the opposition to be false to its ideals and that Barnes's earlier suggestion that new elections be held was under active consideration. And yet this acknowledgment that Barnes's cables were indeed being read in Washington, if perhaps not always answered on time, included a warning that Barnes must not intrigue with the opposition. Vyshensky had raised the issue of Barnes's "sabotage," and Byrnes cautioned that now was not the time to give any appearance of American bad faith.[52] But before Barnes could respond, Cohen cabled his objections to Byrnes's goal of fresh elections. Such a demand, Cohen advised, would merely confirm Soviet suspicions of Western interference. Even were new elections to be held, they would be conducted by the same regime responsible for the earlier balloting, a situation not likely to inspire confidence in their result. Since Vyshensky had concluded that his efforts in Sofia were a failure, might it not be better to ask the Russian how the impasse might now be resolved?[53] Upon reflection, Byrnes cabled his agreement with Cohen's suggestion. Time was now of the essence, Byrnes concluded, since "we have had the definite impression from recent reports that the situation is deteriorating in Bulgaria."[54] Yet when Cohen approached Vyshensky to argue for a new Soviet initiative, the Russian refused. Moscow had attempted to fulfill its responsibilities in good faith, he responded, having met failure because of "impossible and insulting" demands of the opposition, which was abetted by the American representative, Maynard Barnes. Until the Bulgarian opposition reconsidered, Vyshensky concluded, "the situation would remain as it had been before." A chastened Cohen cabled, "He made it plain that the Soviet Government is not prepared to put forward any new suggestion but let events in Bulgaria take their course.[55]

In calmer times, Byrnes and his department might well have admitted defeat, putting the issue of Bulgaria aside and focusing on other crucial issues in East-West relations. But such was not to be. Perhaps the criticism of the Moscow Conference and its results inspired one last effort to justify the hopes with which the secretary had left Moscow in late December. Whatever the motivation, a new proposal was immediately prepared in Washington. Realizing that Soviet assistance was increasingly unlikely, the State Department now appealed directly to the Bulgarian cabinet without prior consultation with Moscow. Such an appeal might capitalize upon the known disagreements between Zveno ministers and the Communists, leading to some opening through which opposition representatives might enter the cabinet to pursue their basic demands. Perhaps a "mistake" similar to that made by Stainov during the August elections might facilitate compromise. Undoubtedly Byrnes must have realized that in this last attempt he was ranging well beyond the letter of the Moscow agreement in an effort to recapture its spirit.

On February 22, the Bulgarian representative in Washington, Lieutenant-General Vladimir Stoichev, was summoned to receive an important State Department message. Delivered by Cohen, the aide-memoir began with an admonition that some misunderstanding appeared to exist within certain quarters in Bulgaria concerning America's interpretation of the Moscow agreement. America, the note continued, had never intended that the Bulgarian opposition enter the Bulgarian cabinet without prior understanding on mutually acceptable changes and policies: "It was never the understanding of the United States Government that pressure was to be exerted on the opposition to nominate two candidates for PRO FORMA inclusion into the Government without regard to the conditions of their participation. Although the Moscow Agreement did not set forth any specific conditions for the inclusion of the two representatives of the opposition, it did, in the view of the United States Government, anticipate that the participation of these representatives would be on the basis of conditions mutually agreeable to both the Bulgarian Government and the opposition."[56]

The precise impact of this message on the various members of the Bulgarian cabinet remains a subject of conjecture, awaiting a future opening of Bulgarian archives. Yet indirect evidence suggests that a heated debate quickly ensued. A recent account of the political fluctuations within the Zveno party cryptically notes that in early 1946, "the position of even the Fatherland Front nucleus around [Zveno Prime Minister] K. Georgiev had weakened."[57] Equally suggestive of an intense dispute within the cabinet is the fact that not until five days had passed did the Bulgarians seek advice from the Soviet Union as to how this surprising communiqué should be handled.[58] Uncertainty prevailed in Moscow as well, with the angry Soviet response being delayed until March 7. And when Moscow finally delivered its answer to Washington, the wisdom of attempting to bypass the Soviet authorities was confirmed. America, the sharp reply asserted, had distorted the terms of the Moscow agreement in the hope of buttressing the position of the Bulgarian opposition. The American aide-memoir delivered to the Bulgarians did "not correspond with the taken in Moscow decision concerning Bulgaria, since nothing is said in the decision of the Moscow Conference that the representatives of the opposition have to enter the Bulgarian Government on the basis of some mutually acceptable conditions." The American note, Moscow charged, "moves the opposition to a breach of the decision taken with the participation of the representative of the United States at the Moscow Conference."[59]

This unambiguous Soviet response terminated all remaining doubts in Washington as to where fault lay for the nonfulfillment of past agreements over Bulgaria. And yet it also confirmed the existence of some room for maneuver and compromise within the Bulgarian cabinet. Despite Soviet refusals to modify their own strict interpretation of the Moscow agreement, pressure from Zvenoist ministers in Sofia produced renewed talks with the opposition on March 24. The following day, Barnes cabled the State Department that significant progress had been made: Prime Minister Georgiev had offered the Ministry of Justice and a position as assistant minister of the interior to the opposition. Even here compromise was possible because "important members of 'Zveno,' Georgiev's party, secretly [are] disposed to support Petkov in this demand." Chances for a positive outcome would be greatly augmented, Barnes advised, if Byrnes himself would send an encouraging message to the Bulgarian cabinet, telling of America's deep satisfaction as to progress made.[60] As Barnes informed Byrnes, this request for further direct American involvement had been initially shown to Foreign Minister Stainov and to Georgiev and was dispatched to Washington only after incorporation of several changes suggested by the two Zvenoist ministers. Petkov had also been informed of the possibility of American encouragement.[61] On March 26, as requested, a message of appreciation was cabled by Byrnes to Barnes for oral transmission to the prime minister, the regency, and the opposition. "You may add," Byrnes stated, "that it is my earnest hope that these negotiations will result in the establishment of a reorganized Govt in accordance [with the] Moscow Agreement and that the U.S. Govt will thus be enabled to extend recognition to such Govt at an early date."[62]

If the clear steps forward in implementing the Moscow agreement raised hopes in both Washington and Sofia, they engendered outrage in Moscow. As a precaution against a Soviet veto of any government-opposition compromise, Barnes had advised his superiors in Washington that the Russians be informed before sending the message of encouragement to Sofia. It seems unlikely that his advice was followed. On March 28, the Soviet ambassador to Bulgaria, Stepan Kirsanov, demanded that the cabinet withdraw all concessions to the opposition and resist any further calls for negotiations.[63] That same day Georgiev told Barnes that there had been a misunderstanding and that he had never offered to extend the Ministry of Justice to the opposition.[64] Three days later a new Bulgarian cabinet was formed which significantly increased the formal power of the Communists. Georgiev retained his position as prime minister, but creation of a new position of vice-prime minister and its assignment to a Communist portended significant limitations of his power. Retaining control of the Ministry of the Interior, and thereby the dreaded militia, the Communists gained the important Ministry of Finance. Petko Stainov, the Zvenoist foreign minister, was replaced by a more complacent member of his party, Georgi Kulishev. No seats were awarded to the opposition.

In tandem with steps taken to diminish Zveno's influence within the cabinet, the Communists began a new campaign designed to weaken Zveno's position within the Fatherland Front and the Bulgarian military. Purges of district and local administrators were initiated, with total loyalty to the Front's program being the price of retention. The number of labor-cultural brigades sent into the villages to ensure "harmony" among the people was expanded threefold.[65] At the Tenth Plenum of the Central Committee, Communist party chief Georgi Dimitrov called for the expulsion of intransigent elements from Zveno, cautioning that the Fatherland Front was prepared to function even in the absence of any members of that party.[66] In the summer of 1946, General Biriuzov, who had been recalled to Moscow the preceding spring for reassignment as deputy commander of Soviet ground forces, returned to assist in the purge of Zvenoists and anti-Fatherland Front elements from the Bulgarian army. On July 2, the Bulgarian government declared that henceforth the responsibilities of the Ministry of War would be executed by the entire cabinet, and by the end of the month Zvenoist War Minister Velchev had dropped from sight. The ensuing purge of the military removed about 30 percent of the Bulgarian officer corps for holding views contrary to policies of the Fatherland Front.[67] As Barnes now cabled from Sofia, the anti-Zveno attacks were aimed not only at former Foreign Minister Stainov and the editor of the Zvenoist paper but also at Georgiev himself. Barnes noted, "It is believed that Prime Minister Georgiev also a Zveno member will soon be forced to let Communists know that these attacks on Zveno must cease or that Zveno will depart from Govt."[68] By now, all prospects for fulfilling the terms of the Moscow agreement had long evaporated, as had all prospects for a democratic Bulgaria. The time had arrived for another agonizing reappraisal of American policy toward the Balkans.

8 The Decision to Recognize

The spring 1946 Soviet notes rejecting a compromise solution for Bulgaria and the failure of Prime Minister Georgiev to arrange an agreement in Sofia reached a State Department already deeply divided over the nature of the Soviet threat in Europe and how best it might be met. Early in the new year, President Truman had directly challenged the optimistic assumptions underlying Byrnes's negotiating stance at the Moscow Conference, remarking to his secretary of state that "unless Russia is faced with an iron fist and strong language another war is in the making. Only one language do they understand—'how many divisions have you.' "[1] The following month, in what was to become known as the famous "Long Telegram," the U.S. chargé in Moscow, George Kennan, provided a more elegant and sophisticated explanation of the ceaseless Soviet campaign against the democratic future of Europe. Focusing on the historic and psychological factors governing the totalitarian policies of the Kremlin, Kennan rejected the notion that Russia would seek compromise with the West or act on behalf of limited objectives: "In summary, we have here a political force committed fanatically to the belief that with US there can be no permanent *Modus Vivendi,* that it is desirable and necessary that the internal harmony of our society be disrupted, our traditional way of life be destroyed, the international authority of our state be broken, if Soviet Power is to be secured."[2] Kennan's interpretation received instant acclaim in Washington, as described by Hugh De Santis: "Telegram number 511 from Moscow rocked the State Department. 'Magnificant' Matthews gushed, the best Kennan had ever done. It 'hits the nail on the head,' Henderson added. For Kohler it dashed any lingering hope of U.S.-Soviet cooperation. Acheson called it 'truly remarkable.' Byrnes sent a message of commendation. . . . Secretary of the Navy Forrestal was so impressed that he had it reproduced and distributed to members of the Truman Cabinet involved with foreign affairs and to upper-echelon officers in the military establishment."[3] As W. W. Rostow, then an assistant division chief in State recalls, "An increasing proportion of the relevant Foreign Service Officers came to Kennan's conclusion about a split Europe. Advocates of Kennan's position tended to regard the offering of positive proposals to Moscow as a waste of time at best, dangerous at worst."[4] One month later, the theme of a Europe half free and half enslaved was brought forcefully to the attention of the American public in Winston Churchill's stirring speech at Fulton, Missouri, with its ringing condemnation of an "Iron Curtain" having rent the Continent.

As the tide of opinion both in Washington and around the nation grew increasingly resigned to a postwar division of Europe which would confirm Communist political power in states occupied by Soviet forces, the State Department prepared to meet its Soviet antagonist at the upcoming Paris Peace Conference. The Moscow Foreign Ministers' Conference of 1945 had agreed that peace agreements with the defeated Axis satellites would be submitted to a convocation of world nations, and by spring 1946 preliminary discussions were well under way. Now might be the final opportunity to reach a compromise of key issues dividing the Allies, reversing the clear trend toward a Europe sharply separated into antagonistic spheres of influence. In lieu of an overall settlement of existing disagreements, the peace conference would be forced to discuss the fate of each former Axis nation separately, confirming the status quo for the foreseeable future. The fate of democracy in Bulgaria and in other East European states lay, in part, with the procedural decision as to whether the peace conference would confront the total picture of Europe's future or would focus upon each state as a self-contained whole.

On April 20, 1946, a meeting crucial for America's approach to the peace conference for Europe took place within the State Department. Present were Secretary Byrnes, Undersecretary Acheson, and Assistant Secretary for Economic Affairs Will Clayton. Cast as protagonists for a last-ditch attempt to avert the division of Europe, the latter two officials presented a detailed plan to postpone negotiation of individual peace agreements until a more comprehensive framework of East-West economic and political cooperation was in place. Acheson and Clayton recommended that Byrnes open the Paris Peace Conference due shortly to convene with an American initiative designed to resolve current pan-European disputes. Starting with a clear affirmation of America's willingness to participate in the long-range economic and political reconstruction of all of Europe, Byrnes was advised to "propose formulas consistent with such a general European settlement, covering specific issues involved in the treaty negotiations (for example, the control of the Danube) and major issues outside the area of treaty negotiations, notably the major unsettled issues in Germany and Austria. He would propose the setting up of a regional United Nations security council to oversee the execution of the settlements

arrived at . . . [and] the creation of an all-European economic organization designed to accelerate lagging reconstruction and to achieve
greater long-run economic unity in Europe, with subcommissions for
fuel and power, trade and transport, finance, the coordination of plans,
and so on." Although Acheson and Clayton could not guarantee that
the USSR would prove receptive to such proposals, they argued that a
postponement of the normal nation-by-nation negotiations of final
peace settlements offered the only alternative to ratification of the
existing division of Europe. But by now even Byrnes despaired of
achieving an equitable agreement with the USSR. As the author of the
Acheson-Clayton proposal subsequently recalled: "Byrnes did reject
the plan by pocket veto. He proceeded with the treaty negotiations one
by one, in effect trading to Moscow essentially what it wanted in the
East for Trieste and Western interests in the Italian Treaty negotiations."[5] Bulgaria, of course, lay east of Trieste.

If the decision to proceed country-by-country at the Paris Peace
Conference in essence determined the overall future of Bulgaria, it did
not require that America forego all efforts for possible changes that
might enhance prospects for the democratic opposition American had
long championed. In late June, Barnes cabled Byrnes his congratula-
tions on a decision at Paris that Soviet troops would at least leave
Bulgaria once a treaty of peace was signed.[6] But such small concessions could not disguise the eventual fate awaiting the state given
America's apparent willingness to forego its past policy of nonrecognition and nonnegotiation until the Sofia government admitted opposition delegates. In July, Byrnes gave tangible proof to the new policy of
conceding Soviet control in Bulgaria by informing Barnes that in a
recent conversation he had advised Molotov that America's nonrecognition of Bulgaria would not delay negotiation of the Bulgarian peace
even though "there might be difficulties in connection with ratification
if [the] Moscow Agreement [was] not carried out."[7] For Barnes, undoubtedly unaware of the abortive efforts of Acheson and Clayton, this
willingness to extend de facto recognition to the unreconstituted Sofia
government portended a significant reversal of past policy. Referring
to an extensive list of recent telegrams he had sent detailing the increasing oppression in Bulgaria, Barnes sadly concluded that if his
secretary was determined to proceed with the Bulgarian peace, fairness
argued that the Bulgarian opposition be so informed: "Should we
allow opposition to prepare [for] participation in [the upcoming] election for GNA [Grand National Assembly] without this knowledge, I
am sure strong body of opinion in Bulgaria would feel we had 'let
down' democratic elements of [the] country."[8]

The elections to which Barnes referred were destined to be the most important of the postliberation public political events because this new assembly would be empowered to draft the future constitution. And as the Sofia regime prepared for the balloting, a new wave of domestic arrests and raids against the opposition was authorized. In early July, British Foreign Secretary Ernest Bevin informed Byrnes by personal letter that he had recently confronted the Speaker of the Bulgarian parliament about conditions in Sofia. "I told M. Kolarov that the reports we had received . . . indicated that the Government were [*sic*] now conducting what amounted to a war against the Opposition. They were assisted in this activity by an armed militia which was being used by one Party as a terrorist instrument against its political opponents."[9] By now, the ever-vigilant Bulgarian militia had expanded its efforts against foreign missions, detaining employees of the United States and arresting some. Outraged by such activities, General Robertson, who had replaced General Crane the preceding spring, requested that the War Department consider the possibility of bringing the offending militiamen before an international tribunal: "I therefore believe that . . . I should be directed to tell Bulgarian and Russian authorities that my Govt is looking into [the] question of citing before War Crimes, Nuremberg, any official responsible for further acts . . . against US military personnel on Control Commission under armistice terms." Both Barnes and the top British representatives concurred in this request, Robertson concluded.[10]

Six days later, Barnes cabled a new list of outrages. Two key members of the Petkov Agrarian leadership had just been arrested, eight hundred Bulgarian advocates who had signed a protest over the illegal detention of fellow countrymen had been seized with two hundred of them already assigned to concentration camps, and all but one opposition newspapers had been subject to closure.[11] "Generals Robertson and Oxley, and my British opposite number agree with me that during past few months democratic freedoms have been so completely stamped out in Bulgaria that our continued presence in ACC without some form of protest . . . would be shameful."[12]

By the end of July, as the campaign against the opposition continued, the Bulgarian government introduced a proposal foreseeing a national referendum on the fate of the monarchy to be held prior to the fall election for the Great National Subrania, which would function as a constitutional assembly. The opposition initially opposed a referendum as unnecessary, but Petkov and his followers soon decided to use the required political activities as a means for testing their own political strength.[13] In mid-July, the Supreme Union Council of the Petkov

Agrarians resolved to support the government's appeal for a republic as long as it would be a republic of law in which the rights of all citizens might be formally guaranteed. In sharp contrast to Communist calls for a People's Democratic Republic, Petkov advocated a return to the statutes of the liberal Turnovo Constitution of the past century, purged of its reference to the monarchy. In rapid succession, the leadership of the opposition Democratic and Radical parties announced their support for the constitution as proposed by Petkov, and even the leading organs of Zveno wavered, casting the party's support for the Communists only at the last moment. In late August, as the election campaign reached its climax, the opposition Socialist party issued a joint declaration with the Petkov Agrarians calling for a free, independent, and democratic republic "under which all the fundamental rights and freedoms of Bulgarian citizens will be established and guaranteed."[14]

The renewed vigor with which the opposition used the impending referendum to disseminate its own democratic slogans produced an immediate reaction from the Bulgarian Communists and their Fatherland Front allies. A plenum of the Communist Central Committee resolved "to expose without quarter the enemies of the people and their agents who hide under various disguises—from Colburg democrats, Nikola Petkov . . . oppositionalists and those dressed in Fatherland Front clothing [but] who conspire against the Fatherland Front power, and [against] advocates of fascism." A common position was worked out by the Fatherland Front parties, and thousands of progovernment meetings were scheduled for the urban and rural districts. According to surviving records, nearly fifteen hundred special committees were created in the Plovdiv region alone, and sixteen thousand public gatherings attended by more than seventy thousand individuals were held. As further guarantee that the official philosophy would be heard, twelve thousand agitation groups formed which issued ninety-eight thousand copies of pro-government appeals and fifteen thousand flyers.[15]

The referendum, held in early September, produced few surprises because all parties, pro-government and opposition, had announced for a republic. With slightly over 4.5 million eligible to vote, 4.131 million went to the polls, approving a republic by an overwhelming majority.[16] On September 15 the republic was declared, and the following day the royal family departed via Turkey for Egypt.[17] More important than the results were the unambiguous signs that terror and intimidation remained an essential aspect of Bulgarian politics. Not until after the referendum campaign ended did the opposition decide to chance participation in the coming ballot for the Grand National Assembly.

The intensity of the pressure exerted by the militia paradoxically opened a new opportunity for Byrnes and Barnes to seek Prime Minister Georgiev's assistence in assuring future free elections. By now, the purge of Zveno members had embraced the editor of the party's main paper, *Izgrev,* with a second Zveno journal, *Vreme,* ceasing publication. Two members of Zveno's Central Committee resigned, and "purification" of local committees was ordered.[18] Equally ominous for Zveno's future were Communist plans to permit voters to distinguish among representatives of the Fatherland Front parties in the next election. Although a common list would be used, different colors before each candidate's name would allow voters to select from the parties they favored.[19] Given the intense antagonisms between many Zveno members and the Communists, the latter might well use the tight control over both the balloting and tabulation of results to deny Zveno significant representation in the new assembly. Thus a strange and partial coincidence of interest continued between American proponents of the Moscow agreement and the now-threatened leader of Zveno, Georgiev. Since the prime minister was in Paris during August 1946 for the peace discussions, Barnes requested authorization from Washington to take leave in the French capital. Although stating that he did not "wish to intrude" on Secretary Byrnes's busy schedule, Barnes prepared a lengthy memorandum for his superior. Emphasizing that militia activities in Bulgaria violated the armistice provisions America was bound to uphold, Barnes, shortly after arriving in Paris, advised Byrnes to have a "frank talk" with Georgiev and Kulishev. A ten-point list of recently violated political and civil liberties was appended to provide a basis of discussion.[20] Four days later, the secretary invited the two Bulgarians and Barnes to a one-and-one-half-hour talk.

In this first meeting with the American secretary, Georgiev, though hesitant to speak in detail, confirmed that the Communists were exerting the heavy pressure on the cabinet. He acknowledged that "political conditions in Bulgaria were unsatisfactory . . . [and] admitted inconveniences and even great difficulties caused by the [the] Communists." Turning to the failure of the Moscow agreement, Georgiev confessed that though his own interpretation of its meaning was midway between that of the United States and the USSR, the "Russians had placed very narrow interpretation on [the] Moscow accord." Given the continuing political tensions in Bulgaria, Georgiev concluded, there existed little chance of broadening the Sofia cabinet before the future elections.[21]

Even though Georgiev's frankness about Communist activities revealed a sincerity rare among Bulgarian leaders, the overall meeting and the absence of a pledge to promote free elections fell far short of

Barnes's expectations. As Barnes had told Byrnes earlier, the prospect of a negotiated peace with the existing cabinet and the de facto recognition such would imply cast doubt upon the wisdom of opposition plans to contest the next election.[22] With Georgiev's refusal to sponsor an effort to broaden the cabinet before the balloting, Barnes focused his efforts on gaining at least a personal promise from the prime minister on behalf of free elections. And following two more meetings with Georgiev, this modest result was achieved. Two days before his return to Sofia, and after private discussions with Molotov, Georgiev handed Barnes a six-point aide memoire promising a final discussion with the opposition so as "to create a more favorable atmosphere in connection with the coming elections." These elections, Georgiev stated, "will give the opposition an opportunity to enter the Sobranye [sic] and exercise from within it their role. The Government is resolved to take appropriate measures to insure free elections for all Bulgarian citizens." Satisfied with this pledge, Barnes advised his superiors that further talks with the Bulgarians would only create the impression that Washington was moving toward a softer position on the points already discussed.[23]

Although the conversations with Georgiev had not produced a new opportunity to implement the Moscow agreement—an unlikely event given the political tensions in Bulgaria—they had produced a major tactical gain for the West. Georgiev had given his personal pledge to the cause of freer elections, and even a moderate weakening of existing political restrictions in Bulgaria would undoubtedly allow numerous opposition candidates to secure positions in the new assembly. Given the growing American propensity to extend formal recognition to Bulgaria once the peace was signed, the presence of an elected opposition would constitute the sole hope that at least a modicum of democracy would remain in Bulgaria. Of equal significance, Georgiev's promise as set forth in the aide memoire might serve as a new vehicle for U.S. protests if these promises were not kept. Well aware that protests forwarded to Moscow under the provisions of the Yalta or Moscow agreements were no longer of use, Barnes and Byrnes now possessed a new "agreement" allowing a direct challenge to Bulgaria's political development if outrages should continue.

As time quickly showed, the modest pledges made by Georgiev remained unfulfilled. On September 13, Barnes cabled Byrnes that despite Georgiev's return to Sofia, political conditions had not eased: "The Communists are now so distrustful of Zveno, the Prime Minister's party, and so confident that with Russian backing they can exercise completely free hand, as to be planning elimination of Zveno from the Government. In this situation Prime Minister seems to be more concerned with saving his own political hide if possible, than in carrying out his promise to assure free elections.[24] It was now clear that Barnes had correctly interpreted the precarious position of Georgiev and his party and had used this understanding to extract Georgiev's promise of freer elections while in Paris. What Barnes had not judged correctly was the direction Georgiev would jump when the final crunch became imminent. Thus little remained for the Americans except a return to the familiar if unsuccessful tactics of protest.

In early October, Maynard Barnes delivered a personal letter from Secretary Byrnes to Georgiev objecting to the failure to implement the pledges contained in Georgiev's Paris aide memoire. A vague threat was included, referring to Byrnes's earlier remarks that in absence of free elections it would be most difficult to gain U.S. Senate ratification of future U.S.-Bulgarian peace. A similar protest was being delivered to the control commission, Byrnes's letter concluded, a step Georgiev applauded.[25] This protest, forwarded by General Robertson to General Biriuzov, insisted upon freedom of the press, noninterference of the militia in the electoral campaign, and convocation of all Bulgarian political leaders in the presence of the ACC to discuss the deteriorating political situation.[26] Expressing "extreme surprise" that America would consider bringing such problems to the ACC, Biriuzov refused to place these demands upon the council's agenda.[27] From this point forward, even the official statements of Byrnes concerning the forthcoming Bulgarian elections were subjected to censorship by Soviet authorities in Bulgaria.[28] As the Soviets had planned, the Bulgarian elections for the Grand National Assembly would take place under a careful Communist eye, without Western interference.

In mid-September, a meeting of the Fatherland Front accepted the common list for the parliamentary election, but with each candidate color-coded as to party. Well aware that any attempt to register single candidates loyal to the opposition would invite the same repression that had accompanied the fall 1945 elections, Petkov's Agrarians in conjunction with the opposition Socialists and a group of "Independent Intellectuals" mimicked the Front example, advancing a common opposition list to ensure registration in all electoral districts. The smaller Democratic party sought a place on this list but failed to gain approval from the larger parties. For both the Front and the opposition, the nature of the future Bulgarian constitution remained a key means by which distinctions in their respective positions could best be laid before the voters, and in early October, all party presses controlled by the Front published a draft calling for a people's republic in which all power would lodge in the hands of the people and labor would constitute the prime principle of social and economic organization.[29] In contrast, Petkov took up the banner for the opposition, demanding a republic based on freedom and equality in which both social justice and private ownership would be safeguarded.[30] On October 27, at the conclusion of a long and often bloody campaign, four million Bulgarians again tramped to the polls in an exercise destined to bring surprises to every participating party. In numerous areas of the state, entire Fatherland Front committees deserted the government for the opposition. In the city of Vidin, the leadership and the nominated candidates of Zveno passed to Petkov's side as did numerous Obbov Agrarians in Ruse, Pleven, Varna, and other cities.[31] Turnovo, Ruse, and Varna districts witnessed major defections from the government, and, according to Communist sources, Zveno adherents in various locales led an open campaign against the Reds.[32]

On the morning following the election, the government published figures it had tabulated showing the Fatherland Front as the recipient of slightly more than 70 percent of all ballots cast. More surprising was the poor showing of the Front's non-Communist members, who polled a scant 717,000 votes. Zveno was credited by the electoral commission with a mere 1 percent of the vote—a disastrous showing which effectively ended its meaningful participation in Bulgaria's future. The Obbov Agrarians, who claimed to be the legitimate heirs of the largest political movement in twentieth-century Bulgaria, were given but 13 percent of the total vote, a sharp contrast to the proportion accorded the Communists.[33] The combined vote for all the non-Communist members of the Fatherland Front was more than half a million fewer than the vote listed for the opposition—a repudiation of amazing dimension given government control over means of coercion during the lengthy campaign. The handwriting was clearly on the wall for the non-Communist allies.

The opposition bloc of Agrarians, Socialists, and Intellectuals emerged as the second strongest force in Bulgarian politics, receiving in excess of 1.2 million votes, or about 28 percent of all votes counted. When translated into deputies, this meant that the opposition received 100 delegates in the Grand National Assembly with the Communists taking 276, the Obbov Agrarians 63, and Zveno and the Front Socialists 5 each.[34] As a result of the election, despite the continuation of violence during the voting, the opposition finally abandoned its position as a persecuted minority to become the second largest party in the Bulgarian parliament, a showing likely to be augmented in the future through defections from the Zveno and Obbov ranks. By early November, even Obbov himself, long the trusted Communist henchman in efforts to destroy the followers of Petkov, was secretly in touch with Barnes and discussing the merits of a new coalition between Agrarians and Communists.[35] Obbov's position had become most difficult, Barnes noted: "If he doesn't join Petkov he will gradually lose his Agrarian following . . . to Petkov. If he breaks with Communists now he will be even more hated by them than Petkov, Lulchev and Stoyanov."[36] In combination with the evident dissatisfaction of Zveno over the voters' rejection of their past loyalty to the Communists, the overall result of the election provided the first hope to Barnes that, even if America extended recognition, democracy in Bulgaria might be firmly enough rooted in the new parliament to survive.[37] By now Barnes, too, had realized the inevitability of recognition as the Paris Peace Conference reached its conclusion, consoling himself that the opposition's strong showing made such an event less disastrous. As he cabled Washington in early November: "In my telegram . . . I expressed opinion that if elections were to give opposition sufficiently strong representation in GNA to preclude measures that might silence this representation, recognition of Bulgarian Govt by US would be made easier and adoption by US of positive policy based on real and live factors in internal political life of country would be facilitated. Elections have given opposition sizable representation in GNA. They have revealed there are only two strong currents [of] political opinion in country—Communist opinion and Agrarian opinion." Barnes found it inconceivable that the Communists would apply strong-arm methods against the opposition now that they had been accepted into the parliament and had received nearly one and a quarter million votes. But as time would show, Barnes's optimism was more indicative of his own democratic consciousness than of Bulgarian realities. Still, even at the height of renewed hope on the morrow of the surprise elections, Barnes seemed to sense that the future was fraught with uncertainty. It might be argued, he cabled home, that Communist indications of a willingness to work with the opposition would be mere window dressing, to be removed once recognition by the West was gained. A better indication of the Communist position might be modification of some of the harsher laws previously used against the opposition: "With moderation [of] these laws to [the] benefit of the opposition, road to recognition should be somewhat cleared." Perhaps, Barnes suggested, the flexibility of the Sofia regime might be expanded via discussions between Washington and Moscow.[38]

On January 4 of the new year, Barnes informed Georgiev, who had recently been demoted to foreign minister, of his views on Bulgaria's future. The elections, he noted, had given the opposition a voice within the parliament, and America could now be expected to sign a peace treaty by mid-February. Recognition undoubtedly would follow shortly after Senate ratification: "I told the FonMin that it was my personal view that relatively satisfactory results of election, despite fraud, and restraint involved made it possible for us now to concentrate on elimination of ACC as [a] wall between US and Bulgaria, free Bulgaria from occupying military forces, to seek conditions that would permit US Govt directly to influence Bulgarian Govt in way of truly democratic methods and real economic and social rehabilitation."[39]

On January 20, 1947, Secretary Byrnes signed the Bulgarian peace treaty. In early February, the Allied Control Commission held its last scheduled session although the respective military missions remained awaiting final ratification of the peace. When formal recognition was extended to Bulgaria by the United Kingdom on February 11, only Washington remained without regular relations, a situation understood by all to be of temporary duration. By now, Secretary Byrnes had resigned, being replaced by General Marshall.

On the eve of his resignation, Byrnes and Barnes exchanged a last lengthy series of cables discussing the future of U.S.-Bulgaria relations. The ratification of the Bulgarian peace treaty would not necessarily lead to full diplomatic recognition, Byrnes noted, although political and practical reasons made such recognition likely. The termination of the Allied Control Commission once the ratified articles were deposited in Moscow as scheduled would deprive America of all facilities to influence Bulgaria's development. Thus recognition could be expected "provided situation in Bulg does not deteriorate in meantime."[40] Barnes accepted the propriety of Byrnes's position, although he objected to the secretary's suggestion that Barnes himself be appointed as the new U.S. chargé in Sofia. Assignment of such a rank, Barnes rejoined, would imply a lowering of assignment, giving support to recent charges that he had exceeded his status and power during the preceding two years.[41]

Since Barnes had earlier denied all interest in becoming the first ambassador to postwar Bulgaria, his lengthy ties with Sofia were rapidly drawing to a close. On January 28 Barnes informed the Bulgarian government that recognition would follow Senate ratification of the peace "provided the situation in Bulgaria does not deteriorate in the meantime."[42] And yet the next day Barnes, although in basic support of the U.S. position, reflected once more on the uncertain future which recognition would bring. Calling Washington's attention to a new purge campaign directed against a little-known group called the Neutral Officers, Barnes concluded: "Repeatedly I ask myself [the] question—will recognition open [the] floodgates of new purge and blood bath? Frankly I do not know [the] answer."[43] Unknown even to Barnes, the Neutral Officers would soon implicate the opposition in treason.

According to Bulgarian accounts, the Neutral Officers were a small group formed in 1945 by reactionary leaders of the Bulgarian army; seventeen officers were identified as members in early 1946.[44] Although such a small organization seemed unlikely to draw government attention—the later head of the U.S. mission even doubting its existence—the initial investigation revealed the government's intention to link the officers with Petkov and the opposition.[45] In early February, State prosecutors announced that the alleged conspiracy involved the opposition, and shortly thereafter the Communist-dominated Grand National Assembly removed the immunity of Agrarian deputy Petar Koev, a longtime personal aide to party chief Petkov.[46] The final purge of the opposition was now in progress although its precise dimensions remained unknown to Barnes right up to his own departure from Sofia in late April.

John E. Horner, Barnes's replacement as American political representative, promptly informed Washington of growing political tensions. Besides reports of a new terror, the political infighting on the assembly floor had reached thundering proportions, and opposition demands that Bulgarian Communism be banned as a fascist movement had been advanced.[47] The decision to debate the merits of the Communist and opposition constitutional drafts had resulted in the closure of the opposition journals.[48] On June 5, the day the U.S. Senate provided final ratification of the peace, the antiopposition movement reached its climax. Following a report by a minor Communist deputy that a letter had been received from the public prosecutor in which Petkov was accused of planning the overthrow of the government, the immunity of the Agrarian leader was removed and he was arrested at once.[49] A search of Petkov's house brought to light letters from twenty-three other opposition deputies promising support, and they too were expelled from the assembly.[50] The campaign was reaching its end.

On June 7, two days after Petkov's arrest and following a face-to-face meeting with the new Bulgarian prime minister, Georgi Dimitrov, in which Dimitrov stated "with a straight face" that the timing of Petkov's incarceration and the U.S. Senate's ratification of the peace was coincidental, Horner fired off an angry cable to Washington.[51] Berating the department in a style that would have done Barnes credit, Horner advised his superiors to reconsider their plans for recognition:

"To recognize present Bulgarian regime without assiduous effort to obtain specific assurances in advance on such of these questions as Department considers of basic importance would seem [a] great mistake. It would mean writing off Bulgaria."[52]

But by now, Washington's policy of concentrating upon the containment of Communism outside the borders of Eastern Europe aside from Greece and Turkey was too firmly in place to allow a major policy review for the sake of a nation in which America had experienced nothing but failures for the past three years. A quickly convened secretary of state's staff meeting presided over by Dean Acheson resolved that "the U.S. should not alter its present plan to recognize the Bulgarian government following the coming into force of the peace treaty." This same session rejected a plea by Maynard Barnes that he be permitted to return to Sofia to seek Petkov's release.[53] Five days later, President Truman signed the peace treaties for Bulgaria, Rumania, and Hungary, publicly expressing his regret and outrage "that the governments of these countries not only disregarded the will of the majority of the people but have resorted to measures of oppression against them." But despite continued repression, Truman concluded, restoration of normal relations would facilitate the withdrawal of Soviet forces and the termination of the Soviet-dominated control commissions.[54] America had made up her mind to recognize.

Although the Truman administration did not hesitate to carry out its recognition decision, it did attempt to intercede on behalf of Petkov and his past efforts to gain a democratic Bulgaria. The August 16 announcement of Petkov's conviction for treason drew a sharp protest. General Robertson was instructed to petition the Soviet head of the control commission for an immediate meeting for a full review of the Petkov case. Referring to the overriding importance of Petkov to the Bulgarian opposition, Robertson's letter once more invoked the Yalta agreement as the basis for his concern.[55] A similar protest was delivered by the British. Until the proposed meeting of the ACC was arranged, Robertson demanded, the Soviets should suspend fulfillment of Petkov's death sentence.[56] Four days later, Cherepanov as acting chairman of the ACC responded that a special meeting lay outside his jurisdiction because the Petkov affair was "purely an internal Bulgarian matter."[57] Immediately upon receipt of Cherepanov's refusal, a second protest was delivered in Moscow, rebutting Cherepanov's claim that this issue fell exclusively within the domain of Bulgarian domestic affairs and requesting consultation at once as provided for in the Yalta agreement.[58] When this note, too, was rejected, U.S. Ambassador Walter Bedell Smith delivered a second message to Soviet officials, stressing the abiding U.S. belief in the principles of the Yalta accord: "The Petkov case, involving the leader of the principal opposition party obviously vitally affects the existence of representative government in Bulgaria. Thus it is clearly within the purview of the Yalta Agreement. . . . The contention that the matter is of purely internal Bulgarian concern cannot relieve the Yalta Powers from their commitment to concert their policies in regard to developments of this nature."[59] But as had been anticipated, this protest also failed to win acceptance in the Soviet capital. On September 23, Nikola Petkov went to his death.

If the death of Petkov was a mortal blow to Western hopes for a democratic Bulgaria, the nature of the execution and the trial revealed an ugliness not seen since the defeat of Germany. Throughout the trial, constant reference was made to hundreds of thousands of telegrams sent by rallies at which the heaviest penalty was demanded. The death sentence was carried out not by firing squad as normal but by hanging, and Petkov's body was placed in an unmarked grave. Petkov's Agrarian party was declared outlawed by the rump Grand National Assembly, with membership to be considered a major criminal offense.[60]

In early September, before Petkov's death, a final approval of American policy toward Bulgaria was taken within the State Department. It was recalled that past Secretary Byrnes had informed the Bulgarians of America's intent to establish diplomatic relations following Senate ratification provided the situation within that country had not deteriorated. At issue was whether the action taken against Petkov, in conjunction with recent evidence that Bulgaria was providing assistance to the guerrillas in Greece, required modification of U.S. policy. Not surprisingly, it was resolved to continue the policy of recognition. As the memorandum of the session remarked, nonrecognition would remove all possibility that America might have a future impact upon Bulgaria's political evolution: "A contrary policy of nonrecognition, which would entail the withdrawal of American representation from that country, would play into Soviet hands and would deny us the means of continuing our efforts (1) to make our weight felt in Bulgaria, (2) to protect American interests there and (3) to obtain information with regard to events in that strategically important area."[61] At a press conference held on October 1, the acting secretary of state, Robert Lovett, announced that the issue of diplomatic relations between America and Bulgaria had been settled and an ambassador designated.[62] The signed peace treaty had been deposited in Moscow as required, the Allied Control Commission officially disbanded, and the state of war long over.[63] Within the constraints of the peace, a sovereign Bulgaria under the careful control of the Communist party emerged on the European political scene. The way was now clear for the rump Parliament to vote on a new constitution. The People's Republic of Bulgaria was declared in December 1947.[64]

Conclusion

The decision to extend recognition to Bulgaria, although derived from sound arguments, soon proved incapable of reestablishing even a modicum of American influence in Sofia as Bulgaria continued her course toward socialism. In 1949, Bulgaria became a founding member of the Soviet-sponsored Council of Mutual Economic Assistance (CMEA), having rejected participation in Marshall Plan aid. In 1955, Bulgaria became a founding member of the Warsaw Pact. By this latter date, the American presence in Bulgaria had ceased, the result of an official break in diplomatic relations during the Bulgarian purge trials in 1950. Contrary to the initial hopes of Secretary of State Byrnes, Bulgaria's isolation from the West remained an insufficient incentive for amelioration of the increasingly harsh strictures now imposed on all facets of domestic life.

When the historian reflects upon the goals, practices, and failures of American policy toward Bulgaria in the period 1943–47, several conclusions come rapidly to mind. Initial American interest in Bulgaria emerged not from a prewar cultural kinship nor from extensive economic ties but rather from the strategic geographic location of this small country at a time of global conflict. Bulgaria's proximity to Greece, Turkey, and the Middle East justified efforts by the Western Allies to deny this land to any unfriendly power or alliance. When the first stages of the OSS plan suggested that America might gain a predominat hand in arranging terms for Bulgaria's exodus from the war, it seemed logical that postwar planners within the State Department would attempt to promote a regime in Sofia supportive of the democratic ideals that had inspired American participation in the global struggle. Surprised by the unexpected Soviet occupation in view of past Russian willingness to advance American claims toward Bulgaria, the State Department confirmed the dominance of the War Department in times of conflict, acquiescing to an inferior position on the Bulgarian control commission until termination of the major goal of defeating Germany. Yet by now, America's involvement in charting the likely future of Bulgaria was too firmly established among decision makers in Washington to permit simple acceptance of growing Soviet domination. Laboring under difficult circumstances, America devoted considerable attention to the establishment of democratic values in Bulgaria from the spring of 1945 until the final peace two years later.

Throughout this period, general appeals for democratic reorganization went hand in hand with a judicious appraisal of alternate tactics that might promote reform within a state occupied by Soviet tropps and possessed of a determined Communist party. As several State Department documents testify, the lessons learned in Bulgaria held insights into general Soviet policy in Eastern Europe.

One of the more surprising discoveries of studying American policy toward Bulgaria is the considerable efforts expended to direct the future of a nation whose postwar future could be of little practical concern for the West even if Western values were rejected. One is hard put to account for such expenditure of energy except in terms of a deep commitment within the American policy-making establishment to democratic values in and of themselves and the self-evident importance of their extension wherever possible. And yet when formulating specific policies tailored to a given Bulgarian problem, Washington refused to lapse into moral outrage which might have imperiled East-West cooperation on the larger issues of the day. Secretary Byrnes's decision to maintain diplomatic and economic pressure upon Bulgaria while awaiting an initiative from the non-Communist members of the Sofia cabinet for domestic reform was wisely calculated to avoid raising problems in the Balkans into a full-scale conflict with Moscow. Clearly, American-Russian relations could not be hostage solely to events in this small Balkan land, no matter how outrageous they might be. Even at the point of maximum confrontation over the Balkans, the London Conference, Byrnes linked activities in Bulgaria to similar patterns displayed by other East European countries in an effort to achieve a general softening of the Soviet yoke. Thus a sense of balance and an understanding of the possible accompanied the abiding American commitment to democracy in Bulgaria. And when prospects for both reform in Bulgaria and improvement in East-West relations waned in 1946, the State Department wisely decided to concentrate finite resources on containing Soviet expansion in areas where the Red Army was not in occupation. In 1947, despite the bloody purge of Nikola Petkov and the repression of the Bulgarian opposition, the United States pragmatically opted for recognition as the sole hope of retaining some influence in Sofia.

The lengthy course of America's relations with monarchial, coalition, and totalitarian Bulgaria puts to rest the frequently cited "non-policy" Washington supposedly followed toward Eastern Europe in the wartime and postwar period. In the last resort, the "loss" of Bulgaria derived not from a lack of interest or effort but from a well-reasoned assessment of American capabilities and strategic priorities.

It was not a determined policy that was lacking; it was a sizable contingent of American troops that might enforce policy decisions far from home. Historians may argue over decisions to concentrate military commitments in Italy and Western Europe in preference to the Balkans, but these decisions were conscious ones with an eye on available U.S. forces, strategic objectives, and the possibility of resurrecting domestic American isolationism as the price of overextension. These were sins, if sins they were, of commission not omission. Only with the precipitous decline of Western (British) influence in Greece did an expansion of America's role in the Balkans ensue, and by then Bulgaria was well ensconced within the Soviet orb.

The pages of American diplomacy toward Bulgaria reveal the professionalism and distinctive abilities of the diplomats assigned to support U.S. policy in an uncertain land. Maynard Barnes and General John Crane were well qualified and well suited for their appointments, both having gained significant experience in the Balkans and in Bulgaria before the outbreak of hostilities. Their understanding and their influence upon the domestic evolution of revolutionary Bulgaria earned well-deserved Soviet protests as a hindrance to Moscow's own shifting plans for socialist reorganization. Although Barnes and Crane frequently came into conflict with their superiors in Washington and sometimes exaggerated the importance of Bulgaria in the overall postwar scheme of things, neither went "native" in a pattern seen among diplomats assigned to cultures imperfectly understood in Washington. The traits of the "Ugly American" were equally foreign to their personalities and deportment.

An interesting sidelight to America's protracted involvement in Bulgaria is the evidence that Moscow's policy toward this state displayed major change and uncertainty, belying later Western assumptions that Eastern Europe somehow constituted a natural Soviet sphere of influence. In 1943 and 1944, Moscow was more than willing to advance an American OSS plan which promised that the postwar reconstruction of Bulgaria would occur without the stultifying presence of Soviet troops. Once the OSS plan had failed, the behavior of Soviet forces in the Bulgarian invasion and in the early period of occupation suggested the dominance of military goals over more subtle designs of Soviet global politics. The degree of support for the continuing war effort apparently functioned as the key criterion according to which Soviet assistance was extended or denied to domestic Bulgarian political movements. Precise determination of the moment when strategic political aims replaced tactical military objectives in Soviet policy must await future documents from Moscow, although existing evidence strongly sug-

gests the failure of the 1945 London Conference as the turning point.
The return of Georgi Dimitrov to Sofia shortly thereafter demonstrated
a firm Soviet commitment to the totalitarian pretensions of the Bulgarian Communist party thereafter.

For the contemporary Western diplomat, American policy toward
Bulgaria holds another lesson: the futility of economic inducements or
pressure as a means of affecting policy within a revolutionary socialist
state. Despite Secretary Byrnes's efforts to restrict Bulgaria's economic trade with the West pending political reorganization coupled
with subtle hints that American aid might greet increased democratiza-
tion, the Bulgarian Communists continued to plot their own course.
Similar failures were to greet similar inducements offered the USSR,
Poland, and Czechoslovakia in the same period. A far wiser policy was
that pursued by Maynard Barnes in seeking out non-Communist and
pro-nationalist political movements which might provide an alternative
to left-wing dictatorship. Unfortunately, the superior organization and
élan of the Bulgarian Communists, the presence of a Soviet army of
occupation, and the structural weaknesses of Zveno doomed Barnes's
efforts to failure. America's continued inability to profit from such
mistakes was perhaps most eloquently noted by a contemporary diplomat, Henry Kissinger, when recounting in *Year of Upheaval* his own
negotiations with North Vietnam some three decades later: "No other
society has considered it a national duty to contribute to the rebuilding
of a defeated enemy; after the Second World War we made it a central
element of our foreign policy. In Vietnam we thought it a device to
induce an undefeated enemy to accept compromise terms. The reverse
side of our faith in what we considered positive goals is a difficulty in
coming to grips with irreconcilable conflict, with implacable revolutionary zeal, with men who prefer victory to economic progress and
who remain determined to prevail regardless of material cost."[1] Such
words could well have been penned by American diplomats evicted
from Bulgaria in the depths of the Cold War.

Notes

INTRODUCTION

1. Quoted in Daniel Yergin, *Shattered Peace*, p. 4.
2. Vojtech Mastny, *Russia's Road to the Cold War*, p. xvii, emphasis added.
3. Thomas G. Paterson, *On Every Front*, Hugh De Santis, *The Diplomacy of Silence*.
4. George F. Kennan, *Memoirs, 1925–1950*, p. 290.

1. WARTIME PLANNING FOR BULGARIA

1. Ilcho Dimitrov, "Colonel Donovan's Mission to Sofia," pp. 3–7.
2. See the diary entry of Prime Minister Filov for this date in Frederick B. Chary, trans. and ed., "The Diary of Bogdan Filov, 1941" (Spring 1974): 63.
3. Dimitrov, "Donovan's Mission," p. 8.
4. Chary, trans. and ed., "Diary of Filov, 1941," p. 64.
5. Dimitrov, "Donovan's Mission," p. 10.
6. Sir George Rendel to Foreign Office, January 22, 1941, FO 371.29721, as cited in Dimitrov, "Donovan's Mission," p. 11. Filov's reluctance to bend to the German will received further confirmation in his diary entry for July 16, 1944: "We entered the Tripartite Pact so as to avoid direct participation in the war, so Bulgaria would not become a theatre of war" (quoted in Colonel Ivan T. Ivanov, "Angliiskata i sever-oamerikanskata strategiia na Balkanite prez liatoto na 1944 g. i opitite na Bulgarskata burzhoaziia za izlizane ot voinata," p. 9.
7. Vitka Toshkove, "Politikata na SASht kum Bulgariia (septemvri 1939–sep-temvri 1944)," p. 260.
8. Marshall L. Miller, *Bulgaria during the Second World War*, p. 111; Voin Bozhinov, *Politicheskata kriza v Bulgariia prez 1943–1944*, p. 43.
9. See Chary, trans. and ed., "Diary of Filov, 1943" (Spring 1976): 40.
10. Vitka Toshkova, "Vunshnata politika na pravitelstvo na Dobri Bozhilov (sep-temvri–mai 1944 g.)," pp. 19, 20. In 1942, Germany broke the Bulgarian diplomatic code, periodically circulating copies of intercepted messages in a top secret booklet nicknamed "the Brown Friend." See Miller *Bulgaria*, p. 110.
11. Berry to Secretary of State Cordell Hull, May 20, 1943, Record Group 59, 874.00/740, Decimal Files, U.S. Department of State, National Archives (hereafter cited as DSNA). See also Toshkova, "Politikata na SASht kum Bulgariia," p. 261.
12. Chary, trans. and ed., "Diary of Filov, 1943," pp. 30, 34, 38.
13. See Nicolas Balabanov, "A Year in Ankara," (December 1964): 48–49. For a good summary of Boris's disillusions concerning Germany, see Hans-Joachim Hoppe, *Bulgarien—Hitlers eigenwilliger Verbuendeter*, pp. 143–46.

14. Quoted in Robert Dallek, *Franklin D. Roosevelt and American Foreign Policy, 1932–1945*, p. 396.

15. William D. Leahy, *I Was There*, p. 159.

16. Dallek, *Roosevelt*, pp. 409–10, 415.

17. Robert Murphy, *Diplomat among Warriors*, pp. 186–88; Giuseppe Mammarella, *L'Italia dopo il fascismo, 1943–68*, pp. 32–37.

18. See Angel Kouyoumdjisky's account of his first meeting with General Donovan in "Details sur le mission de A. Kouyoumdjisky en Turquie du 17 novembre 1943 au 22 mars 1944 adressés au secretary of state," April 20, 1944, Record Group 59, 874.00/4-2044, DSNA.

19. JCS 436, "O.S.S. Plan to Detach Bulgaria from the Axis," August 2, 1943, ABC 384 Bulgaria (August 3, 1943), Record Group 165, Modern Military Branch, National Archives (hereafter cited as MMBNA).

20. Minutes of the JCS 99th Meeting, August 3, 1943, U.S. Joint Chiefs of Staff Geographic File, 1942–45, CCS 092 Bulgaria, Record Group 218, MMBNA (hereafter cited as JCS Geographic File).

21. Notes on JSP 95th Meeting, August 18, 1943, ABC 384 Bulgaria, MMBNA.

22. Memorandum for the director of Strategic Services, August 24, 1943, JCS Geographic File, MMBNA.

23. Anthony Cave Brown, *The Last Hero*, p. 353. The suggested operations to arrange the withdrawal of Hungary and Rumania from the war were more limited in scope in deference to the competing claims of British and Soviet secret services and floundered because of Washington's inability to ensure these states against the inevitable Soviet invasion. See ibid., pp. 382–93, 399–403.

24. Memorandum from the director of Strategic Services, November 25, 1943, ABC 384 Bulgaria.

25. "Le mission de A. Kouyoumdjisky en Turquie," pp. 1–2; Telegram from JCS to General Royce, 16 November 1943, JCS Geographic File, MMBNA.

26. In the fall of 1943, the Soviets gave initial approval to Allied activities in the Balkans. When asked if they might have any objections to British and American military actions there, the Soviet ambassador to London, Ivan Maisky, replied that Moscow "would be very glad if we invaded the Balkans" (Notes of a conversation with Maisky, September 14, 1943, Dalton Papers, as cited in Elisabeth Barker, *British Policy in South-East Europe in the Second World War*, p. 136).

27. Ibid., pp. 132–33; Sir Ernest Llewellyn Woodward, ed., *British Foreign Policy in the Second World War*, 5:20.

28. FO 371/37153, R 2129, as quoted in Charles A. Moser, *Dimitrov of Bulgaria*, p. 165.

29. Barker, *British Policy*, pp. 134–35.

30. Ibid.

31. Aide-Memoire, the British Embassy to the Department of State, August 16, 1943, U.S. Department of State, *Foreign Relations of the United States, 1943*, 1:497 (hereafter cited as *FRUS* followed by appropriate year).

32. Barker, *British Policy*, p. 119.

33. Memorandum for the President, January 19, 1944, *FRUS, Conference at Cairo and Teheran, 1943*, p. 871.

34. Francis L. Loewenheim et al., eds., *Roosevelt and Churchill*, p. 385.

35. Barker, *British Policy*, p. 119. For a brief assessment of OSS capabilities in Istanbul see U.S. Office of the Assistant Secretary of War, History Project, Strategic Service Unit, *The Overseas Target*, 2:269.

36. Bickham Sweet-Escott, *Baker Street Irregular*, p. 194.

37. "Summary of the Proceedings of the Fifth Session of the Tripartite Conference," October 23, 1943, *FRUS, 1943*, 1:619.

38. "Record of the Proceedings of the Foreign Ministers' Conference Held in Moscow from 19th October to 30th October 1943; Annex 7 of the Secret Protocol," Public Records Office. General Correspondence, Political: Russia, 1906–1945, FO 371/37031. N 6921/5412/6, pp. 10–11.

39. "Report Received from the British Chiefs of Staff," October 20, 1943, JCS Geographic File, MMBNA.

40. Memorandum of the British Chiefs of Staff, Cairo, December 3, 1943, *FRUS, Conference at Cairo and Teheran*, pp. 782–83.

41. Sir John Slessor, *The Central Blue*, p. 596.

42. Harriman to Hull, January 6, 1944, *FRUS, 1944*, 1:580–82. See also V. Toshkova, "Bulgariia v Balkanskata politika SASht (septemvri 1943–iuni 1944 g.)," p. 36.

43. Georgi Dimitrov, "Krizis v Bolgarii," *Pravda*, December 27, 1943, as reprinted in Georgi Dimitrov, *Suchineniia*, 11:127, 132–33.

44. Hoppe, *Bulgarien*, p. 149, p. 241, n. 13; Toshkova, "Vunshnata politika na pravitelstvo na Dobri Bozhilov," p. 8.

45. Chary, trans. and ed., "Diary of Filov, 1943," p. 47.

46. Quoted in Hoppe, *Bulgarian*, pp. 149–50.

47. Chary, trans. and ed., "Diary of Filov, 1943," p. 47.

48. Quoted in Hoppe, *Bulgarian*, p. 241, n. 14.

49. Andreas Hillgrueber, ed. and annot., *Staatsmaenner und Diplomaten bei Hitler*, 2:338, 332.

50. Toshkova, "Vunshnata politika na pravitelstvo na Dobri Bozhilov," p. 21; Chary, trans. and ed., "Diary of Filov, 1943," pp. 49, 52.

51. "Le mission de A. Kouyoumdjisky en Turquie," Annexe 2, p. 9, Annexe 3, pp. 10, 3; Report of the Office of Strategic Services, March 23, 1944, ABC 384 Bulgaria, MMBNA.

52. "Le mission de A. Kouyoumdjisky en Turquie," Annexe 6, pp. 16–19.

53. Quoted in Bozhinov, *Politicheskata Kriza v Bulgariia prez 1943–1944*, p. 45.

54. Nicolas Balabanov, "A Year in Ankara" (December 1965):52.

55. Ibid., p. 50.

56. "Apercu sur la situation politique, militaire et economique de la Bulgarie par Angel Kouyoumdjisky depuis ler décembre 1943 au 11 mars 1944," March 27, 1944, Record Group 59, 874.00/4-2044, DSNA, p. 15.

57. "Le mission de A. Kouyoumdjisky en Turquie," p. 3; JCS 436, March 23, 1944, p. 2, ABC 384 Bulgaria, MMBNA.

58. "Le mission de A. Kouyoumdjisky en Turquie," p. 4, and Annexe 10, pp. 26–30.

59. Bozhinov, *Politicheskata kriza v Bulgariia prez 1943–1944*, pp. 38–40, 52, quoting materials from Bulgarian Archives.

60. V. Toshkova, *Bulgariia i tretiiat Raikh*, pp. 173–74, n. 134; Angel Nakov, *Bulgaro-Suvetski otnosheniia, 1944–1948*, p. 14.

61. L. B. Valev et al., eds., *Sovetsko-Bolgarskie otnosheniia i sviazi*, p. 591.

62. Toshkova, "Vunshnata politika na pravitelstvo na Dobri Bozhilov," p. 22.

63. "Le mission de A. Kouyoumdjisky en Turquie," Annexe 11, p. 32.

64. JCS 436, March 23, 1944, p. 3, ABC 384 Bulgaria, MMBNA.

65. "Le mission de A. Kouyoumdjisky en Turquie," Annexe 11, p. 35; Balabanov, "A Year in Ankara" 5 (December 1965): 52.

66. Loewenheim, et al., eds., *Roosevelt and Churchill*, pp. 434–38, 458–59. For an exhaustive account of all documents relating to the Bulgarian venture in Roosevelt's personal files at Hyde Park see Frederick B. Chary, "Prezident Ruzevelt i Bulgarskite sondazhi za mir, 1944 g.," pp. 269–75.

67. See the extensive correspondence between Secretary Hull and various U.S. ambassadors and with President Roosevelt in *FRUS, 1944*, 1:580–93.

68. Undersecretary of State Edward Stettinius to Harriman, February 10, 1944, *FRUS, 1944*, 3:300–301.

69. Bozhinov, *Politcheskata kriza v Bulgariia prez 1943–1944*, p. 52.

70. Roosevelt to Churchill, Febraury 25, 1944, *FRUS, 1944*, 3:302.

71. MacVeagh to Hull, March 7, 1944, *FRUS, 1944*, 3:311.

72. Stettinius to MacVeagh, March 9, 1944, *FRUS, 1944*, 3:312.

73. Balabanov, "A Year in Ankara" (December 1965): 51.

74. Memorandum for Chief, Civil Affairs Division, War Department General Staff, October 16, 1943, Civil Affairs Division 014 Bulgariam Record Group 165, MMBNA.

75. Report by General Hilldring, director of the Civil Affairs Division, Febraury 23, 1944, ibid.; Hull to Leahy, March 14, 1944, JCS Geographic File, MMBNA.

76. Report by General Hilldring.

77. Stettinius to Ambassador in the United Kingdom John Winant, March 4, 1944, *FRUS, 1944*, 3:309.

78. Memorandum, Division of Political Studies, December 29, 1943, 768.74158/ 12-2943, DSNA.

79. CAC-70a, Febraury 24, 1944, U.S. Department of State, Documents of the Interdivisional Country and Area Committee, 1943–44, microfilm T 1221, reel 1, DSNA.

80. "Summary of Recommendations, Treatment of Enemy States, Bulgaria," July 24, 1944, U.S. Department of State, Records of Harley A. Notter, 1939–45, Record Group 59, Records of Policy and Planning Committees, Box 145, Lot 60D–224 (hereafter, Records of Harley Notter), followed by box number DSNA.

81. EUR-13, July 15, 1944, Records of Harley A. Notter, Box 137, DSNA.

82. Hoppe, *Bulgarian*, p. 242, n. 26; Chary, trans. and ed., "Diary of Filov, 1944" (Spring 1977): p. 66, n. 11.

83. Hillgrueber, ed. and annot., *Staatsmaenner*, 2:370–84.

84. Quoted from unpublished portions of the diary of Regent Nikola Mikhov in the Bulgarian Archives by V. D. Voznesenskii, "Zakliuchitel'nye etap politicheskogo krizisa v Bolgarii (aprel'–9 sentiabriia 1944 g.)," p. 31.

85. V. D. Voznesenskii, "SShA, Angliia i vykhod Bolgarii iz voiny v 1944

godu," p. 102. The decision to send the "unofficial" Kiselov instead of a delegation to Cairo was made at a March 21 meeting between Filov, Bozhilov, Kiselov, and Shishmanov. See Bozhinov, *Politcheskata kriza v Bulgariia prez 1943–1944*, p. 51.

86. Berry to Hull, March 25, April 10, 1944, *FRUS, 1944*, 3:317–20; Lawrence Steinhardt, U.S. ambassador in Turkey, to Hull, May 16, 1944, ibid., p. 329.

87. Report by the Combined Civil Affairs Committee, April 1, 1944, JCS Geographic File, MMBNA.

88. Memorandum, Surrender Terms for Bulgaria, June 28, 1944, U.S. Department of State, Records of Philip E. Mosely, U.S. Political Adviser, 1943–45, International Conferences, Commissions and Expositions, European Advisory Commission, Record Group 59, Box 2, File 110 (hereafter Records of Philip E. Mosely), DSNA.

89. U.S. Department of State, *Bulletin* 255 (13 May 1944), p. 425.

90. Valer et al., eds., *Sovetsko-Bolgarskie otnosheniia i sviazi*, p. 591. The Soviet government naturally kept its American ally fully informed of its efforts to force Bulgaria from her Axis commitments. See the numerous exchanges between Moscow and Washington in *FRUS, 1944*, 3:323–24 and 330–33.

91. USSR, *Vneshniaia politika Sovetskogo soiuza v period otechestvennoi voiny*, pp. 185–86, 188–89.

92. Toshkova, "Vunshnata politika na pravitelstvo na Dobri Bozhilov," p. 32. Toshkova had full access to the Central State Historical Archives upon which this account is based.

93. Valev et al., eds., *Sovetsko-Bolgarskie otnosheniia i sviazi*, p. 594.

2. DIPLOMACY OF THE BULGARIAN SURRENDER

1. Curtis H. Martin, "United States Diplomacy and the Issue of Representative Government in the Former German Satellite States, 1943–1946," p. 46, n. 6.

2. De Santis, *Diplomacy of Silence*, p. 84.

3. For a discussion of unconditional surrender and the Casablanca Conference see Dallek, *Roosevelt and Foreign Policy*, pp. 373–76; Winston Churchill, *The Second World War: The Hinge of Fate*, p. 686.

4. Harriman to Hull, January 11, 1944, *FRUS, 1944*, 4: 134–35.

5. Cordell Hull, *The Memoirs of Cordell Hull*, 2:1570.

6. Harriman to Hull, January 6, 1944, *FRUS, 1944*, 1:581.

7. Hull, *Memoirs*, 2:1573–74.

8. Ibid.; Hull to Harriman, January 25, 1944, *FRUS, 1944*, 1:582.

9. Hull to Winant, March 28, 1944, *FRUS, 1944*, 1:586.

10. Kennan, *Memoirs*, pp. 164–66.

11. Murphy, *Diplomat among Warriors*, p. 232.

12. Ray S. Cline, *Washington Command Post*, p. 323.

13. Kennan, *Memoirs*, p. 172.

14. Documents of the Post–War Programs Committee, 1944, PWC–37, WS–58b, February 21, 1944, DSNA. The Joint Chiefs did not give final approval to WS–58b until March 20, 1944, although provisional approval had been granted by the Civil Affairs Division (Memorandum of the Civil Affairs Division, March 20, 1944, JCS Geographic file, JCS 773, MMBNA.

15. Stettinius to Winant, March 4, 1944, *FRUS, 1944,* 3:308–10; Joint Chiefs of Staff to Hull, February 5, 1944, ibid., 1:167–70; Stettinius to Harriman, March 4, 1944, ibid., 3:308.

16. Winant to Hull, March 13, 1944, ibid., p. 313.

17. Harriman to Hull, March 17, 1944, ibid., pp. 316–17.

18. De Santis, *Diplomacy of Silence,* p. 109.

19. Hull, *Memoirs,* 2:1427–29; Report to the secretary of state by Stettinius of his mission to London, April 7–29, 1944, May 22, 1944, *FRUS, 1944,* 1:1–30.

20. Memorandum by the Division of Southern European Affairs, March 1944, ibid., 3:304–5.

21. "Memorandum: Surrender Terms for Satellite States particularly Bulgaria," June 19, 1944, Records of Philip E. Mosely, Memorandum of Conversation, April 18, 1944, 740.0011 Stettinius Mission/141, Decimal Files, DSNA.

22. "British Interests in South Eastern Europe: Bulgaria," 740.0011 Stettinius Mission/141, Decimal Files, DSNA.

23. Memorandum: Surrender Terms for Bulgaria, June 20, 1944, paraphrased by E. Allen Lightner, Jr., secretary, U.S. Delegation, EAC, Records of Philip E. Mosely, DSNA.

24. Winant to Hull, May 8, 1944, *FRUS, 1944,* 3:327.

25. "Declaration by the American, British and Soviet Governments Regarding the Four Satellites," U.S. Department of State, *Bulletin* 255 (May 13, 1944): 425.

26. "Proposed Terms of Surrender for Bulgaria," June 8, 1944, Documents of the Interdivisional Country and Area Committees, 1943–46, CAC 229, DSNA.

27. Joint Chiefs of Staff to Hull, July 3, 1944, JCS Geographic File, MMBNA. Admiral Leahy to Hull, August 2, 1944.

28. Hull to Winant, July 5, 1944, *FRUS, 1944,* 3:341; "Surrender Terms for Bulgaria," July 13, 1944, Records of Philip E. Mosely, DSNA.

29. Winant to Hull, July 13, 1944, *FRUS, 1944,* 3:345.

30. Winant to Hull, August 25, 1944, ibid., pp. 367–70. The final enabling clause was added at the request of the British. See "Draft Armistice for Bulgaria," Eden memo for the prime minister, August 30, 1944, PM/44/598, PREM 3/79/2, Public Records Office (hereafter PRO).

31. "American Participation in Occupation of Bulgaria," April 28, 1944, Records of Harley A. Notter, DSNA.

32. "Long Range Interests and Objectives of the United States," July 24, 1944, Ibid.

33. "Summary of Recommendations for Rumania," July 26, 1944, Ibid.

34. Memorandum (in Russian), August 29, 1944, Records of Philip E. Mosely, DSNA.

35. Lawrence S. Wittner, *American Intervention in Greece, 1943–1949,* p. 5.

36. Eden to Clark Kerr, May 5, 1944, FO 371/44000, as quoted in Barker, *British Policy,* p. 140.

37. Woodward, *British Foreign Policy,* 3:116.

38. Loewenheim et al, eds., *Roosevelt and Churchill,* pp. 502–3.

39. "War and Peace Aims of the United States," March 1, 1944, Records of Harley A. Notter, DSNA.

40. De Santis, *Diplomacy of Silence,* pp. 116–17; Woodward, *British Foreign Policy,* p. 117; Loewenheim, et al., eds., *Roosevelt and Churchill,* pp. 526–27, 531–32.

41. Stalin to Churchill, n.d., FO 371/ 43636, as quoted in Barker, *British Policy,* p. 142.

42. Loewenheim, et al., eds., *Roosevelt and Churchill,* p. 121; Woodward, *British Foreign Policy,* pp. 122–23; De Santis, *Diplomacy of Silence,* p. 117.

43. USSR, *Vneshnaia politika Sovetskogo soiuza v period otechestvennoi voiny,* 2:188–89.

44. Toshkova, "Vunshnata politika na pravitelstvo na Dobri Bozhilov," p. 31.

45. USSR, *Vneshnaia politika Sovetskogo soiuza v period otechestvennoi voiny,* 2:189–90.

46. Valev et al., eds., *Sovetsko-Bolgarskie otnosheniia i sviazi,* p. 594.

47. Toshkova, "Vunshnata politika na pravitelstvo na Dobri Bozhilov," p. 32.

48. Quoted in Angel Nakov, "Antisovetskaia politika Bolgarskikh pravitel'stva nakanune deviatogo sentiabria 1944g.," p. 568.

49. Quoted from the unpublished diary of Purvan Draganov by Ivan T. Ivanov, "Angliiskata i severoamerikanskata strategiia na Balkanite prez liatoto na 1944g. i opitite na Bulgarskata burzhoaziia za izlizane ot voinata," p. 9.

50. Nakov, "Antisovetskaia politika Bolgarskikh pravitel'stva nakanune deviatogo sentiabria 1944 g.," p. 572; Angel Nakov, *Internatsional'naia missiia Sovetskikh vosik v Bolgarii,* p. 16.

51. Bozhinov, *Politicheskata kriza v Bulgariia prez 1943–1944,* p. 79, quoting the archives of the Bulgarian Foreign Ministry.

52. Ibid., p. 102.

53. Toshkova, "Vunshnata politika na pravitelstvo na Dobri Bozhilov," p. 30.

54. Bozhinov, *Politicheskata kriza v Bulgariia prez 1943–1944,* p. 50.

55. V. A. Matsulenko, *Razgrom nemetsko-fashistskikh voisk na Balkanskom napravlenii,* p. 8.

56. Toshkova, "Vunshnata politika na pravitelstvo na Dobri Bozhilov," p. 31.

57. Bozhinov, *Politicheskata kriza v Bulgariia prez 1943–1944,* p. 62.

58. Hoppe, *Bulgarien,* pp. 156–57.

59. Ilcho Dimitrov, "Vunshnata politika na pravitelstvo na Ivan Bagrianov (1 iune–1 septemvri 1944g.)," p. 254.

60. V. D. Voznesenskii, "Deviatoe sentiabria 1944 g., v Bolgarii" (May–June 1974):104.

61. Dimitar R. Petroff, "The Bagrianov Cabinet," p. 52. Petroff was Draganov's private secretary.

62. Chary, trans and ed., "Diary of Filov, 1944" (Spring 1977):96.

63. Nakov, "Antisovetskaia politika Bolgarskikh pravitel'stva nakanune deviatogo sentiabria," p. 571.

64. Bozhinov, *Politicheskata kriza v Bulgariia prez 1943–1944,* pp. 79–80.

65. Nakov, *Internatsional'nais missiia Sovetskikh voisk v Bolgarii,* p. 16.

66. Bozhinov, *Politicheskata kriza v Bulgariia prez 1943–1944,* p. 82.

67. Nakov, "Antisovetskaia politika Bolgarskikh pravitel'stva nakanune deviatogo sentiabria 1944g.," pp. 572–73.

68. Chary, trans. and ed., "Diary of Filov, 1944," p. 97.

69. USSR, *Suvetsko-Bulgarskite otnosheniia*, pp. 22–24; Bozhinov, *Politicheskata kriza v Bulgariia prez 1943–1944*, p. 83.

70. Nakov, "Antisovetskaia politika Bolgarskikh pravitel'stvo nakanune deviatogo sentiabria 1944 g.," p. 574, citing the unpublished Draganov diary and the Central State Historical Archives.

71. Ibid., p. 573.

72. Matsulenko, *Razgrom nemetsko-fashishtskikh voisk na Balkanskom napravlenii*, p. 5.

73. Albert Seaton, *The Russo-German War, 1941–45*, p. 471. U.S. intelligence reported rumors of war in Turkey and "an unusual concentration of Turkish troops along the Bulgarian border in Thrace" (Intelligence report from JICAME, July 26, 1944, Record Group 226, Document 84830, MMBNA).

74. USSR, *Suvetsko-Bulgarskite otnosheniia*, p. 25.

75. V. Toshkova, "Khitleristki planove za prevrat v Bulgariia (avgust–septemvri 1944 g.)," p. 34.

76. The Soviet ambassador in Ankara pointedly informed his American counterpart that the resignation of the Bozhilov government was the result of Soviet pressures (Lawrence Steinhardt to Cordell Hull, May 24, 1944, *FRUS, 1944*, 3:329–30.

77. Berry to Hull, June 8, 15, 1944, ibid., pp. 335, 337.

78. Berry to Hull, June 15, 1944, 874.00/6-1544, Decimal Files, DSNA; July 6, 1944 *FRUS, 1944*, 3:344.

79. Hull to Admiral Leahy, July 26, 1944, JCS Geographic File, MMBNA; Toshkova, "SASht i izlizaneto na Bulgariia ot Tristranniia pakt (iune–septemvri 1944 g.)," pp. 207–8; Berry to Hull, July 21, 1944, *FRUS, 1944*, 3:348–49. On June 25, the Bagrianov cabinet had ordered the removal of all occupation troops from territories to which Bulgaria had no permanent claim excepting certain key defensive units. The order apparently was temporarily blocked by the regents. See Bozhinov, *Politicheskata kriza v Bulgariia prez 1943–1944*, p. 92.

80. Hull to Berry, July 26, 1944, *FRUS, 1944*, 3:353.

81. Toshkova, "SASht i izlizaneto na Bulgariia ot Tristranniia pakt," p. 208.

82. Admiral Leahy to Hull, August 2, 1944, JCS Geographic File, MMBNA.

83. Stettinius to Admiral Leahy, August 5, 1944, JCS Geographic File, MMBNA; Stettinius to Harriman, August 4, 1944, *FRUS, 1944*, 3:354; Stettinius to Winant, August 12, 1944, ibid., p. 335; Winant to Feodor T. Gousev, August 5, 1944, Records of Philip E. Mosely, DSNA.

84. Toshkova, "SASht i izlizaneto na Bulgariia ot Tristranniia pakt," p. 208.

85. For Moshanov's background see Bozhinov, *Politicheskata kriza v Bulgariia prez 1943–1944*, p. 103; Nissan Oren, *Bulgarian Communism*, pp. 120, 130n, 147, 243–44, 246, 247.

86. Voznesenskii, "Deviatoe sentiabria 1944g., v Bolgarii" (July–August 1974):112.

87. Ibid., p. 113; Toshkova, "SASht i izlizaneto na Bulgariia ot Tristranniia pakt," p. 210; Balabanov, "A Year in Ankara" (December 1966):35. There appears to be some confusion as to whether the first meeting with the British ambassador took place on August 15 or 16.

88. Aide-Memoire of the British Embassy to the Department of State, August 20, 1944, *FRUS, 1944,* 3:358–60.

89. Bozhinov, *Politicheskata kriza v Bulgariia prez 1943–1944,* p. 105, citing the archives of the Bulgarian Foreign Ministry; Voznesenskii, "Deviatoe sentiabria 1944 g., v Bolgarii" (May–June 1974):103.

90. Ivanov, "Angliiskata i severoamerikanskata strategiia na Balkanite," p. 8.

91. V. D. Voznesenskii, "Zakliuchitel'nyi etap politicheskogo krizisa v Bolgarii (aprel'–9 sentiabria 1944 g.)," p. 44, quoting portions of Nikola Mikhov's unpublished diary.

92. Toshkova, "SASht i izlizaneto na Bulgariia ot Tristranniia pakt," p. 211; Voznesenskii, "Deviatoe sentiabria 1944 g., v Bolgarii" (May–June 1974):109.

93. For an appraisal of Bagrianov's speech which, Burton Berry noted, "confirms the view . . . that this Government will not commit Bulgaria further to the German cause" see Berry to Hull, August 18, 1944, *FRUS, 1944,* 3:357–58. Filov's angry response noted, "The speech of Bagrianov is unconditional capitulation before the possible victors. . . . He throws in his hand too early. . . . I feel a great internal struggle; I am not able to side with the politics and methods of Bagrianov" quoted in Voznesenskii, "Deviatoe sentiabria 1944 g., v Bolgarii" (May–June 1974):106. See also Toshkova, "Khitleristka planove za prevrit v Bulgariia," pp. 30–42.

94. Hoppe, *Bulgarien,* p. 168; Nakov, "Antisovetskaia politika Bolgarskikh pravitel'stva nakanune deviatogo sentiabria 1944 g.," p. 575; Ilcho Dimitrov, "Poslednato pravitelstvo na Burzhoazna Bulgariia," p. 6.

95. "Operations of the Bulgarian Forces in the War against Germany, 1944–1945," Geog. 1. Bulgaria 370.2, MMBNA. Apparently Regents Filov and Cyril again blocked the withdrawal from Macedonia. See Ivanov, "Angliiskata i severoamerikanskata strategiia na Balkanite," p. 12; Iv. Marinov, "Pet dni v pravitelstvo na K. Muraviev," p. 85. Marinov was a division commander in Macedonia.

96. Nakov, "Antisovetskaia politika Bolgarskikh pravitel'stvo nakanune deviatogo sentiabriia 1944 g.," pp. 570–71.

97. Toshkova, "SASht i izlizaneto na Bulgariia ot Tristranniia pakt," pp. 214–15; Harold Shantz, chargé, to Hull, Memorandum: Subject: Bulgarian Armistice Mission in Cairo, September 5, 1944, 740.00119 E.W./9-544, Decimal Files, DSNA.

98. Bozhinov, *Politicheskata kriza v Bulgariia prez 1943–1944 g.,* p. 110; Ilcho Dimitrov, *Burzhoaznata opozitsiia v Bulgariia 1939/1944,* p. 223. Voznesenskii, "Deviatoe sentiabria 1944 g., v Bolgarii" (July–August 1974):119.

99. For examples see n. 98, above.

100. Shantz to Hull, Memorandum, September 5, 1944, RG59, 740.00119 E.W./9-544, DSNA. For a review of Bulgarian charges that the British attempted to impose extremely harsh conditions on Moshanov, see Voznesenskii, "Deviatoe sentiabria 1944 g., v Bolgariia" (July–August 1974):118; Voin Bozhinov, "Politikata na SASht spriamo Bulgariia prez 1944 g.," p. 78, n. 48.

101. Dimitrov, *Burzhoaznata opozitsiia v Bulgariia 1939/1944,* p. 224.

102. For the military particulars of the Soviet invasion see M. M. Minasian, *Osvobozhdenie narodov iugo-vostochnoi Evrope,* pp. 221–26.

103. Nakov, "Antisovetskaia politika Bolgarskikh pravitel'stva nakanune deviatogo sentiabriia 1944 g.," p. 583.

104. Bozhinov, *Politicheskata kriza v Bulgariia 1943–1944*, p. 134; I. V. Ganevich, *Deiatel'nost' Bolgarskoi kommunisticheskoi partii po ukrepleniiu diktatury proletariata, sept. 1944–1948*, pp. 13–37.

105. Cordell Hull complained to his ambassador in Turkey that the Soviets had given only about one hour notice before their declaration of war. See Hull to Lawrence Steinhardt, September 9, 1944, *FRUS, 1944*, 3:407–8. The British "astonishment" at the Soviet declaration was delivered personally to Foreign Minister Molotov by Ambassador Clark Kerr. See Harriman to Hull, September 7, 1944, ibid., pp. 401–3.

106. CCS 507/4, September 1, 1944, and JCS 921/5, September 2, 1944, JCS Geographic File, MMBNA.

107. U.S. Chief of Staff to Hull, September 9, 1944, JCS Geographic File, MMBNA.

108. The Soviet representative on the European Advisory Commission (Gousev) to the American representative on the European Advisory Commission (Winant), September 9, 1944, *FRUS, 1944*, 3:405–6.

109. Winant to Hull, September 12, 1944, ibid., p. 417.

110. Ibid.

111. Redraft of Article 13, September 15, 1944, Records of Philip E. Mosely, DSNA.

112. Winant to Hull, September 19, 1944, *FRUS, 1944*, 3:426.

113. Ibid., pp. 426–27; Winant to Hull, September 20, 1944, ibid., p. 431.

114. JCS 921/8, September 26, 1944, JCS Geographic File, MMBNA. The approval was sent to Hull the same day (*ibid.*).

115. Winant to Hull, September 23, 1944, *FRUS, 1944*, 3:435; Hull to Winant, September 26, 1944, ibid., pp. 438–39; JCS 921/10, October 3, 1944, JCS Geographic File, MMBNA.

116. Winant to Hull, October 10, 1944, *FRUS, 1944*, 3:443.

117. See Albert Resis, "The Churchill-Stalin Secret 'Percentages' Agreement on the Balkans, Moscow, October 1944.

118. "Anglo-Soviet Political Conversation at Moscow, October 9–October 17, 1944," pp. 12–13, 55–58, FO, PREM 3/434/4. The Americans, however, did reconfirm a willingness to allow a temporary augmentation of Soviet power while the war against Germany lasted in line with Winant's compromise draft. See "Eden Memo to Prime Minister," October 6, 1944, FO, PM /44/645, PREM 3/79/2.

119. Winant to Hull, October 18, 1944, *FRUS, 1944*, 3:467.

120. Resis, "Churchill-Stalin Secret 'Percentages,' " p. 385.

121. Winant to Hull, October 12, 1944, *FRUS, 1944*, 3:452.

122. Winston S. Churchill, *The Second World War: Triumph and Tragedy*, p. 250.

123. "Eden Memo to Prime Minister," October 6, 1944, FO, PM/ 44/645, PREM 3/79/2.

124. Winant to Hull, October 22, 1944, *FRUS, 1944*, 3:473.

125. Maynard Barnes to the secretary of state, January 12, 1945, *FRUS, 1945*, 4:143.

3. PERCEPTIONS OF REVOLUTIONARY BULGARIA

1. For a review of initial, uncertain assessments of Soviet policy in Bulgaria see Harriman to Hull, September 7, 12, 19, 1944, *FRUS, 1944,* 3:401–3, 413, 826–28; Berry to Hull, September 25, 1944, ibid., pp. 435–36; Maynard Barnes, American representative in Bulgaria, to Hull, December 1, 1944, ibid., pp. 495–96; Memorandum by the deputy of the Office of European Affairs, M. Freeman Matthews, to Cordell Hull, October 16, 1944, ibid., pp. 1016–19; "Russia—Seven Years Later," September 1944, reprinted in Kennan, *Memoirs,* pp. 503–31; De Santis, *Diplomacy of Silence,* pp. 123–30; Peter Gosztony, "Der 9 September 1944," pp. 85–106; Alexander C. Kirk, U.S. political adviser, Allied Forces Headquarters, to Hull, September 16, 1944, Record Group 59, 740.0011 EW/ 9-1644, Decimal Files, DSNA; Stoian Pinter, "Nachalna deinost na suiuznata kontrolna komisiia v Bulgariia (oktomvri 1944–ianuare 1945 g.)"; Field Marshal Lord Wilson, *Eight Years Overseas, 1939–1947,* pp. 234–35.

2. Barnes to Hull, January 8, 1945, *FRUS, 1945,* 4:139.

3. There are numerous Bulgarian studies of the birth and evolution of the Fatherland Front. A standard analysis is Diniu Sharlanov, *Otechestveniiat front, 1942–1944.* In English, the standard work remains Oren, *Bulgarian Communism;* see esp. pp. 201–2. The size and significance of the "resistance movement" remains a topic of debate. See ibid., pp. 200–220.

4. The membership of the Bulgarian Communist party in September 1944, is listed as between fifteen and twenty-five thousand, depending on the source consulted. The lower figure is given by Oren, p. 257. The higher is offered in Institut istorii Bolgarskoi kommunisticheskoi partii pre TsK BKP, *Istoriia Bolgarskoi Kommunisticheskoi partii,* p. 471; Voin Bozhinov, *Zashtitata na natsionalnata nezavisimost na Bulgaria, 1944–47,* pp. 8–9. Although the Agrarians undoubtedly had a larger following, the organized peasant movement had been badly split in the 1930s, with the largest branch remaining outside the wartime Fatherland Front. Zveno and the Social Democrats represented smaller movements.

5. Nissan Oren, *The Revolution Administered,* p. 73.

6. Dimo Kazasov, *Burni godini, 1918–1944,* p. 757. Oren bases much of his account of this period in *Bulgarian Communism* on Kazasov's book, arguing that "his account retains a degree of objectivity absent in official Communist writings" (Oren, p. 232, n. 27). Since Oren's book appeared in 1971, a much fuller discussion has appeared in a work by Tsola Dragoicheva, member of party Politbureau and, after 1944, chairman of the National Committee of the Fatherland Front. Although Dragoicheva in both word and deed had never been above deception, her memoirs add new insights to this confused period. See Tsola N. Dragoicheva, *Pobeda.*

7. Kazasov, *Burni godini,* pp. 757–58, 760; Dragoicheva, *Pobeda,* pp. 562–63. Bagrianov had tried to split the Fatherland Front ever since coming to power in early June 1944. See Bozhinov, *Politicheskata kriza v Bulgariia prez 1943–1944,* p. 5.

8. Dragoicheva, *Pobeda,* pp. 555–56. Emphasis added.

9. Kiril Lazarov, "Obaianie i ocharovanie," pp. 405–6. Lazarov had been a member of the Bulgarian Communist party since 1915 and was at this time attached to the Bulgarian section of Radio Moscow.

10. Quoted in Filo Khristov, "Pobedite na suvetskata armiia i tiakhnoto znachenie za razmakha na vuoruzhenata borba i uspekha na devetoseptemvriiskato narodno antifashistko vustanie," p. 11. See also Dimitrov, *Suchineniia*, 11:147–48.

11. Khristov, "Pobedite," p. 11.

12. Dragoicheva, *Pobeda*, pp. 557, 565.

13. Ibid., p. 570. For confirmation that only Communist members of the Fatherland Front were invited into the Muraviev cabinet, see Dimitrov, "Poslednato pravitelstvo na burzhoazna Bulgariia," p. 570.

14. Dragoicheva, *Pobeda*, p. 570. See also Marinov, "Pet dne v pravitelstvota na K. Muraviev," p. 89. Dragoicheva, *Pobeda*, pp. 570, 573–75, 579. These figures may exaggerate actual forces available to the insurgents. See Oren, *Bulgarian Communism*, pp. 217–20.

16. Dragoicheva, *Pobeda*, pp. 580, 587, 594.

17. At the end of July, Marshal Tolbukhin, commander of the Third Ukranian Front, met with Georgi Dimitrov in Moscow for discussions. See A. S. Zheltov, "Vinage zaedno," p. 51.

18. G. K. Zhukov, *Vospominaniia i razmyshleniia*, pp. 595–97.

19. V. A. Matsulenko, *Razgrom nemetsko-fashistskikh voisk na Balkanskom napravlenii*, pp. 100–101; Minasian, *Osvobozhdenie narodov iugo-vostochnoi Evropy*, p. 221; Seaton, *Russo-German War*, pp. 487–88; A. I. Antonov, *Istoriia velikoe otechestvennoi voiny Sovetskogo soiuza 1941–1945 v shesta tomakh*, 3 p. 302.

20. Antonov, *Istoriia velikoe otechestvennoi vainy Sovetskogo*, p. 302.

21. S. S. Biriuzov, *Surovye gody*, p. 437. Soviet intelligence overflights of Bulgaria had been forbidden by the Supreme Command, limiting additional information on possible Bulgarian troop movements. See ibid., p. 431.

22. S. M. Shtemenko, *The Last Six Months*, p. 169.

23. Speaking of this preparatory period, General-Colonel A. Zheltov, head of the Third Ukrainian Front's Military Soviet, recalls that "it is necessary to emphasize the fact that we did not know how the Bulgarian army would conduct itself." See Zheltov, "Osvobozhdenia Bolgarii," p. 61. Stalin, too, in late August, argued that further information was required on the Bulgarian domestic situation prior to invasion. See Shtemenko, *Last Six Months*, pp. 168–69.

24. See Valev et al., eds., *Sovetsko-bolgarskie otnosheniia i sviazi*, pp. 600–601.

25. Bozhinov, *Politicheskata kriza v Bulgariia prez 1943–1944*, p. 122.

26. Dimitrov, *Burzhoaznata opozitsiia v Bulgariia 1939/1944*, p. 218.

27. Marinov, "Pit dni v pravitelstvo na K. Muraviev," pp. 88–89; Bozhinov, *Politicheskata kriza v Bulgariia prez 1943–1944*, pp. 92–93.

28. Marinov, "Pit dni v pravitelstvo na K. Muravier," pp. 89–90, 92. The fact that War Minister Marinov subsequently played a major role in the September 9 coup casts some doubts on his motives in this period. His assessment of the dangerous military situation on September 5, however, appears to have been sincere and was accepted by other cabinet members equally aware of the dilemma. See also Bozhinov, *Politicheskata kriza v Bulgariia prez 1943–1944*, p. 123.

29. See the account of the September 5–6 Politbureau meeting in Dragoicheva, *Pobeda*, pp. 594–601. The text of the Soviet message is given in Bozhinov, *Politicheskata kriza v Bulgariia prez 1943–1944*, pp. 125–26.

30. Dragoicheva, *Pobeda*, p. 601.
31. Shtemenko, *Last Six Months*, pp. 171–72, emphasis added; Antonov, *Istoriia*, pp. 302–5.
32. Biriuzov, *Surovye gody*, p. 442. The undefended status of the capital is confirmed by Antonov, *Istoriia*, p. 306.
33. Voznesenskii, "Deviatoe sentiabria 1944 g., v Bolgarii" (July–August 1974):123.
34. Zheltov, "Osvobozhdenie Bolgarii," p. 63. Zheltov promptly issued a general proclamation to the Bulgarian people denying that the Red Army had any intentions of changing the existing social order: "Private property of the citizens remains everywhere inviolable." See Minasian, *Osvobozhdenie narodov*, p. 226.
35. Antonov, *Istoriia*, p. 306. Chief of Staff Sergei Biriuzov was dispatched to Sofia to organize the Bulgarian army in support of the Yugoslav effort. See Biriuzov, *Surovye gody*, p. 443.
36. Oren, *Bulgarian Communism*, pp. 251–58; Ganevich, Deiatel'nost' pp. 13–42.
37. I have relied primarily upon the account given in Oren, *Bulgaria Communism*, pp. 251–58. Georgiev had been minister of railroads in the late 1920s and prime minister in 1934. For a theoretical discussion of the social and political nature of the September 9 uprising, see Ganevich, *Deiatel'nost'* p. 37, and Dimitur Ganev, "Doklad o polozhenii v Bolgarii," a speech delivered in Moscow on September 22, 1944.
38. Bulgaria, *Ustanoviavane i ukrepvane na narodnodemokratichnata vlast*, p. 51 (hereafter *UUNV*).
39. Biriuzov, *Surovye gody*, p. 442; USSR, *Sovetsko-Bolgarskie otnosheniia, 1944–1948 g.*, p. 15. On September 20, Marshal Tolbukhin suggested that Soviet military advisers be dispatched to Bulgarian units; the first took their positions in early October. See Biriuzov, *Surovye gody*, pp. 193–94.
40. The central importance of a major Bulgarian military effort as a means of consolidating domestic politics of the Fatherland Front was stressed by Georgi Dimitrov on numerous occasions. See Dimitrov's letter of August 27, 1944, in Dimitrov, *Suchineniia*, 11:147–48: "After the harm which Bulgaria . . . brought to our neighboring states, to our liberator, Russia, to the liberation effort of the United Nations, we must firmly realize that the future of our state will depend first of all on those real contributions which now as a people and state will be added to the common war effort" (ibid., p. 152). See also "Memo from the U.S. Embassy Moscow to the State Department, 26 April, 1945, subject: Transmitting Summary of Lecture entitled 'The New Bulgaria' delivered in Moscow on March 9, 1945 by [Vasil] Kolarov," Record Group 59, 874.00/4-2645, DSNA.
41. Antonov, *Istoriia*, p. 420.
42. Mito Isusov, "Stopanski razkhodi," p. 56. Minasian states that 339,760 Bulgarian soldiers were involved in the struggle against the Germans after September 9, with almost 200,000 participating at the front, and sustaining 32,000 deaths (*Osvobozhdenie narodov*, p. 240).
43. Ganevich, *Deiatel'nost*, pp. 13–14.
44. Biriuzov, *Surovye gody*, p. 446.

45. Boris Iordanov, "Osobenosti na rabotnicheskiia kontrol nad proizvodstvoto na kapitalisticheskata promishlenost v Bulgariia (1944–1947g.)," p. 44.

46. Maynard B. Barnes obituary, *New York Times,* August 5, 1970, p. L35. Barnes was not the first official U.S. representative to enter Bulgaria after the September 9 uprising. There were several OSS missions, an investigatory commission on atrocities led by General William B. Hall which arrived in early October, and a commission under General Egmont F. Koenig which verified Bulgaria's withdrawal from Greek Macedonia in early November.

47. Maynard B. Barnes, "The Current Situation in Bulgaria," lecture, National War College, Washington, D.C., June 3, 1947, p. 6.

48. Ibid., pp. 3–4. Emphasis added.

49. Biriuzov, *Surovye gody,* p. 495.

50. Barnes, "Current Situation in Bulgaria," p. 11; Cyril E. Black, "The Start of the Cold War in Bulgaria: A Personal View," p. 171. Black, now a distinguished professor of European History at Princeton, arrived in Sofia five days before and functioned as his adviser and translator. See Moser, *Dimitrov of Bulgaria,* p. 227.

51. The base for this precaution are given in Memorandum: The British Embassy to the Department of State, October 3, 1944, *FRUS, 1944,* 4:245.

52. Minutes of the State Department Policy Committee, PC-8, November 8, 1944, Records of Harley A. Notter, Box 137, Lot 60D-224, This directive substantially repeated the document tentatively approved earlier by the Policy Committee and printed in *FRUS, 1945,* 4:143. Barnes revealed his full awareness of the directive by requesting permission to read it to General Biriuzov. See Barnes to the secretary of state, January 12, 1945, *FRUS, 1945,* 4:143.

53. Black, "Start of the Cold War," p. 171.

54. Memo from Operations Division, WDGS Mediterranean Section, November 26, 1944, OPD 336 Bulgaria, Record Group 165, MMBNA. The actual number of military representatives varied over the next three years.

55. Memo from J. E. Hull, Maj. General, Ass't Chief of Staff OPD to Major General John Crane, November 17, 1944, ibid.

56. U.S. delegation, Allied Central Commission Bulgaria, "History of the Allied Control Commission, Bulgaria, vols. 1–2 to 31 March 1946," Office of the Chief of Military History MMBNA. See Chapter 5 for a full discussion of these functions.

57. Biriuzov, *Surovye gody,* pp. 5–8, 428.

58. A. I. Cherepanov, "Burnye gody v Bolgarii (1944–1947)" (September–October 1976):105.

59. Barnes to secretary of state, December 7, 13, 1944, *FRUS, 1944,* 3:498–99, 502–3.

60. Bulgaria *Vunshna politika,* 1:8–9.

61. Biriuzov, *Surovye gody,* p. 433.

62. S. S. Biriuzov, "Bratiia po dukh i borba," p. 31; Nakov, *Bulgaro-Suvetski otnosheniia,* p. 99.

63. For a listing of Soviet colonels dispatched to regional commands in November 1944, see A. I. Suchkov, "Iz moite spomena za Bulgariia," p. 169. Suchkov was Biriuzov's chief of staff.

64. Stoian Tanev, "Pomoshtta na Suvetskota voenno komanduvane za pol-

itscheskoto ukrepvane na narodnodemokratichnota vlast v Bulgariia (septemvri 1944–1947 g.)," p. 75.

65. Ibid., p. 69.

66. Biriuzov, *Surovye gody*, pp. 484–85.

67. Cherepanov, "Burnye gody v Bulgarii," p. 106.

68. Biriuzov, *Surovye gody*, p. 485.

69. Nakov, *Bulgaro-Suvetski otnosheniia*, p. 84.

70. Biriuzov, *Surovye gody*, p. 486.

71. Suchkov, "Iz moite spomena za Bulgariia," p. 164.

72. Cherepanov, "Burnye gody v Bulgarii," p. 105.

73. *Rabotnichesko delo* (Sofia), November 15, 1944.

74. USSR, *Sovetsko-Bolgarskie otnosheniia, 1944–1948 a.*, p. 70. This letter is dated November 29, 1944.

75. Cherepanov, "Burnye gody v Bulgarii," p. 108. Emphasis added.

76. Barnes to the secretary of state, December 9, 1944, Records of the Department of State, National Archives, Decimal File, 700.00119 Control (Bulgaria)/12-944.

77. Suchkov, "Iz moite spomena za Bulgeriia," pp. 167–68.

78. Barnes to secretary of state, December 27, 1944, *FRUS, 1944,* 3:511.

79. Message from AFMQ, Caserta, to the War Department, December 2, 8, 1944 (emphasis added); "Cable from OSS Caserta to the War Department," December 14, 1944, CAD 334 ACC Bulgaria, Record Group: 165, MMBNA.

80. Barnes to the secretary of state, December 29, 1944, *FRUS, 1944,* 3:513–14.

81. Cable from ACC Bulgaria US Delegation to War Department, December 30, 1944; cable from Major-General Crane to AFHQ Caserta," February 27, 1945, CAD 334 ACC Bulgaria, Record Group 165, MMBNA.

82. Barnes to the secretary of state, January 18, 1945, *FRUS, 1945,* 4:144. The British delegation was also unaware of the details of the Eden-Molotov agreement until receipt of appropriate documents in mid-January. The British Foreign Office expressed outrage that the Americans had been shown these documents, sending a "rocket" to Houstoun-Boswall in protest of his revealing "ultra secret documents" to the Americans. See Alexander Kirk, American representative on the Advisory Council for Italy, to the secretary of state, February 1, 1945, Record Group 59, 874.01/2-145, DSNA.

83. Memo from Harrison A. Gerhardt, Colonel, General Staff Corps, to Assistant Secretary of State James C. Dunn, January 22, 1944, Record Group, 740.00119 Control (Bulgaria) 1-2245, DSNA.

84. Grew to Barnes, January 26, 1945, *FRUS, 1945,* 4:148–51; Kennan to the secretary of state, January 30, 1945, ibid., pp. 151–52, repeated to Sofia. Kennan had signed the Bulgarian armistice on October 28 in the absence of Harriman. There remains to this day confusion as to what was known in Washington about the secret Eden-Molotov agreement. Although the State Department was aware that Eden had granted Russian predominance, the basis for Hull and Winant's message in late October 1944 that a revision of the control commission statute might be required after completion of the war against Germany, it is not apparent that Eden's promise restricting the taking of Allied seats in the commission was known. Returning to Washington for consultation in late October, Ambassador Harriman informed the State Department Policy Committee that at the Churchill-Stalin meetings in October 1944, "it was

agreed that the Soviets should have a free hand in Rumania, Hungary and Bulgaria during the war. Eden endeavored to persuade Molotov to agree that after the close of hostilities in Europe, the three participants on the Control Commission in these countries should have an equal status, but he was unsuccessful." When one of the members of the Policy Committee (Savage) suggested at the October 25 meeting called to affirm policy for Bulgaria that spheres of influence perhaps ought to be addressed in the resulting document, the consensus of opinion was "to state our policy in regards to their essential characteristics and to see that this policy is made effective." Thus no mention was made of spheres or of the uncertain Eden-Molotov promises in the resulting document forwarded to President Roosevelt in early November and to Barnes. See Minutes, Department of State Policy Committee, October 25, 1944, Records of Harley A. Notter, box 145. It appears that Barnes and Crane first discovered exactly what was at stake.

85. Barnes to secretary of state, December 1, 1944, January 8, 1945, *FRUS, 1944*, 3:495, ibid. *1945*, 4:139.

86. Bulgaria, *Istoriia na Bulgarskata komunisticheska partiia: za sistemata na partiinata prosveta* (Sofia, 1978), p. 325.

87. Cherepanov, "Burnye gody v Bulgarii," p. 106.

88. Diniu Sharlanov and Penka Damianova, *Miastoto i roliato na otechestveniia front v sistemata na narodnata demokratsiia*, pp. 39–40.

89. Bulgaria, *Ustanoviavane i ukrepvane na narodnodemokratichnata vlast*, pp. 470–71.

90. Bozhinov, *Zashtitata na natsionalnata nezavisimost na Bulgariia, 1944–1947*, p. 16.

91. Institut istorii Bolgarskoi kommunisticheskoi partii pre TsK BKP, *Istoriia Bolgarskoi kommunisticheskoi partii*, p. 471.

92. Bulgaria *Istoriia na Bulgarskata komunisticheska partiia*, p. 319.

93. Tanev, "Pomoshtta na Suvetskota," pp. 68, 79.

94. Barnes to secretary of state, December 8, 15, 1944, *FRUS, 1944*, 3:500, 503.

95. A. V. Blagodatov, "Ramo do ramo," p. 177; V. V. Sosnovikov, "Obiknakh tazi strana," pp. 99–100; Ivan Filchev, *Bulgaro-Suvetskata boina druzhba prez otechestvenata voina (1944–1945)*, p. 50.

96. Quoted in Ignat Lalov, M. Kostadinova, T. Tashev, *Pomoshtnik komandirite v otechestvenata voina*, p. 49; also ibid., p. 53.

97. Ibid., pp. 51, 67.

98. Ibid., p. 63.

99. Ganevich, *Deiatel'nost'* p. 79.

100. Lalov, Kostadinova, and Tashev, *Pomoshtnik Komandirite*, p. 101.

101. Resolution 4 is published in *UUNV*, pp. 323–24.

102. Lalov, Kostadinova, and Tashev, *Pomoshtnik Romandirite*, p. 101.

103. Cherepanov, "Burnye gody v Bulgarii," p. 110.

104. Biriuzov, *Surovye gody*, p. 501.

105. Cherepanov, "Burnye gody v Bulgarii," p. 110.

4. YALTA AND THE POSTPONEMENT OF ELECTIONS

1. De Santis, *Diplomacy of Silence*, pp. 106–30.

2. Kennan, "Russia—Seven Years Later," in *Memoirs*, p. 521.

3. Kennan to the secretary of state, October 20, 1944, *FRUS, 1944*, 4:924.

4. Acting secretary of state to Kennan, November 3, 1944, ibid., pp. 253–54. This message was repeated to Caserta and to the U.S. representative to Rumania, Burton Berry, who was en route to Bucharest. See also Berry to the secretary of state, December 4, 1944, ibid., p. 275.

5. See n. 33, Chapter 2, above.

6. "Briefing Book Paper: Principal Bulgarian Problems, Summary," *FRUS, 1945, Conferences at Malta and Yalta*, p. 240. Emphasis added.

7. Barnes to the secretary of state, December 27, 1944, *FRUS, 1944*, 3:512.

8. Minutes of the Department of State Policy Committee, October 25, 1944, General Records of Harley A. Notter, box 145.

9. Minutes of the Department of State Policy Committee—PC-8 (second revision), November 1, 1944, ibid.

10. Martin, "United States Diplomacy," p. 103, emphasis added by Martin.

11. Deputy director of the Office of European Affairs to the secretary of state, January 8, 1945, *FRUS, 1945, Conferences at Malta and Yalta*, pp. 93–96.

12. Martin, "United States Diplomacy," p. 110.

13. Harley A. Notter, *Postwar Foreign Policy Preparation, 1939–1945*, p. 373.

14. "Memorandum for the President; Establishment of an Emergency High Commission for Liberated Europe," Edward R. Stettinius, secretary of state, to President Roosevelt, January 18, 1945, *FRUS, 1945, Conferences at Malta and Yalta*, p. 98.

15. "Emergency High Commission for Liberated Europe," ibid., pp. 99–100.

16. "Declaration on Liberated Europe," Ibid., pp. 98–99; Martin, "United States Diplomacy," p. 113.

17. James F. Byrnes, *Speaking Frankly*, p. 23.

18. "Agreed minutes," Meeting of the Foreign Ministers, H.M.S. *Sirius* in Grand Harbor, February 1, 1945, *FRUS, 1945, Conferences at Malta and Yalta*, p. 503; Martin, "United States Diplomacy," p. 111.

19. Notter, *Postwar Foreign Policy*, p. 394.

20. Martin, "United States Diplomacy," p. 118. Byrnes, *Speaking Frankly*, pp. 32–33.

21. "Text Proposed by the United States for a Declaration on Liberated Europe," Yalta, February 9, 1945, *FRUS, 1945, Conferences at Malta and Yalta*, p. 863.

22. "Page minute," Meeting of the Foreign Ministers, Yalta, February 10, 1945, ibid., p. 873.

23. "Declaration on Liberated Europe," as released to the press by the U.S. State Department on March 24, 1947, *FRUS, 1945, Conference of Berlin*, 2:1569.

24. See "Memorandum for the President, Establishment of an Emergency High Commission for Liberated Europe," Stettinius to President Roosevelt, January 18, 1945, *FRUS, 1945, Conferences at Malta and Yalta*, pp. 97–100.

25. "Declaration on Liberated Europe," *FRUS, 1945, Conference of Berlin*, 2:1569.

26. Quoted in Martin, "United States Diplomacy," pp. 121, 126. See Daniel Yergin, *Shattered Peace*, p. 63, for an alternate view.

27. Memorandum to secretary of state (E. Stettinius) from President Roosevelt, February 28, 1945, as quoted in Lynn E. Davis, *The Cold War Begins*, pp. 259–60.

28. Barnes to Stettinius, February 27, 1945, *FRUS, 1945*, 4:163.

29. Acting secretary of state (Grew) to Barnes, March 3, 1945, ibid., p. 169.

30. Barnes to Stettinius, March 9, 1945, ibid., p. 171.

31. Barnes to Stettinius, March 2, 1945, ibid., pp. 167–68.

32. Oren, *Bulgarian Communism*, p. 255.

33. Bozhinov, *Zashtitata na natsionalnata nezavisimost na Bulgariia 1944–1947*, p. 16.

34. Sharlanov and Damianova, *Miastato i roliata na otechestveniia front v sistemata na narodnata demokratsiia*, p. 40.

35. Petur D. Ostoich, *BKP i izgrazhdaneto na narodno-demokraticheskata durzhava*, p. 78.

36. *UUNV*, pp. 122–23, 150.

37. Ostoich, *BPK i izgrazhdaneto*, p. 76–77.

38. Sharlanov and Damianova, *Miastoto i roliata*, pp. 44–46.

39. B. Iordanov, "Partiiata i rabotnicheskiiat kontrol nad kapitalisticheskata promishlenost v Bulgariia (1944–1947g.)," p. 110–11.

40. Bozhinov, *Zashtitata na natsionalnata nezavisinost na Bulgariia* p. 17.

41. Institut istorii Bolgarskoi kommunisticheskoi partii pri TsK BKP, *Istoriia Bolgarskoi kommunisticheskoi partii*, p. 471.

42. Oren, *Revolution Administered*, p. 15, n. 8.

43. Moser, *Dimitrov of Bulgaria*, pp. 16–187.

44. Mito Isusov, *Politicheskite partii v Bulgariia, 1944–1948*, pp. 74–77.

45. *Zemedelsko zname*, September 14, 1944.

46. Isusov, one of the more reliable of contemporary Bulgarian historians, correctly affirms this as the party's constituent congress. See Isusov, *Politicheskite partii v Bulgariia*, pp. 79–80. K. Kukov, in *Razgrom na burzhoaznata opozitsiia (1944–1947 g.)*, p. 24, maintains that the conference was in violation of party rules and traditions and its members were hand-picked by Gemeto.

47. Isusov, *Politicheskite partii v Bulgariia*, pp. 79–80; Kukov, *Razgrom na burzhoaznata opozitsiia*, p. 24; Moser, *Dimitrov of Bulgaria*, p. 192.

48. Kukov, *Razgrom na burzhoaznata opozitsiia* pp. 27–28.

49. Moser, *Dimitrov of Bulgaria*, p. 194.

50. Ibid., pp. 200–201, citing Gemeto's unpublished memoirs.

51. Quoted in Dr. Georgi Dimitrov, "Bravest Democrat of All," p. 208.

52. Isusov, *Politicheskite partii v Bulgariia*, pp. 75–77. These figures, purporting to come from Bulgarian Central Party Archives, must be used with care because Communist historians have placed a premium on underemphasizing Agrarian strength.

53. I. Dimitrov, "Naroden Suiuz 'Zveno' (1 oktomvri 1944–19 fevruari 1949 g.)," p. 5.

54. There remains considerable debate as to the exact size of National Union-Zveno during this period. Dimitrov (ibid., p. 6) suggests that membership was but one-tenth that offered by *Izgrev*. I. V. Ganevich places membership at 50,000 (*Deiatel'nast Bolgarskoi kommunisticheskoi partii*, p. 91).

55. Dimitrov, "Naroden Suiuz 'Zveno', p. 7, quotation on p. 5.

56. See the "Program of the Fatherland Front" in *UUNV*, p. 133; Ostoich, *BKP i izgrazhdaneto*, p. 145.

57. "Nepublikuvani radiogrami na Georgi Dimitrov i TsK na BRP(k) (avgust–dekemvri 1944 g.)," p. 61.

58. *Rabotnicheski delo*, December 4, 5, 7, 1944.

59. *Zemedelsko zname*, December 6, 1944.

60. *Izgrev*, December 7, 1944.

61. *Rabotnicheski delo*, December 12, 1944.

62. Kukov, *Razgrom na burzhoaznata opozitsiia*, p. 58.

63. Moser, *Dimitrov of Bulgaria*, p. 211 citing Gemeto's unpublished diary.

64. Barnes to Stettinius, January 9, 1945, *FRUS, 1945*, 4:140.

65. Moser, *Dimitrov of Bulgaria*, pp. 212–13; Isusov, *Politicheskite partii v Bulgariia*, pp. 83–84; Kukov, *Razgrom na burzhoaznata opozitsiia*, pp. 60–61.

66. Moser, *Dimitrov of Bulgaria*, p. 215; Isusov, *Politicheskite partii v Bulgariia*, p. 84.

67. Kukov, *Razgrom na burzhoaznata opozitsiia*, p. 65.

68. Isusov, *Politicheskite partii v Bulgariia*, p. 84.

69. *Rabotnicheski delo*, March 7, 1945.

70. *Otechestvan front*, March 14, 1945.

71. *UUNV*, pp. 523, 559.

72. Kukov, *Razgrom na burzhoaznata opozitsiia*, p. 69.

73. Barnes to Stettinius, March 2, 1945, *FRUS, 1945*, 4:167–68.

74. Barnes to Stettinius, March 7, 8, 1945, ibid., p. 170, 874.00/3-845, CS/MAS, Decimal Files, DSNA.

75. *Otechestven front*, March 10, 1945.

76. Barnes to Stettinius, March 9, 1945, *FRUS, 1945*, 4:171–72.

77. *UUNV*, pp. 470–471, 541. This law was published in the state registry journal, *Durzhaven vestnik*, over the signature of Prime Minister Georgiev on March 17, although the document was dated January 26, 1945.

78. *Otechestven front*, March 10, 1945.

79. Houstoun-Boswall to Foreign Office, February 28, 1945, as reprinted in an annex to the British Embassy to the Department of State, March 11, 1945, 874.00/3-1445, Decimal Files, DSNA.

80. Harriman to the People's Commissar of Foreign Affairs of the Soviet Union (Molotov), March 14, 1945, *FRUS, 1945*, 5:513.

81. Molotov to Harriman, March 17, 1945, ibid., p. 517.

82. Grew to Harriman, March 26, 1945, ibid., pp. 522–24.

83. See Chapter 2 above.

84. Roosevelt to Churchill, March 11, 1945, *FRUS, 1945*, 5:509–10. See also Davis, *The Cold War Begins*, pp. 256–66.

85. Memorandum by Charles E. Bohlen to Stettinius, April 19, 1945, *FRUS, 1945*, 5:834.

86. Grew to Harriman, March 29, 1945, ibid., 4:179–80.

87. Winant to Stettinius, April 13, 1945, ibid., p. 185.

88. Harriman to Stettinius, April 15, 1945, ibid., p. 186.

89. Ostoich, *BPK i izgrazhdaneto*, p. 145.

90. Barnes to Stettinius, May 12, 1945, *FRUS, 1945*, 4:213. In mid-March 1945, a major regional conference of the Agrarian party meeting in Plovdiv resolved that

elections be held in Bulgaria "only after the normalization of the situation" within the state. See Isusov, *Politcheskite partii v Bulgariia,* p. 87. For reports on Foreign Minister Petko Stainov's efforts to delay the impending elections until the fall of 1945, see Barnes to Stettinius, April 11, 1945, 874.00/ 4-1145, Decimal Files, DSNA.

91. Harriman to Stettinius, April 15, 1945, *FRUS, 1945,* 4:186.

92. Memorandum by Charles E. Bohlen to Stettinius, April 19, 1945, ibid., 5:834–35.

93. *UUNV,* pp. 580–96, 611, 628–29.

94. AFHQ Caserta to War Department, April 6, 1945, CAD 334 ACC Bulgaria, Record Group 165, MMBNA.

95. Barnes to Stettinius, May 31, 1945, *FRUS, 1945,* 4:241.

96. Isusov, *Politcheskite partii v Bulgariia,* p. 87–88.

97. Barnes to Stettinius, April 27, 1945, *FRUS, 1945,* 4:200.

98. Barnes to Stettinius, April 25, 1945, 874.00/ 4-2545, Decimal Files, DSNA.

99. Kukov, *Razgrom na burzhoavznata opozitsiia,* pp. 78–79.

100. Isusov, *Politcheskite partii v Bulgariia,* p. 92.

101. Barnes to Stettinius, May 13, 1945, *FRUS, 1945,* 4:214.

102. Kukov, *Razgrom na burzhoavznata opozitsiia,* pp. 80–81.

103. Barnes to Stettinius, May 11, 1945, 874.00/5-1145, Decimal Files, DSNA.

104. Isusov, *Politcheskite partii v Bulgariia,* pp. 94–95.

105. Dimitrov, "Bravest Democrat of All," p. 208.

106. Barnes to Stettinius, May 11, 1945, 874.00/5-1145, Decimal Files, DSNA.

107. Isusov, *Politcheskite partii Bulgariia,* p. 97, n. 333, citing the archives of the Bulgarian Academy of Science. I have found no confirmation of this meeting in the U.S. Archives or Diplomatic Post Records.

108. Barnes to Stettinius, June 10, 1945, Records of the Foreign Service Posts, RG 84, Decimal file 800, Washington National Records Center.

109. See Moser, *Dimitrov of Bulgaria,* pp. 225–48.

5. CAMPAIGN FOR TRIPARTITE ADMINISTRATION

1. Crane to AFHQ Caserta, March 17, 1945, CAD 334, ACC Bulgaria, Record Group 165, MMBNA.

2. Memorandum by Fleet Admiral William D. Leahy, chief of staff to the commander in chief of the army and navy, to secretary of state, May 28, 1945, *FRUS, 1945,* 4:233; Winant to Stettinius, June 11, 1945, ibid., pp. 827–28.

3. Crane to AFHQ Caserta, April 6, 1945, CAD 334, ACC Bulgaria, Record Group 165, MMBNA.

4. U.S. delegation, Allied Control Commission Bulgaria, "History of the Allied Control Commission, Bulgaria, vols. 1–2 to 31 March 1946," Office of the Chief of Military History, MMBNA 8–3.3, AA, 1 (hereafter "History of ACC, Bulgaria"), pp. 2, 2–3, 20. Earlier intelligence operatives in postarmistice Bulgaria had served with the OSS.

5. Memorandum for Coordinator of War Department Libraries, March 29, 1945, OPD 336 Bulgaria, Record Group 165, MMBNA; "Memorandum from J. B.

Crawford, acting chief, European Section Theatre Group, OPD: Subject, Roster of Personnel (ACC, Bulgaria)," June 11, 1945, ibid.

6. Cable from OSS Caserta to War Department, November 30, 1944, CAD 334, ACC Bulgaria, Record group 165, MMBNA; "History of ACC, Bulgaria," p. 80.

7. "Lt. Colonel John Bakeless," n.d., ABC 336 Rumania, September 26, 1943, Record Group 165, MMBNA.

8. "History of ACC, Bulgaria," p. 63.

9. Ibid., pp. 63–65.

10. Ibid., pp. 63–64.

11. Ibid., pp. 66, 70, 71.

12. Ibid., pp. 72–73.

13. Ibid., pp. 73–74.

14. Ibid., p. 17.

15. Ibid., pp. 18–20.

16. Crane to AFHQ Caserta, January 27, 1945, OPD 336 Bulgaria, Record Group 165, MMBNA.

17. "History of ACC, Bulgaria," pp. 22–23.

18. Barnes to James F. Byrnes, February 4, 1946, *FRUS, 1946*, 6:69–70.

19. Cable from U.S. representative, Allied Control Commission for Bulgaria, to AGWAR retransmitted by AFHQ Caserta, February 26, 1945, CAD 334 ACC Bulgaria, Record Group 165, MMBNA.

20. Cherepanov, "Burnyi gody v Bolgarii (1944–1947 gg.)" 19 (September–October 1976): 105.

21. S. S. Biriuzov, *Sovetskii soldat na Balkanakh*, p. 251.

22. Cherepanov, "Burnyi gody v Bolgarii," p. 102.

23. Ibid., pp. 102, 103.

24. A. I. Cherepanov, "Nezabravimi sreshti," p. 152.

25. *Rabotnichesko delo*, November 15, 1944.

26. USSR, *Sovetsko-Bolgarskie otnosheniia, 1944–1948 gg.*, p. 70.

27. Suchkov, "Iz moite spomeni za Bulgariia," pp. 159–64, 165, 167.

28. Nakov, *Bulgaro-Suvetski otnosheniia 1944–1948*, p. 132.

29. R. I. Ablova, *Sotrudnichestvo Sovetskogo i Bolgarskogo narodov v bor'be protiv fashizma (1941–1945g.)*, p. 400.

30. Biriuzov, *Sovetskii soldat na Balkanakh*, p. 254.

31. Cherepanov, "Burnyi gody v Bolgarii," p. 106.

32. Biriuzov, *Sovetskii soldat na Balkanakh*, p. 256.

33. Suchkov, "Iz moite spomeni za Bulgariia," pp. 167–68.

34. Woodward, *British Foreign Policy*, 3:566, n. 1.

35. Kennan to Stettinius, April 17, 1945, Record Group 59, 740.00119 Control (Bulgaria)/4-1745, Decimal Files, DSNA.

36. Woodward, *British Foreign Policy* 3:566, n. 1.

37. "Statutes of the Allied Control Commission in Hungary," *FRUS, 1945*, 4:802–3.

38. Woodward, *British Foreign Policy*, 3:566, n. 1.

39. Harriman to Stettinius, February 27, 1945, Record Group 59, 740.00119 Control (Bulgaria)/2-2745, Decimal Files, DSNA. For details on the rights of Soviet

representatives in Italy see David Key (U.S. chargé in Italy) to Secretary of State James Byrnes, April 18, 1946, *FRUS, 1946*, 6:98–99.

40. Woodward, *British Foreign Policy*, 3:562.

41. Grew to Harriman, June 12, 1945, *FRUS, 1945*, 4:254. Emphasis added.

42. Grew to Barnes, March 10, 1945, ibid., pp. 172–73.

43. Barnes to Stettinius, March 13, 1945, ibid., p. 173.

44. Memorandum of conversation by Mr. Charles E. Bohlen, assistant to the secretary of state, April 20, 1945, ibid., 5:232.

45. As quoted in De Santis, *Diplomacy of Silence*, p. 139.

46. "United States Participation in Allied (Soviet) Control Commission, Bulgaria," Memorandum by the United States representative in Bulgaria (Maynard Barnes), April 20, 1945, *FRUS, 1945*, 4:192.

47. Ibid., pp. 195, 197.

48. "Memorandum: The Current Situation in Bulgaria: Summary," Crane to the Secretariat, JCS, May 2, 1945, ABC 336 Rumania, September 26, 1943, Record Group 165, MMBNA.

49. Memorandum by the acting secretary of state (Joseph Grew) to President Truman," May 1, 1945, *FRUS, 1945*, 4:202–3.

50. Memorandum of conversation by the acting secretary of state (Joseph Grew) with President Truman, General Schuyler, and General Crane, May 2, 1945, RG 59, 711.00/5-245, DSNA; Harry S. Truman, *Year of Decision*, pp. 283–84.

51. Memorandum by the United States representative on the Allied Control Commission for Bulgaria (Major General John Crane) to President Truman, May 3, 1945, *FRUS, 1945*, 4:206–7.

52. Cable from Major-General Crane to AFHQ Caserta, May 18, 1945, CAD 334 ACC Bulgaria, Record Group 165, MMBNA.

53. Cable from Lieutenant General McNarney to War Department, May 19, 1945, CAD 334 ACC Bulgaria, Record Group 165, MMBNA.

54. Marshall to commanding general, AFHQ Caserta, May 19, 1945, CAD 334 ACC Bulgaria, Record Group 165, MMBNA. Lynn Davis mistakenly argues that a "lack of urgency" characterized the State and War departments' approach to ACC reforms in the period following Crane's visit to Washington and that refusal to approve Crane's May 18 plan of action reflected indecision among the diplomats. In fact, the only uncertainty concerned which East European state to select as the initial target of reform, Hungary being quickly chosen, as Marshall's return cable indicates. See Davis, *Cold War Begins*, p. 278. Her mistake apparently derives from examining only the OPD memorandum dealing with the incident to the exclusion of the cables.

55. Crane to AFHQ Caserta, May 20, 1945, CAD 334 ACC Bulgaria, Record Group 165, MMBNA.

56. Harriman to Molotov, January 20, 1945, *FRUS, 1945*, 4:800; John Balfour, British chargé in U.S.S.R., to Harriman, January 20, 1945, ibid., pp. 800–801.

57. Molotov to Harriman, January 20, 1945, ibid., 4:801–4.

58. Grew to Harriman, May 28, 1945, *FRUS, Conference of Berlin (Potsdam), 1945*, 1:368, n. 5.

59. Grew to Harriman, June 8, 1945, ibid., 1:372, n. 6; Grew to Harriman, June 12, 1945, ibid., p. 364, n. 4.

60. Barnes to Stettinius, June 6, 7, 11, 16, 1945, *FRUS, 1945,* 4:249, 251–52, 258–60.

61. Barnes to Grew, June 23, July 9, 1945, *FRUS, Conference of Berlin (Potsdam), 1945,* 1:383, 403.

62. Crane to McNarney, July 10, 1945, ibid., p. 404.

63. Crane to the Joint Chiefs of Staff, July 11, 1945, ibid., pp. 405–6.

64. Ibid., p. 405.

65. Barnes to Grew, July 12, 1945, ibid., p. 407.

66. H. F. Arthur Schoenfeld, U.S. representative in Hungary, to Grew, July 13, 1945, ibid., p. 408.

67. "Proposal by the United States Delegation: Revised Allied Control Commission Procedures in Rumania, Bulgaria and Hungary," Babelsberg, July 31, 1945, ibid., 2:732; Eleventh Plenary Meeting, Babelsberg, July 31, 1945, ibid., p. 525.

68. Eleventh Meeting of the Foreign Ministers, Babelsberg, August 1, 1945, ibid., pp. 554–55.

69. Ibid., pp. 554–56.

70. "Letter Transmitted on July 12 to the Representatives of the US and UK Governments on the Allied Control Commission in Hungary," ibid, p. 689. The first English translation of the Soviet proposal as presented to General Key in Budapest was apparently in error, and the official document used at Potsdam replaced the phrase suggesting that "agreement by the Western representatives would henceforth be required for ACC directives. The Potsdam document read "coordination," a term much closer to the language used in similar draft revisions sent to Sofia and Bucharest. See Schoenfeld to Byrnes, July 13, 1945, *FRUS, 1945,* 4:835.

71. Protocol of the Proceedings of the Berlin Conference, Berlin, August 1, 1945, *FRUS, Conference of Berlin (Potsdam), 1945,* 2:1494. Emphasis added.

72. Alexander C. Kirk, United States political adviser to the Supreme Allied Commander, Mediterranean, to Byrnes, August 21, 1945, *FRUS, 1945,* 4:300–302.

73. U.S. delegation, Allied Control Commission Bulgaria, "History of Allied Control Commission Bulgaria, Minutes of Plenary Meetings," Office of the Chief of Military History, 8-3.3, AA, vol. 2, MMBNA (hereafter ACC Bulgaria, Minutes of Plenary Meetings).

74. "History of ACC, Bulgaria," p. 13.

75. Transcript of the Eighth Plenary Meeting of the ACC Bulgaria, November 27, 1945, British Minutes, ACC Bulgaria, Minutes of Plenary Meetings.

76. U.S. Department of State, *Bulletin* 279 (October 29, 1944), p. 493.

77. Transcript of the Third Plenary Meeting of the ACC Bulgaria, September 25, 1945, British Minutes, ACC Bulgaria, Minutes of Plenary Meetings.

78. Transcript of the Sixth Plenary Meeting of the ACC Bulgaria, October 30, 1945, ibid.

79. Transcript of the Seventh Plenary Meeting of the ACC Bulgaria, November 20, 1945, ibid.

80. Transcript of the Eighth Plenary Meeting of the ACC Bulgaria, November 27, 1945, ibid.

81. Transcript of the Twenty-Second Plenary Meeting of the ACC Bulgaria, July 25, 1946, ibid.

82. Transcript of the Extraordinary Session of the ACC Bulgaria, October 24, 1946, ibid.

83. Transcript of the Twenty-Fifth Plenary Session of the ACC Bulgaria, November 14, 1946, ibid.

84. Ablova, *Sotrudnichestvo,* p. 401.

85. Transcript of the Twenty-Second Plenary Meeting of the ACC Bulgaria, July 25, 1946, Soviet Minutes, ACC Bulgaria, Minutes of Plenary Meetings.

86. Transcript of the Ninth Plenary Meeting of the ACC Bulgaria, December 18, 1945, British Minutes, ibid.

87. "History of the ACC, Bulgaria," p. 50.

88. Transcript of the Twenty-Third Plenary Meeting of the ACC Bulgaria, August 29, 1946, and Twenty-Fourth Plenary Meeting, September 12, 1946, British Minutes, ACC Bulgaria, Minutes of Plenary Meetings.

89. U.S. Department of State, *Bulletin* 279 (October 29, 1944), p. 492.

90. Transcript of the Fourth Plenary Meeting of the ACC Bulgaria, October 2, 1945, British Minutes, ACC Bulgaria, Minutes of Plenary Meetings.

91. Ibid.

92. Transcript of the Eleventh Plenary Meeting of the ACC Bulgaria, January 17, 1946, ibid.

93. Transcript of the Twenty-First Plenary Meeting of the ACC Bulgaria, July 13, 1946, British and Soviet Minutes, ibid.

94. Barnes to Byrnes, February 4, 1946, *FRUS, 1946,* 6:69–71.

6. PLANNING FOR POSTWAR BULGARIA

1. Quoted in De Santis, *Diplomacy of Silence,* p. 139.

2. Memorandum for the Secretary of War from Mr. Grew, Acting Secretary of State, May 12, 1945, reprinted in Joseph C. Grew, *Turbulent Era,* 2:1456.

3. Quoted in Yergin, *Shattered Peace,* p. 81.

4. Grew, *Turbulent Era,* 2:1454, 1474–76.

5. Truman, *1945,* p. 283; Grew *Turbulent Era,* 2:1454–55.

6. Grew, *Turbulent Era,* 2:1464, 1468–73.

7. For a recent account of Byrnes's early influence upon Truman see Robert L. Messer, *The End of an Alliance,* pp. 31–70.

8. Richard L. Walker, "E. R. Stettinius, Jr., p. 76.

9. Grew, *Turbulent Era,* 1446.

10. "Recommended Policy on the Question of Establishing Diplomatic Relations and Concluding Peace Treaties with the Former Axis Satellite States," June 29, 1945, *FRUS, Conference of Berlin (Potsdam) 1945,* 1:357, 362.

11. Harriman's message is given in ibid., p. 358, n. 5; Barnes to Grew, June 23, 1945, ibid., pp. 382–84.

12. See Grew to Barnes, June 21, 1945, ibid., p. 380.

13. Memorandum by the acting director of the Office of European Affairs (J. Hickerson), July 14, 1945, ibid., pp. 413–14.

14. Barnes to Stettinius, May 21, 1945, *FRUS, 1945,* 4:219. According to a report entitled "Monetary Situation in Bulgaria and Its Affects on the American Section of

ACC," dated Sofia, May 15, 1945, and lodged in the Post Records of the American mission, the official rate of exchange at the time was 120 leva to the dollar although the black market exchange was much higher. See Records of the Foreign Service Posts of the Department of State, Record Group 84 (711.9, 800 box, 80, Sofia), Washington National Records Center (hereafter Records of Foreign Service Posts, Sofia).

15. Quoted in Crane to the Joint Chiefs of Staff, July 24, 1945, *FRUS, Conference of Berlin (Potsdam), 1945,* 2:713.

16. Notes of a conversation between deputy people's commissar of foreign affairs USSR (A. Vyshensky) and the political representative of Bulgaria in the USSR (D. Mikhalchev), Moscow, January 11, 1945, USSR, *Sovetsko-Bolgarskie otnosheniia, 1944–1948,* pp. 94–95; Stainov to Biriuzov, March 1, 1945, ibid., pp. 100–102; Mikhalchev to Stainov, March 5, 1945, ibid., p. 107.

17. Stainov to Biriuzov, April 12, 1945, ibid., pp. 129–30.

18. Barnes to Grew, June 23, July 23, 1945, *FRUS, Conference of Berlin (Potsdam), 1945,* 1:382–84, 708–9; quotation p. 383.

19. Isusov, *Politicheskite partii v Bulgariia,* pp. 96–97; Barnes to Stettinius, June 13, 1945, 874.00/6-1345, Decimal Files, DSNA. For a historic sketch of Obbov see Moser, *Dimitrov of Bulgaria,* pp. 33, 56, 65, 67, 137. Barnes saw Obbov as a "stooge" to whom even the Bulgarian foreign minister referred as a "worn-out prostitute" (Barnes to Stettinius, June 16, 1945, *FRUS, 1945,* 4:257).

20. Ostoich, *BKP i izgrazhdaneto na narodno demokraticheskata durzhava,* pp. 155–56.

21. President of the Democratic party, A. Girginov, to the minister-president of Bulgaria, July 29, 1945, Records of Foreign Service Posts, Sofia.

22. Barnes to Stettinius, June 16, 1945, *FRUS, 1945,* 4:259–60.

23. Isusov, *Politcheskite partii v Bulgariia,* p. 98.

24. Barnes to Byrnes July 7, 1945, 874.00/7-745, Decimal Files, DSNA.

25. Barnes to Byrnes, July 14, 1945, 874.00/7-1445, Decimal Files, DSNA. The independent minister of finance, Petko Stoianov, and the Socialist minister of social welfare, Grigor Cheshmedzhiev, were considered to be Petkov supporters.

26. "Yugov's Proposal to Petkov," July 12, 1945, Records of Foreign Service Posts, Sofia.

27. "Counter-Proposal of Petkov to Yugov," July 13, 1945, ibid.

28. Barnes to Grew, July 17, 1945, *FRUS, Conference of Berlin (Potsdam), 1945,* 2:694.

29. Grew to Barnes, July 18, 1945, *FRUS, 1945,* 4:267.

30. Barnes to Grew, July 23, 25, 27, 31, 1945, *FRUS, Conference of Berlin (Potsdam), 1945,* 2:708, 717, 724–25, 734.

31. Grew to Byrnes, August 1, 1945, ibid., pp. 734–35. Grew's cable to the secretary of state followed a top-level review of policy during a meeting of the Secretary's Staff Committee at which the ongoing Bulgarian crisis was introduced as "Urgent Business." The discussion concerned Barnes's recommendation that America and Britain issue an immediate statement that no Bulgarian government emerging from unfree elections would be granted Western recognition. Byrnes's advice was sought on this point. See Minutes of the Secretary of State's Staff Committee, August 1, 1945, Lot 122, Secretary's Staff Committee, DSNA.

32. See Messer, *End of an Alliance;* Patricia D. Ward, *The Threat of Peace;* and Byrnes, *Speaking Frankly.*

33. Byrnes, *Speaking Frankly,* pp. 23, 67.

34. Grew to Truman, June 30, 1945, *FRUS, Conference of Berlin (Potsdam), 1945,* 1:201–2, 198, n. 1.

35. Herbert Feis, *Between War and Peace,* p. 64.

36. Messer, *End of an Alliance,* p. 56.

37. "Implementation of the Yalta Declaration on Liberated Europe," July 17, 1945, *FRUS, Conference of Berlin (Potsdam), 1945,* 2:643–44.

38. Third Meeting of the Foreign Ministers, Babelsberg, July 2O, 1945, ibid., pp. 155–66.

39. Byrnes, *Speaking Frankly,* p. 74.

40. Protocol of proceedings, Berlin, August 1, 1945, *FRUS, Conference of Berlin, (Potsdam) 1945,* 2:1492.

41. U.S. Department of State, *Bulletin* 320 (August 12, 1945), p. 211.

42. Barnes to Byrnes, August 11, 1945, *FRUS, 1945,* 4:282.

43. Barnes to Grew, July 30, 1945, *FRUS, Conference of Berlin (Potsdam), 1945,* 2:728–32.

44. Barnes to Byrnes, July 28, 1945, *FRUS, 1945,* 4:272.

45. Byrnes to the American political representative in Hungary (H. F. Arthur Schoenfeld), August 23, 1945, ibid., p. 854.

46. Memorandum by the assistant secretary of state (James Dunn) to Byrnes, August 9, 1945, ibid., p. 281.

47. Byrnes to Barnes, August 11, 1945, ibid., p. 283.

48. Byrnes to Barnes, August 11, 1945, 874.00/8-1145, Decimal Files, DSNA.

49. Barnes to Byrnes, August 14, 1945, *FRUS, 1945,* 4:284–85; Barnes to his Excellency Kimon Georgiev, August 14, 1945, Records of Foreign Service Posts, Sofia.

50. Barnes to Byrnes, August 15, *FRUS, 1945,* 4:287; *Rabotnichesko delo,* August 16, 1945.

51. Kukov, *Razgrom na burzhoaznata opozitsiia,* p. 94; Winant to Byrnes, August 17, 1945, 874.00/8-1745, Decimal Files, DSNA; Barnes to Byrnes, August 15, 1945, 874.00/8-1545, Decimal Files, DSNA. Barnes's note to the Bulgarian prime minister as published in *FRUS* does not support this charge. See Barnes to Byrnes, August 14, 1945, *FRUS, 1945,* 4:284–85.

52. Chairman of the State Council (Kimon Georgiev) to General-Colonel Biriuzov, August 16, 1945, USSR, *Sovetsko-Bolgarskie otnosheniia, 1944–1948,* pp. 169–70.

53. Barnes to Byrnes, August 16, 1945, *FRUS, 1945,* 4:290.

54. See Records of the Secretary's Staff Committee, 1944–47, National Archives Microfilm Publication M1054. As Charles Bohlen later noted, "Byrnes' personal style was to operate as a loner, keeping matters restricted to a small circle of advisers (of which I think I could call myself one)" (*Witness to History, 1929–1969,* p. 256).

55. Byrnes to Barnes, August 18, 1945, *FRUS, 1945,* 4:294.

56. Barnes to Georgiev, Stainov, the Regents, and the ACC, August 20, 1945, Records of Foreign Service Posts, Sofia. For Byrnes's view of the respective ACCs

and their mission, see letter cited in note 45 above. The contemporary Bulgarian scholar Stoian Tanev maintains that this message again demanded postponement of the elections. See "Pomoshtta na Suvetskoto voenno," p. 76.

57. Letter from the Office of the British Political Representative, Sofia, August 21, 1945, Records of Foreign Service Posts, Sofia.

58. For the coordination of U.S. and British views in the days preceding the August elections see Barnes to Byrnes, August 17, 1945, 874.00/ 8-1745, Decimal Files, DSNA; Winant to Byrnes, August 22, 1945, 874.00/8-2245, ibid.; Byrnes to the British chargé in Washington (John Balfour), August, 20 1945, *FRUS, 1945,* 4:297.

59. Barnes to Byrnes, August 22, 1945, *FRUS, 1945,* 4:302.

60. Transcripts of the Meetings of the Allied Control Commission, Bulgaria, 22–24 August, 1945, Records of Foreign Service Posts, Sofia (hereafter Transcripts of ACC Bulgaria, August 22–24, 1945).

61. Barnes to Byrnes, August 22, 23, 1945, *FRUS, 1945,* 4:3O4–5.

62. Transcripts of ACC Bulgaria, August 22–24, 1945.

63. Ostoich, *BKP i izgrazhdaneto,* p. 161.

64. Isusov, *Politicheskite partii v Bulgariia,* p. 154. General A. I. Cherepanov, Biriuzov's first deputy, recalls that he, too, was interested in the circumstances of Stainov's comment. Stainov's future replacement as Bulgarian foreign minister, Georgi Kulishev, also a Zveno member, informed Cherepanov that the remarks were not inspired by rashness. Stainov simply had not foreseen the consequences of his statement. See Cherepanov, "Burnye gody v Bolgarii" (November–December 1976):115.

65. Dimitrov, "Naroden suiuz 'Zveno,' " p. 16.

66. Barnes to Stettinius, April 11, 1945, 874.00/4-1145, Decimal Files, DSNA. On August 20, 1945, just two days before Stainov's press conference, Barnes informed the State Department that he possessed a copy of a "secret bulletin" of the Bulgarian cabinet which contained a coded telegram sent to Stainov from a Bulgarian representative in London. The source of this "leak" unfortunately is not included, but Stainov cannot be excluded as the possible contact. See Barnes to Byrnes, August 20, 1945, 874.00/8-2045, Decimal Files, DSNA.

67. Transcripts of ACC Bulgaria, August 22–24, 1945.

68. Barnes to Byrnes, August 23, 1945, *FRUS, 1945,* 4:305.

69. Transcripts of ACC Bulgaria, August 22–24, 1945.

70. Ibid.

71. Ibid.

72. Barnes to Byrnes, August 24, 1945, *FRUS, 1945,* 4:309–10; Transcripts of ACC Bulgaria, August 22–24, 1945.

73. Cherepanov, "Burnye gody v Bolgarii" (November–December 1976):115.

74. Malcolm MacKintosh, "Stalin's Policies toward Eastern Europe, 1939–1948," pp. 239–40.

75. Byrnes to Barnes, August 25, 1945 (two letters), *FRUS, 1945,* 4:311–13.

76. Notes of a conversation of the deputy people's commissar of foreign affairs of the USSR (Vyshensky) with the ambassador of Bulgaria in the USSR (Mikhalchev), Moscow, November 4, 1945, USSR, *Sovetsko-Bolgarskie otnosheniia, 1944–1948,* p. 187.

77. Barnes to Byrnes, August 28, 1945, *FRUS, 1945,* 4:314.

78. Byrnes to Barnes, August 24, 1945, ibid., pp. 308–9.

79. Barnes to Byrnes, August 25, 1945, ibid., pp. 311–12.

80. Byrnes, *Speaking Frankly,* p. 244.

81. Byrnes to Barnes, August 30, 1945, *FRUS, 1945,* 4:317.

82. "Paraphrase of War Dept Cable from US Rep, ACC for Bulgaria to Supreme Allied Commander, Allied Forces Caserta," September 5, 1945, 874.00/9-645, Decimal Files, DSNA.

83. Byrnes to the acting American representative in Rumania (Roy M. Melbourne), August 11, 1945, *FRUS, 1945,* 5:566.

84. Melbourne to Byrnes, August 14, 20, 1945, ibid., pp. 566–67, 574.

85. Byrnes to Winant, August 21, 1945, ibid., pp. 581–83.

86. Byrnes to Melbourne, August 25, 1945, Harriman to Byrnes, September 3, 1945, Byrnes to Winant, September 4, 1945, ibid., pp. 494, 604, 606.

87. Philip Mosely, former political adviser at the European Advisory Council, who attended the Potsdam Conference, recalls that Stalin expressed deep concern over proposed free elections in Eastern Europe: "Any freely elected government would be anti-Soviet and this we cannot permit" (quoted in Philip E. Mosely, "Hope and Failure: American Policy towards East Central Europe, 1941–47," in Stephen D. Kerterz, ed., *The Fate of East Central Europe,* p. 70).

88. Byrnes, *Speaking Frankly,* p. 107. Later Byrnes concluded that the issue of Soviet participation in the future of postwar Japan was the cause of Molotov's intransigence (ibid., p. 108).

89. See "Proposals for a Peace Treaty with Bulgaria," London, September 12, 1945, *FRUS, 1945,* 2:148, and "Proposals for a Peace Treaty with Rumania," London, September 12, 1945, ibid., pp. 149–50.

90. Memorandum by Mr. Cavendish W. Cannon, political adviser to U.S. delegation at the Council of Foreign Ministers, to the secretary of state, September 14, 1945, ibid., p. 183.

91. "Suggested Directive to the Deputies from the Council of Foreign Ministers to Govern Them in the Drafting of a Treaty of Peace with Bulgaria," London, September 19, 1945, ibid., p. 263. An identical statement prefaced the American draft peace for Rumania (ibid., p. 266).

92. Memorandum of Conversation by Charles E. Bohlen, special assistant to the secretary of state, London, September 20, 1945, ibid., p. 268.

93. U.S. delegation, Minutes of the Sixteenth Meeting of the Council of Foreign Ministers, London, September 21, 1945, ibid., p. 304.

94. Byrnes, *Speaking Frankly,* p. 102.

95. Quoted in Ward, *Threat of Peace,* pp. 43–44.

96. Byrnes, *Speaking Frankly,* p. 108.

97. H. Stuart Hughes, "The Second Year of the Cold War: A Memoir and an Anticipation," *Commentary* 48 (August 1969), reprinted in Thomas G. Paterson, ed., *The Origins of the Cold War,* p. 102.

7. SEARCH FOR COMPROMISE

1. Isusov, *Polititcheskite partii v Bulgariia,* pp. 156–59; Ostoich, *BKP i izgrazhdaneto na narodno demokraticheskata durzhava,* p. 162; secretary of the

United States mission in Bulgaria (Milton Rewinkel) to Byrnes, September 10, 17, 1945, *FRUS, 1945,* 4:324, 330–31.

2. Isusov, *Politcheskite partii v Bulgariia,* 168–69.

3. Dimitrov, "Naroden suiuz 'Zveno,' " p. 17.

4. Isusov, *Policheskite partii v Bulgariia,* pp. 158, 169. "Document received from Nikola Petkov on 11 September, and was to be sent to Regents, Russian ACC, and US Delegation on September 12, 1945" (Second Lieutenant Kostanick to Crane, September 26, 1945, Records of Foreign Service Posts, Sofia.

5. Rewinkel to Byrnes, September 14, 18, 1945, *FRUS, 1945,* 4:329–30, 332–33.

6. Acheson to Rewinkel, September 7, 1945, ibid., pp. 319–20.

7. Barnes to Byrnes, October 6, 1945, ibid., pp. 343–44.

8. See *Narodno zemedelsko zname,* September 28, 1945, and *Svoboden narod,* September 16, 1945.

9. Report by Second Lieutenant Huey Kostanick to Major General Crane, September 26, 1945, Records of Foreign Service Posts, Sofia. This report includes a translation of forty-eight telegrams dealing with terror directed against Agrarians.

10. Kukov, *Razgrom na burzhoaznata opozitsiia,* pp. 120–22, 125.

11. Mark Ethridge and Cyril E. Black, "Negotiating on the Balkans, 1945–1947," p. 184.

12. Messer, *End of an Alliance,* p. 135.

13. Byrnes, *Speaking Frankly,* pp. 64–65; Messer, *End of an Alliance,* pp. 133, 135. According to Byrnes's account, it was not until late November that the secretary decided the time was right to request the Moscow Conference (Byrnes, *Speaking Frankly,* p. 109).

14. Barnes to Byrnes, October 30, 1945, *FRUS, 1945,* 4:357.

15. Barnes to Byrnes, October 29, 1945, Byrnes to Barnes, October 31, 1945, ibid., pp. 354–56, 358–59.

16. Byrnes to Harriman, November 6, 1945, ibid., pp. 363–64.

17. Barnes to Byrnes, November 11, 1945, ibid., pp. 369–70.

18. Harriman to Byrnes, November 14, 1945, ibid., pp. 374–75.

19. Barnes to Byrnes, November 12, 14 (two letters), 1945, ibid., pp. 370–71, 375–76, 378–79.

20. Byrnes to Barnes, November 14, 1945, ibid., pp. 376–77. The letter was transmitted to Prime Minister Georgiev on November 16. See Records of Foreign Service Posts, Sofia.

21. Barnes to Byrnes, November 17, 1945, Records of Foreign Service Posts, Sofia.

22. Telegram 133, U.S. Embassy, Moscow, to Sofia, November 20, 1945, ibid.

23. Ostoich, *BKP i izgrazhdaneto na naradno demokricheskata divizhava,* p. 172.

24. Barnes to Byrnes, November 29, 1945, *FRUS, 1945,* 4:398–400.

25. Kennan, *Memoirs,* pp. 287–88.

26. Byrnes, *Speaking Frankly,* pp. 113–14.

27. "Suggested Procedure with Regard to Bulgaria," Memorandum by the U.S. delegation at the Moscow Conference of Foreign Ministers, December, 18, 1945, *FRUS, 1945,* 2:700–701.

28. "Suggested Procedure with Regard to Rumania," Memorandum by the U.S.

delegation at the Moscow Conference of Foreign Ministers, December 18, 1945, ibid., pp. 701–2.

29. Memorandum of Conversation by the U.S. delegation at the Moscow Conference of Foreign Ministers, December 23, 1945, ibid., p. 751.

30. Ibid., pp. 753–56; Byrnes, *Speaking Frankly,* pp. 116–17.

31. Communiqué of the Moscow Conference of the three foreign ministers, Harriman to Grew, December 27, 1945, *FRUS, 1945,* 2:822.

32. Ibid., pp. 821–22.

33. Byrnes, *Speaking Frankly,* p. 122.

34. Barnes to Byrnes, January 4, 1946, *FRUS, 1946,* 6:46–47.

35. *Rabotnichesko delo,* January 7, 1946.

36. Dimitrov, "Naroden suiuz 'Zveno,' " pp. 18–20.

37. Barnes to Byrnes, March 25, 1946, *FRUS, 1946,* 6:87–89; Barnes to Byrnes, March 26, 1946, 874.00/3-2646, ibid., p. 88, n. 19.

38. Radio Sofia (in Greek), January 6, 1946, *British Broadcasting Company Daily Digest of World Broadcast and Radio Telegraph Service.*

39. Foreign Minister P. Stainov to the Bulgarian Foreign Ministry, January 8, 1946, USSR, *Sovetsko-Bolgarskie otnosheniia, 1944–1948,* p. 211. For the bland communiqué following this surprise Bulgarian visit to Moscow see "Communique of the Ministerial Council," January 11, 1946, Bulgaria, *Vunshna politika na narodna republika Bulgariia,* p. 39.

40. Barnes to Byrnes, January 13, 1946, *FRUS, 1946,* 6:50.

41. Kukov, *Razgrom na burzhoaznata opozitsiia,* p. 133.

42. "Concerning the Decision Relative to Bulgaria," TASS, January 13, 1946, as reprinted in USSR, *Sovetsko-Bolgarskie otnosheniia, 1944–1948,* p. 214.

43. Kennan to Byrnes, January 15, 1946, *FRUS, 1946,* 6:55; Barnes to Byrnes, January 15, 1946, ibid., pp. 53–54.

44. Truman, *Year of Decision* p. 552.

45. George Curry, "James F. Byrnes," in Ferrell, ed., *American Secretaries of State and Their Diplomacy,* p. 186; Geir Lundestad, *The American Non-Policy towards Eastern Europe, 1943–1947,* p. 247.

46. Quoted in De Santis, *Diplomacy of Silence,* p. 171.

47. For indications that the remaining problems in Rumania were primarily the result of Rumanian obstinacy see "Memorandum of Conversation by the First Secretary of Embassy in the Soviet Union (Page), Temporarily at Bucharest," January 9, 1946, *FRUS, 1946,* 6:562–68.

48. U.S. representative in Rumania (Burton Berry) to Byrnes, January 9, 1946, ibid., pp. 561–62.

49. "Memorandum of Conversation (Extract)," London, January 22, 1946, ibid., p. 573.

50. Byrnes to Berry, February 12, 1946, ibid., p. 576; Curry, "Byrnes," p. 199.

51. Byrnes to Cohen, January 31, 1946, *FRUS, 1946,* 6:64–65.

52. Byrnes to Barnes, February 2, 1946, ibid., pp. 65–66. Three days earlier, Barnes had complained that Washington seemed to be ignoring him and that he had received no answer to his political advice since December. See Barnes to Byrnes, January 30, 1946, ibid., pp. 62–64.

53. Cohen to Byrnes, February 2, 1946, ibid., pp. 66–68.

54. Byrnes to Cohen, February 5, 1946, ibid., p. 71.

55. Cohen to Byrnes, February 16, 1946, ibid., pp. 76–77.

56. "Aide-Memoire handed by Mr. Benjamin V. Cohen, Counselor of the Department of State to Lt. General Vladimir Stoichev, Bulgarian Representative in Washington on 22 February, 1946," U.S., Department of State, *Bulletin* 350 (March 17, 1946), p. 447.

57. Dimitrov, "Naroden suiuz 'Zveno,' " p. 20.

58. Telegram from the Bulgarian foreign minister to the Bulgarian mission in the USSR, February 27, 1946, USSR, *Sovetsko-Bolgarskie otnosheniia, 1944–1948*, pp. 218–19.

59. Soviet chargé (N. Novikov) to the secretary of state, March 7, 1946, *FRUS, 1946*, 6:84. For the Russian original see USSR *Sovetsko-Bolgarskie ontosheniia, 1944–1948*, pp. 220–22.

60. Barnes to Byrnes, March 25, 1946, *FRUS, 1946*, 6:87–88.

61. Barnes to Byrnes, March 29, 1946, ibid., pp. 92–94.

62. Acheson to Barnes, March 26, 1946, ibid., p. 92.

63. Barnes to Byrnes, March 25, 29 (two letters), April 1, 1946, ibid., pp. 88, 92–98; Dimitrov, "Bravest Democrat of All," p. 209.

64. Barnes to Byrnes, March 29, 1946, *FRUS, 1946*, 6:93.

65. Kukov, *Razgrom na burzhoaznata opozitsiia*, pp. 136–37.

66. Dimitrov, *Suchineniia*, 12:279.

67. Biriuzov, *Sovetskii soldat na Balkanakh*, pp. 311–13. Dimitrov, "Naroden suiuz 'Zveno,' " *Razgrom na burzhoaznata opozitsiia*, p. 148. Filo Khristov, "Deveti septemvri i Bulgarskata narodna armiia," p. 188.

68. Barnes to Byrnes, July 12, 1946, *FRUS, 1946*, 6:118.

8. THE DECISION TO RECOGNIZE

1. Truman, *1945*, p. 552.

2. Kennan to Byrnes, February 22, 1946, *FRUS, 1946*, 6:706.

3. De Santis, *Diplomacy of Silence*, p. 175. See also Yergin, *Shattered Peace*, pp. 170–71.

4. W. W. Rostow, *The Division of Europe after World War II*, p. 42.

5. ibid., pp. 5, 8. Rostow, then assistant chief of the Division of German and Austrian Economic Affairs within the State Department, had drafted the proposal. For the various drafts see ibid., pp. 94–119.

6. Barnes to Byrnes, June 21, 1946, *FRUS, 1946*, 6:106–7.

7. Byrnes to Barnes, July 26, 1946, ibid., p. 125.

8. Barnes to Byrnes, July 31, 1946, ibid., p. 128.

9. Ernest Bevin to Byrnes, July 1, 1946, ibid., p. 109.

10. Barnes to Byrnes, July 6, 1946, ibid., p. 113. A quick reply from Acting Secretary Acheson noted that further charges before the Nuremberg court would require Soviet assent (Acheson to Barnes, July 8, 1946, ibid., pp. 113–14).

11. Barnes to Byrnes, July 12, 1946, ibid., pp. 116–17.

12. Barnes to Byrnes, July 16, 1946, ibid., p. 119.

13. Petkov had argued in the December 7, 1945, issue of *Narodno zemedelsko zname* that the issue of the monarchy was not pressing because the heir apparent was so young.

14. Mito Isusov, "Izborite," pp. 6–7.

15. Quoted in Kukov, *Razgrom na burzhoaznata opozitsiia,* pp. 61–62; see also p. 154.

16. ibid., p. 157; *Rabotnichesko delo,* September 15, 1946. Almost 15 percent of the voters either did not cast ballots, defaced their ballots, or voted to retain the monarchy. See Isusov, "Izborite za Konstitutsionno subrania," p. 8.

17. Kukov, *Razgrom na burzhoaznata opozitsiia,* p. 158; Isusov, "Izborite za konstitutsionno subrania," p. 8.

18. Dimitrov, "Naroden suiuz 'Zveno,' " p. 23.

19. Isusov, "Izborite za konstitutsionno subraniia," p. 8.

20. Barnes to Byrnes, July 31, 1946, *FRUS, 1946,* 6:128; memorandum by Barnes for Byrnes, August 23, 1946, ibid., pp. 133–36.

21. U.S. delegation at the Paris Peace Conference to the acting secretary of state, August 29, 1946, ibid., p. 137.

22. Barnes to Byrnes, July 31, 1946, ibid., pp. 126–28.

23. U.S. delegation at the Paris Peace Conference to the acting secretary of state, August 31, September 3, 1946, ibid., pp. 139–41.

24. U.S. delegation at the Paris Peace Conference to the acting secretary of state, September 13, 1946, ibid., pp. 143–44.

25. Barnes to Byrnes, October 2, 1946, ibid., pp. 150–51; U.S. Department of State, *Bulletin* 383 (November 3, 1946), p. 818; USSR, *Sovetsko-Bolgarskie otnosheniia, 1944–1948,* pp. 246–47.

26. U.S. Department of State, *Bulletin* 383 (November 3, 1946), p. 820; USSR, *Sovetsko-Bolgarskie otnosheniia, 1944–1948,* p. 248.

27. Biriuzov to Major-General Robertson, October 4, 1946, USSR, *Sovetsko-Bolgarskie otnosheniia, 1944–1948,* p. 249; Biriuzov, *Sovetskii soldat na Balkanakh,* p. 316.

28. Barnes to Byrnes, October 22, 1946, *FRUS, 1946,* 6:158–59.

29. Isusov, "Izborite za konstitutsionno pubraniia," pp. 9, 13, 16; *Rabotnichesko delo,* October 4, 1946, printed the Fatherland Front draft constitution.

30. Kukov, *Razgrom na burzhoaznata opozitsiia,* p. 164.

31. Ostoich, *BKP i izgrazhdaneto,* p. 201.

32. Dimitrov, "Naroden suiuz 'Zveno,' " p. 25. Kukov, *Razgrom na burzhoaznata opozitsiia,* pp. 171–72.

33. Barnes to Byrnes, October 29, 1946, *FRUS, 1946,* 6:163–64. Ostoich, *BKP i izgrazhdareto,* p. 203. Kukov, *Razgrom na burzhoaznata opozitsiia,* p. 167.

34. Ostoich, *BKP i izgrazhdaneto,* p. 203.

35. Barnes to Byrnes, November 4, 1946, *FRUS, 1946,* 6:164–66.

36. Barnes to Byrnes, October 24, 1946, ibid., p. 164.

37. At a congress called to discuss the disastrous election results in early November, 1946, remaining Zveno members quickly polarized into left and right factions with Georgiev calling for a compromise position. In December, the left began to form

its own organizations. In early 1949, with its traditional positions long forsaken and the membership discredited, in exile, or in jail, Zveno voted to end its independent existence. See Dimitrov, "Naroden suiuz 'Zveno,' " pp. 27–33.

38. Barnes to Byrnes, November 5, 1946, *FRUS, 1946,* 6:166–67.

39. Barnes to Byrnes, January 4, 1947, *FRUS, 1947,* 4:137.

40. Byrnes to Barnes, January 18, 1947, ibid., p. 140.

41. Barnes to Byrnes, January 20, 1947, ibid., pp. 140–43.

42. Memorandum by the director of the Office of European Affairs (John D. Hickerson) to the secretary of state and undersecretary of state, September 8, 1947, ibid., p. 179.

43. Barnes to Byrnes, January 29, 1947, ibid., p. 145.

44. Kukov, *Razgrom na burzhoaznata opozitsiia,* p. 179.

45. John E. Horner, "The Ordeal of Nikola Petkov and the Consolidation of Communist Rule in Bulgaria," p. 77, n. 12; Barnes to Byrnes, January 4, 1947, *FRUS, 1947,* 4:138–40.

46. Barnes to the secretary of state (George C. Marshall), February 6, 1947, ibid., pp. 148–49.

47. Dimitrov, "Bravest Democrat of All," p. 210.

48. Horner to Marshall, May 3, 8, 1947, *FRUS, 1947,* 4:152–53, 155; Kukov, *Razgrom na burzhoaznata opozitsiia,* p. 185.

49. Horner, "Ordeal of Nikola Petkov," p. 77; Horner to Marshall, June 5, 1947, 874.00/6-547, *FRUS, 1947,* 4:159, n. 1.

50. Horner to Marshall, June 22, 1947, ibid., pp. 164–66; Kukov, *Razgrom na burzhoaznata opozitsiia,* p. 187.

51. Horner, "Ordeal of Nikola Petkov," p. 78.

52. Horner to Marshall, June 7, 1947, *FRUS, 1947,* 4:162.

53. Minutes of the Secretary of State's Staff Meeting, Washington, June 9, 1947, ibid., p. 163.

54. Statement by the President upon Ratification of Peace Treaties, U.S. Department of State, *Bulletin* 415 (June 22, 1947), p. 1214.

55. "Letter from Major-General Robertson to Lieutenant General Cherepanov, August 18, 1947, ibid., 426 (August 31, 1947), pp. 429–30.

56. Horner, "Ordeal of Nikola Petkov," p. 81.

57. "Letter from Lieutenant General Cherepanov to Major-General Robertson," August 22, 1947, U.S. Department of State, *Bulletin* 426 (August 31, 1947), p. 430.

58. U.S. Embassy, Moscow, to USSR Foreign Office, August 23, 1947, ibid., 427 (September 7, 1947), p. 481.

59. Smith to the Soviet Foreign Office, August 30, 1947, ibid., September 14, 1947, p. 532.

60. Horner, "Ordeal of Nikola Petkov," pp. 80–83.

61. Memorandum by the director of the Office of European Affairs (John D. Hickerson) to the secretary of state and undersecretary of state, September 8, 1947, *FRUS, 1947,* 4:181.

62. "Announcement by Acting Secretary of State Lovett," October 1, U.S. Department of State *Bulletin* 432 (October 12, 1947), p. 181, n. 5.

63. "Press Communication," Moscow, September 16, 1947, USSR, *Sovetsko-Bolgarskie otnosheniia, 1944–1948,* pp. 359–60; "Communique", Sofia, September 16, 1947, Bulgaria, *Vunshna politika na narodno republika Bulgariia,* p. 94; U.S. Department of State, *Bulletin* 433 (October 19, 1947), p. 771.

64. Bulgaria, *Istoriia na Bulgarskata komunisticheska partiia,* p. 347.

CONCLUSION

1. Henry Kissinger, *Years of Upheaval,* p. 38.

Bibliography

PRIMARY SOURCES

ARCHIVAL MATERIALS

United Kingdom

Foreign Office. General Correspondence, Political: United States of America. FO 371/ 1919 (3431, 3635, 3835), 1938–45.
Prime Minister. Confidential Papers, 1939–46. PREM 4.
————. Operations Papers, 1938–46. PREM 3.
Public Record Office. General Correspondence, Political: Russia, 1906–45. FO 371.
War Cabinet. Chiefs of Staff Committee, Minutes, 1939–46. Cab. 79.
————. Deputy Chiefs of Staff Committee. Minutes, 1939–47. Cab. 82.
————. Memoranda, 1939–45. Cab. 66.
————. Minutes, 1939–45. Cab. 65.

United States

Records of the Department of State, 1940–47. National Archives, Record Group 59. Decimal Files.
————. Record Group 59. Harley Notter Papers. Advisory Committee on Postwar Foreign Policy (Political Subcommittee, Subcommittee on Territorial Problems, Subcommittee on European Organizations, Interdivisional Committee on Russia and Poland, Subcommittee on Security Problems), Policy Committee, Country-Area Committee, Postwar Programs Committee, Stettinius Record, 1942–45.
————. Lot 122, Secretary's Staff Committee.
Records of the Foreign Service Posts of the Department of State. Record Group 84. Washington National Records Center.
Records of Office of Strategic Services, 1941–1945. National Archives, Record Group 226.
Records of the War Department, General and Special Staffs, Civil Affairs Division, 1941–45. National Archives, Record Group 165.
————. Office of the Chief of Staff, 1941–45. National Archives, Record Group 165.
————. Operations Division, 1941–45. National Archives, Record Group 165.
————. Joint Chiefs of Staff, Geographic File, 1942–45. Record Group 218.
U.S. Delegation, Allied Control Commission, Bulgaria, "History of the Al-

228BIBLIOGRAPHY

lied Control Commission, Bulgaria. Vols. 1–2 to 31 March, 1946," Office
of the Chief of Military History, MMBNA 8.3.3, AA.

PUBLISHED DOCUMENTS

Bulgaria. *Dokumente ueber die feindliche und aggressive Politik der Regierung der Vereinigten Staaten gegenueber der Volksrepublik Bulgarien.* Berlin, 1954.

_____. *Govori Radiostantsiia "Khristo Botev" 23 iuli 1941–22 septemvri 1944.* 7 vols. Sofia, 1948–52.

_____. *The Trial of Nikola D. Petkov, August 5–15, 1947: Record of the Judicial Proceedings.* Sofia, 1947.

_____. *Ustanoviavane i ukrepvane na narodnodemokratichnata vlast: Septemvri 1944–mai 1945: Sbornik dokumenti.* Sofia, 1969.

_____. *Vunshna politika na narodna republika Bulgariia: Sbornik ot dokumenti i materiali v dva toma, I, 1944–1962.* Sofia, 1979.

Campbell, Thomas M., and Herring, George C., eds. *The Diaries of Edward R. Stettinius, Jr., 1943–1946.* New York, 1975.

Dimitrov, Georgi. *Suchineniia.* 14 vols. Sofia, 1951–55.

Etzold, Thomas H., and Gaddis, John L., eds. *Containment: Documents on American Policy and Strategy, 1945–1950.* New York, 1978.

Hillgrueber, Andreas, ed. and annot. *Staatsmaenner und Diplomaten bei Hitler.* 2 vols. Frankfurt am Main, 1970.

Loewenheim, Francis L., et al., eds. *Roosevelt and Churchill: Their Secret Wartime Correspondence.* New York, 1975.

U.S. Department of State. *Department of State Bulletin.* Vols 5–16. 1941–47.

_____. *Foreign Relations of the United States.* Annual vols., 1933–47. Washington, 1950–70.

_____. *Foreign Relations of the United States: The Conferences at Cairo and Teheran, 1943.* Washington, 1961.

_____. *Foreign Relations of the United States: The Conference of Berlin (The Potsdam Conference), 1945.* 2 vols. Washington, 1960.

_____. *Foreign Relations of the United States: The Conferences at Malta and Yalta, 1945.* Washington, 1955.

U.S., Office of the Assistant Secretary of War. *The Overseas Target: War Report of the OSS.* 2 vols. Washington, 1976.

USSR. *Correspondence between the Chairman of the Council of Ministers of the U.S.S.R. and the President of the U.S.A. and the Prime Minister of Great Britain during the Great Patriotic War of 1941–1945.* 2 vols. Moscow, 1957.

_____. *Suvetsko-Bulgarskite otnosheniia: Dokumenti.* Moscow, 1944.

_____. *Sovetsko-Bolgarskie otnosheniia, 1944–1948g.: Dokumenty i materialy.* Moscow, 1969.

_____. *Tegeran, Ialta, Potsdam: Sbornik dokumenty.* Moscow, 1967.

_____. *Vneshniaia politika Sovetskogo soiuza v period otechestvennoi voiny: Dokumenty i materialy.* 2 vols. Moscow, 1944–46.

Valev, L. B., et al., eds. *Sovetsko-Bolgarskie otnosheniia i sviazi: Dokumenty i materialy, Tom 1, Noiabr 1917–SENTIABR' 1944.* Moscow, 1976.

Woodward, Sir Ernest Llewellyn, ed. *British Foreign Policy in the Second World War.* 5 vols. 1970–76.

MEMOIRS

Acheson, Dean. *Present at the Creation.* New York, 1969.

Barnes, Maynard B. "The Current Situation in Bulgaria." Lecture, National War College, Washington, June 3, 1947.

Biriuzov, Sergei S. *Belgradskaia operatsiia.* Moscow, 1964.

_____. *Kogda gremeli pushki.* Moscow, 1961.

_____. *Sovetskii soldat na Balkanakh.* Moscow, 1963.

_____. *Surovye gody.* Moscow, 1966.

Bohlen, Charles. *Witness to History, 1929–1969.* New York, 1973.

Byrnes, James F. *All in One Lifetime.* New York, 1958.

_____. *Speaking Frankly.* New York, 1947.

Churchill, Winston S. *The Second World War: The Grand Alliance.* Boston, 1950.

_____. *The Second World War: The Hinge of Fate.* Boston, 1950.

_____. *The Second World War: Closing the Ring.* Boston, 1951.

_____. *The Second World War: Triumph and Tragedy.* Boston, 1953.

Clay, Lucius D. *Decision in Germany.* Garden City, 1950.

Dalton, Hugh. *The Fateful Years: Memoirs. 1931–1945.* London, 1957.

De Gaulle, Charles. *The Complete War Memoirs.* New York, 1964.

Deakin, F. W. D. *European Resistance Movements, 1939–1945.* New York, 1964.

Deane, John R. *Strange Alliance.* New York, 1947.

Djilas, Milovan. *Conversations with Stalin.* Translated by Michael B. Petrovich. New York, 1962.

Dragoicheva, Tsola N. *Iz moite spomeni.* Sofia, 1979.

_____. *Pobeda.* Sofia, 1979.

Eden, Anthony. *The Reckoning.* Boston, 1965.

Eisenhower, Dwight D. *Crusade in Europe.* London, 1948.

Grew, Joseph C. *Turbulent Era: A Diplomatic Record of Forty Years, 1904–1945.* 2 vols. London, 1953.

Harriman, W. Averill, and Abel, Elie. *Special Envoy to Churchill and Stalin, 1941–1946.* New York, 1975.

Hull, Cordell. *The Memoirs of Cordell Hull.* 2 vols. New York, 1948.

Jebb, Gladwyn. *Memoirs.* London, 1972.

Jones, Joseph M. *The Fifteen Weeks.* New York, 1955.

Kennan, George F. *Memoirs, 1925–1950.* Boston, 1967.

Knatchbull-Higessen, Hugh. *Diplomat in Peace and War.* London, 1949.

Leahy, William D. *I Was There.* New York, 1950.

Maiskey, Ivan. *Memoirs of a Soviet Ambassador, the War: 1939–43*. New York, 1968.
Mikolajczyk, Stanislaw. *The Pattern of Soviet Domination*. London, 1948.
Millis, Walter, ed. *The Forrestal Diaries*. New York, 1951.
Murphy, Robert. *Diplomat among Warriors*. Garden City, 1964.
Rendel, Sir George. *The Sword and the Olive: Recollections of Diplomacy and the Foreign Service, 1913–1954*. London, 1957.
Schmidt, Paul. *Statist auf diplomatischen Buehore 1923–1945*. Bonn, 1958.
Shtemenko, S. M. *The Last Six Months: Russia's Final Battles with Hitler's Armies in World War II*. Translated by Guy Daniels. Garden City, 1977.
————. *The Soviet General Staff at War (1941–1945)*. Moscow, 1970.
Slessor, Sir John. *The Central Blue*. New York, 1957.
Smith, Walter B. *My Three Years in Moscow*. Philadelphia, 1950.
Stettinius, Edward R. *Roosevelt and the Russians: The Yalta Conference*. Edited by Walter Johnson. Garden City, 1949.
Stimson, Henry L., and Bundy, McGeorge. *On Active Service in Peace and War*. New York, 1947.
Sulzberger, C. L. *A Long Row of Candles: Memoirs and Diaries, 1934–1954*. New York, 1964.
Sweet-Escott, Bickham. *Baker Street Irregular*. London, 1965.
Truman, Harry S. *Year of Decision*. New York, 1955.
Wilson, Field Marshal Lord. *Eight Years Overseas, 1939–1947*. London, 1950.
Zhukov, G. K. *Vospominaniia i razmyshlennia*. Moscow, 1969.

NEWSPAPERS

Izgrev (Sofia)
Izvestiia (Moscow)
Narodno zemedelsko zname (Sofia)
New York Times
Otechestvan front (Sofia)
Pravda (Moscow)
Rabotnichesko delo (Sofia)
Svoboden narod (Sofia)
Zemedelsko zname (Sofia)

SECONDARY SOURCES

BOOKS

Ablova, R. I. *Sotrudnichestvo Sovetskogo i Bolgarskogo narodov v bor'be protiv fashizma (1941–1945g.)*. Moscow, 1973.
Alperovitz, Gar. *Atomic Diplomacy: Hiroshima and Potsdam*. New York, 1965.

Antonov, A. I. *Istoriia velikoe otechestvennoi voiny Sovetskogo soiuza 1941–1945 v shesta tomakh.* Moscow, 1962.

Atanasov, Shteriu, et al. *Kratka istoriia na otechestvenata voina.* Sofia, 1958.

Auty, Phyllis, and Clogg, Richard, eds. *British Policy towards Wartime Resistance in Yugoslavia and Greece.* London, 1975.

Barker, Elisabeth. *British Policy in South-East Europe in the Second World War.* London, 1976.

——. *Truce in the Balkans.* London, 1948.

Beloff, Max. *The Foreign Policy of Soviet Russia.* 2 vols. London, 1947, 1949.

Bialer, Seweryn, ed. *Stalin and His Generals.* New York, 1969.

Black, Cyril E. *The Establishment of Constitutional Government in Bulgaria.* Princeton, 1943.

Bozhinov, Voin. *Politicheskata kriza v Bulgariia prez 1943–1944.* Sofia, 1957.

——. *Zashtitata na natsionalnota nezavisimost na Bulgariia, 1944–47.* Sofia, 1962.

Brown, Anthony Cave. *The Last Hero: Wild Bill Donovan.* New York, 1982.

Brzezinski, Zbigniew. *The Soviet Bloc.* Cambridge, 1969.

Bulgaria. *Istoriia na Bulgarskata komunisticheska partiia: Za sistemata na partiinata prosveta.* Sofia, 1978.

——. *Istoriia na Bulgarskata komunisticheska partiia.* Sofia, 1977.

Clemens, Diane Shaver. *Yalta.* New York, 1970.

Cline, Ray S. *United States Army in World War II: The War Department, Washington Command Post: The Operations Division.* Washington, 1955.

Dallek, Robert. *Franklin D. Roosevelt and American Foreign Policy, 1932–1945.* New York, 1981.

Davis, Lynn E. *The Cold War Begins: Soviet-American Conflict over Eastern Europe.* Princeton, 1974.

Deacon, R. A. *A History of the British Secret Service.* London, 1969.

De Santis, Hugh. *The Diplomacy of Silence: The American Foreign Service, the Soviet Union, and the Cold War, 1933–1947.* Chicago, 1980.

Devine, Robert. *Roosevelt and World War II.* Baltimore, 1970.

Dimitrov, Ilcho. *Burzhoaznata opozitsiia v Bulgariia 1939–1944.* Sofia, 1969.

Druks, Herbert. *Harry S. Truman and the Russians, 1945–1953.* New York, 1966.

Feis, Herbert. *Between War and Peace: The Potsdam Conference.* Princeton, 1960.

——. *Churchill-Roosevelt-Stalin: The War They Waged and the Peace They Sought.* Princeton, 1957.

——. *From Trust to Terror: The Onset of the Cold War, 1945–1950.* New York, 1970.

Filchev, Ivan. *Bulgaro-Suvetskata boina druzhba prez otechestvenata voina (1944–1945g.).* Sofia, 1961.

Fleming, D. F. *The Cold War*. 2 vols. Garden City, 1961.

Gaddis, John L. *The United States and the Origins of the Cold War, 1941–1947*. New York, 1972.

Ganevich, I. V. *Deiatel'nost' Bolgarskoi kommunisticheskoi partii po ukrepleniiu diktatury proletariata, (sentiabr') sept., 1944–1948*. Kiev, 1974.

Georgiev, Georgi. *2194 dni. Khronika na edna pobeda, 1939–1945*. Sofia, 1969.

Hahn, Werner. *Postwar Soviet Politics: The Fall of Zhdanov and the Defeat of Moderation, 1946–53*. Ithaca, 1982.

Hart, B. H. Liddell. *History of the Second World War*. London, 1970.

Herring, George C. *Aid to Russia, 1941–1946: Strategy, Diplomacy, and the Origins of the Cold War*. New York, 1973.

Hoppe, Hans-Joachim. *Bulgarien—Hitlers eigenwilliger Verbuendeter*. Stuttgart, 1979.

Howard, Michael. *Grand Strategy*. London, 1972.

———. *The Mediterranean Strategy in the Second World War*. London, 1968.

Iatrides, John O. *Revolt in Athens*. Princeton, 1972.

Inozemtsev, N., et al. *Mezhdunarodnye otnosheniia posle vtoroi mirovoi voiny*. 3 vols. Moscow, 1962.

Institut istorii Bolgarskoi kommunisticheskoi partii pre TsK BKP. *Istoriia Bolgarskoi kommunisticheskoi partii*. Moscow, 1971.

Israelian, V. I. *Diplomaticheskaia istoriia velikoi otechestvennoi voiny*. Moscow, 1959.

Isusov, Mito. *Politicheskite partii v Bulgariia, 1944–1948*. Sofia, 1978.

———. *Rabotnicheskoto klasa v Bulgariia, 1944–1947*. Sofia, 1971.

Ivanov, L. N. *Ocherki mezhdunarodnykh otnoshenii v period vtorai mirovoi voiny*. Moscow, 1958.

Janis, Irving L. *Victims of Groupthink: A Psychological Study of Foreign Policy and Fiascoes*. Boston, 1972.

Kamenov, Evgenii *Ikonomicheskata pomosht na Suvetskiia Suiuz—reshavasht faktor za izgrazhdaneto na sotsializma v Bulgariia*. Sofia, 1955.

Kazasov, Dimo. *Burni godini, 1918–1944*. Sofia, 1949.

Kerterz, Stephen D., ed. *The Fate of East Central Europe*. Notre Dame, 1956.

Kirchev, Ivan. *Otechestvenata voina, 1944–1945*. Sofia, 1946.

Kolko, Gabriel. *The Politics of War: The World and United States Foreign Policy, 1943–1945*. New York, 1968.

Krecker, Lothar. *Deutschland und die Tuerkei im zweiten Weltkreig*. Frankfurt am Main, 1964.

Kukov, Kol'o *Razgrom na burzhoaznata opozitsiia (1944–1947g.)*. Sofia, 1968.

Kuznetsov, P. G. *Marshal Tolbukhin*. Moscow, 1966.

LaFeber, Walter. *America, Russia and the Cold War, 1945–1975*. New York, 1976.

Lalov, Ignat. *Voinishkite komiteti i Bulgarskata narodna prez septemvri 1944*. Sofia, 1959.

Lalov, Ignat; Kostadinova, M.; and Tashev, T. *Pomoshtnik komandirite v otechestvenata voina*. Sofia, 1975.

Lundestad, Geir. *The American Non-Policy towards Eastern Europe, 1943– 1947*. New York, 1978.

Mammarella, Giuseppe, *L'Italia dopo il fascismo, 1943–68*. Bologna, 1970.

Martin, Curtis H. "United States Diplomacy and the Issue of Representative Government in the Former German Satellite States, 1943–1946: A Study of Foreign Policy and the Foreign Policy Process." Ph.D. dissertation, Tufts University, 1974.

Mastny, Vojtech. *Russia's Road to the Cold War: Diplomacy, Warfare, and the Politics of Communism, 1941–1945*. New York, 1979.

Matloff, Maurice. *United States Army in World War II, the War Department: Strategic Planning for Coalition Warfare, 1943–1944*. Washington, 1959.

Matsulenko, V. A. *Razgrom nemetsko-fashistskikh voisk na Balkanskom napravlenii: Avgust–sentiabr' 1944*. Moscow, 1957.

Mayne, Richard. *The Recovery of Europe, 1945–1973*. New York, 1973.

McCagg, William O. *Stalin Embattled, 1943–1948*. Detroit, 1978.

McNeill, William H. *America, Britain and Russia*. London, 1953.

Mee, Charles L., Jr. *Meeting at Potsdam*. New York, 1975.

Messer, Robert L. *The End of an Alliance: James F. Byrnes, Roosevelt, Truman, and the Origins of the Cold War*. Chapel Hill, 1982.

Miller, Marshall L. *Bulgaria during the Second World War*. Stanford, 1975.

Minasian, M. M. *Osvobozhdenie narodov iugo-vostochnoi Evropy*. Moscow, 1967.

Mosely, Philip. *The Kremlin and World Politics*. New York, 1960.

Moser, Charles A. *Dimitrov of Bulgaria: A Political Biography of Dr. Georgi M. Dimitrov*. Ottawa Ill., 1979.

Nakov, Angel. *Bulgaro-Suvetski otnosheniia, 1944–1948*. Sofia, 1978.

———. *Internatsional'naia missiia Sovetskikh vosik v Bolgarii*. Moscow, 1973.

Notter, Harley A. *Postwar Foreign Policy Preparation, 1939–1945*. Washington, 1949.

Oren, Nissan. *Bulgarian Communism: The Road to Power, 1934–1944*. New York, 1971.

———. *The Revolution Administered: Agrarianism and Communism in Bulgaria*. Baltimore, 1973.

Ostoich, Petur D. *BKP i izgrazhdaneto na narodno-demokraticheskata durzhava: 9 septemvri 1944–dekemvri 1947*. Sofia, 1967.

Padev, Michael. *Dimitrov Wastes No Bullets: Nikola Petkov, the Test Case*. London, 1978.

Paterson, Thomas G. *On Every Front: The Making of the Cold War*. New York, 1979.

———. *The Origins of the Cold War*. Lexington, 1974.

———. *Soviet-American Confrontation: Postwar Reconstruction and the Origins of the Cold War.* Baltimore, 1973.

———, ed. *Cold War Critics.* Chicago, 1971.

Petrov, S. *Strategiiata i taktikata na BKP v borbata protiv monarkho-fashizma (1941–1944).* Sofia, 1969.

Petrova, Slavka *Borbata na BKP za ustanoviavane narodnodemokraticheskata vlast, mai–septemvri 1944.* Sofia, 1964.

———. *Devetoseptemvriiska khronika.* Sofia, 1969.

Pogue, Forrest C. *United States Army in World War II, The War Department, The European Theatre of Operations: The Supreme Command.* Washington, 1954.

Quinlan, Paul D. *Clash over Romania: British and American Policies towards Romania, 1938–1947.* Los Angeles, 1977.

Rachev, Stoian. *Angliia i suprotivitelnoto dvizhenie na Balkanite (1940–1945).* Sofia, 1978.

Roberts, Walter F. *Tito, Mihailovic and the Allies, 1941–1945.* New Brunswick, 1973.

Rostow, W. W. *The Division of Europe after World War II: 1946.* Austin, 1981.

Rothschild, Joseph. *The Communist Party of Bulgaria: Origins and Development, 1883–1936.* New York, 1959.

———. *East Central Europe between the Two World Wars.* Seattle, 1974.

Seaton, Albert. *The Russo-German War, 1941–45.* New York, 1970.

Sharlanov, Diniu *Otechestveniiat front, 1942–1944.* Sofia, 1964.

Sharlanov, Diniu, and Damianova, Penka. *Miastoto i roliato na otechestveniia front v sistemata na narodnata demokratsiia.* Sofia, 1968.

Sherwood, Robert. *Roosevelt and Hopkins.* New York, 1948.

Smith, Gaddis. *American Diplomacy during the Second World War, 1941–45.* New York, 1967.

Stafford, David. *Britain and European Resistance, 1940–1945: A Survey of the Special Operations Executive, with Documents.* Toronto, 1980.

Stavrianos, L. S. *The Balkans since 1453.* New York, 1959.

Steel, Ronald. *Walter Lippmann and the American Century.* Boston, 1980.

Stoler, Mark A. *The Politics of the Second Front: American Military Planning and Diplomacy in Coalition Warfare, 1941–43.* Westport Conn., 1977.

Tikhomirov, V. P. *Sotsialisticheskoe pereustroistvo sel'skogokhoziaistva Bolgarii.* Moscow, 1951.

Toshkova, Vitka. *Bulgariia i tretiiat Raikh.* Sofia, 1975.

Trukhanovsky, V. G. *Antoni Eden: Stranitsy Angliiskoi diplomatii, 30–50 e gody.* Moscow, 1974.

———. *British Foreign Policy during World War II.* Moscow, 1970.

———. *Istoriia mezhdunarodnykh otnoshenii i vneshnei politiki SSSR, 1917–1967 gg.* Moscow, 1967.

———. *Uinsten Cherchill: Politicheskaia biografiia.* Moscow, 1969.

Ulam, Adam. *Expansion and Coexistence: The History of Soviet Foreign Policy, 1917–1967*. New York, 1969.
_____. *The Rivals: America and Russia since World War II*. New York, 1971.
Vasilev, I. U. *O Turetskom 'neutralitite' vo vtoroi mirovoi voini*. Moscow, 1951.
Ward, Patricia D. *The Threat of Peace: James F. Byrnes and the Council of Foreign Ministers, 1945–1946*. Kent, 1979.
Watson, Hugh-Seton. *The East European Revolution*. New York, 1961.
Weisband, Edward. *Turkish Foreign Policy, 1943–1945: Small State Diplomacy and Great Power Politics*. Princeton, 1973.
Williams, William Appleman. *The Tragedy of American Diplomacy*. New York, 1962.
Wittner, Lawrence S. *American Intervention in Greece, 1943–1949*. New York, 1982.
Wolfe, Thomas W. *Soviet Power and Europe, 1945–1970*. Baltimore, 1970.
Wolff, Robert Lee. *The Balkans in Our Times*. Cambridge, 1956.
Yergin, Daniel. *Shattered Peace: The Origins of the Cold War and the National Security State*. Boston, 1977.

ARTICLES

Andonov, Vladimir. "Osvoboditelniiat pokhod na Suvetskata armiia v Bulgariia prez purvata polovina na septemvri 1944." *Voennoistoricheski sbornik* 1 (1975): 37–47.
Baisninski, Kostadin, et al. "Duskusiia po vuprosa za burzhoaznata opozitsiia i kharaktera na pravitelstvoto na Muraviev." *Izvsetiia na instituta po istoriia na BKP* 30 (1974): 167–354.
Balabanov, Nicolas. "A Year in Ankara." *Bulgarian Review 4* (December 1964): 47–51.
_____. "A Year in Ankara." *Bulgarian Review 5* December 1965): 49–55.
_____. "A Year in Ankara." *Bulgarian Review 6* (December 1966): 33–42.
_____. "The 5th September 1944 in Ankara." *Bulgarian Review 3* (November 1963): 32–34.
Biriuzov, Sergei S. "Bratiia po dukh i borba." In Ignat Lalov, ed., *Ot Volga do Balkana*, pp. 19–38. Sofia, 1967.
_____. "Ekho geroicheskoi bor'by." *Rabotnichesko delo*, August 31, 1964.
_____. "Osvoboditel'nyi pokhod na Balkany (vospominaniia)." *Novaia i noveishaia istoriia* 6 (1961): 91–101.
_____. "Poiski pravil'nogo resheniia." *Voennoistoricheskii zhurnal* 8 (May 1963): 59–77.
Black, Cyril E. "The Start of the Cold War in Bulgaria: A Personal View." *Review of Politics* 41 (April 1979): 163–202.
Blagodatov, A. V. "Ramo do ramo." In Ignat Lalov, *Ot Volga do Balkana*, pp. 176–82. Sofia, 1967.

Bozhinov, Voin. "Politikata na SASht spriamo Bulgariia prez 1944 g." *Isto-richeski pregled* 22 (November–December 1966): 67–82.

————. "Vunshno-politicheskata polozhenia na Bulgariia v navecherieto i po vreme na devetoseptemvruskata vustanie." *Voennoistoricheski sbornik* 5 (1964): 68–76.

Chary, Frederick B. "Prezident Ruzevelt i Bulgarskite sondazhi za mir, 1944 g." In *Bulgariia v svete ot drevnostta do nashi dni*, pp. 269–75. Sofia, 1979.

————, trans. and ed. "The Diary of Bogdan Filov, 1941–1944." *South-eastern Europe* 1 (1974): 46–71; 3 (1976): 17–60; 4 (1977): 48–107.

Cherepanov, A. I. "Burnye gody v Bolgarii (1944–1947)." *Novaia i noveishaia istoriia* 20 (September–October 1976), 101–11; (November–December 1976), 107–22.

————. "Nezabravimi sreshti." In Ignat Lalov, *Ot Volga do Balkana*, 149–58. Sofia, 1967.

Curry, George. "James F. Byrnes." In *The American Secretaries of State and Their Diplomacy*, ed. Robert H. Ferrell and Samuel Flagg Bemis, 14:87-317. New York, 1965.

Danov, A. I. "Georgi Dimitrov i otechestvenata voina na Bulgarskiia narod (1944–1945)." *Izvestiia na instituta po istoriia na BKP* 28 (1972): 95–138.

De Santis, Hugh. "Conflicting Images of the USSR: American Career Diplomats and the Balkans, 1944–1946." *Political Science Quarterly*, 94 (Fall 1979): 475–94.

Dimitrov, Dr. Georgi. "Bravest Democrat of All." *Saturday Evening Post*, December 6, 1947, pp. 28–29, 208–10.

Dimitrov, G. "Vzaimodeistvieto mezhdu Bulgarskata norodna armiia i voiskata na 3-ti Ukrainski front prez otechestvenata voina na Bulgariia." *Voennoistoricheski sbornik* 44 (January-February 1975): 48–60.

Dimitrov, Ilcho. "Colonel Donovan's Mission in Sofia." *Bulgarian Historical Review* 6, no. 4 (1978): 3–13.

————. "Naroden suiuz 'Zveno' (1 oktomvri 1944–19 fevruari 1949 g.)." *Istoricheski pregled* 26 (September–October 1970): 3–33.

————. "Poslednato pravitelstvo na burzhoazna Bulgariia." *Istoricheski pregled* 20 (September–October 1964): 3–33.

————. "Vunshnata politika na pravitelstvo na Ivan Bagrianov (1 iune–1 septemvri 1944g.)." *Godishnik na Sofiiskiia universitet* 41, istoriia (1967): 182–274.

Doinova, Tsvetnan. "Dokumentalnite materiali za otechestvenata voina 1944–1945 g. v tsentralniia durzhaven arkhiv na NR Bulgariia." *Voennoistoricheski sbornik* 33 (May–June 1964): 51–57.

Doronchenkov, A. I. "Po vuprosa za otnosheniiata mezhdu Suvetskata armiia i Bulgarskiia narod v purvite godini sled osvobozhdenieto na Bulgariia ot fashizma (1944–1947)." *Voennoistoricheski sbornik* 40 (January–February 1971): 3–15.

Dragoliubov, Petko. "Izbornite borbi i rabotata na BKP v narodnoto subranie

(1945–1949)." *Izvestiia na instituta po istoriia na BKP* 13 (1965): 209–68.

——. "Kum vuprosa za roliata i miastoto na komitetite na otechestveniia front v sistemata na narodnato vlast." *Izvestiia na instituta po istoriia na BKP* 12 (1964): 119–52.

Ethridge, Mark, and Black, Cyril E. "Negotiating on the Balkans, 1945–1947." In Raymond Dennett and Joseph E. Johnson, *Negotiating with the Russians*, pp. 171–206. Boston, 1951.

Gaddis, John Lewis. "Containment: A Reassessment." *Foreign Affairs* 55 (July 1977): 873–88.

Ganev, Dimitur. "Doklad o polozhenii v Bolgarii." *Izvestiia na instituta po istoriia na BKP* 42 (1980): 459–67.

Giurova, S. "Bor'ba Plevenskoi oblastnoi organizatsii BRP(k) protiv oppozitsii vo vremia referenduma i vyborov v velikoe narodnoe sobranie." *Izvestiia na instituta po istoriia na BKP* 36 (1977): 333–66.

Gornenski, Nikifor. "Podgotovka i izvurshvane na devetoseptemvriiskoto vustanie." *Istoricheski pregled* 4 (1959): 42–64.

——. "Ukazaniiata na zadgranichnoto biuro na TsK na do partiiata prez vreme na podgotovkata i provezhdaneto na devetoseptemvriiskoto vustania." *Voennoistoricheski sbornik* 5 (1964): 113–20.

Gosztony, Peter. "Der 9 September 1944: Einer Studie zur Frage der Neutralitaet und Wehrbereitschaft am Beispiel der September-Ereignisse 1944 in Bulgarien." In *Neutrale Kleinstaaten in zweiten Weltkrieg*, pp. 85–106. Muensingen, 1973.

Horner, John E. "The Ordeal of Nikola Petkov and the Consolidation of Communist Rule in Bulgaria." *Survey* 1 (Spring 1974): 75–83.

Hughes, H. Stuart. "The Second Year of the Cold War: A Memoir and an Anticipation." *Commentary* (August 1969): 27–32. Reprinted in Thomas G. Paterson, ed., *The Origins of the Cold War*, pp. 100–113. Lexington, 1974.

Iordanov, Boris. "Osobenosti na rabotnicheskiia kontrol nad proizvodstvoto na kapitalisticheskata promishlenost v Bulgariia (1944–1947g.)." *Istoricheski pregled* 29 (January–February 1973): 43–54.

——. "Partiiata i rabotnicheskiiat kontrol nad kapitalisticheskata promishlenost v Bulgariia (1944–1947)." *Istoricheski pregled* 25 (March–June 1969): 106–21.

Isusov, Mito. "Dvizhenieto za kooperativno obrabotvane na zemiata v Bulgariia." Istoricheski pregled 25 (March–June 1969): 147–171.

——. "Formirane na opozitsionnite politicheski sili v Bulgariia (1944–1945g.)." *Izvestiia na instituta po istoriia na BKP* 27 (1972): 123–68.

——. "Izborite za konstitutsionno subrania i razpolozhenieto na politicheskite silov Bulgariia prez 1946g." *Istoricheski pregled* 32 (July–August 1976): 3–30.

——. "Otechestveniiat front i opitite za deformirane na novata parlamentarna sistema v Bulgariia (1945–1946g.)." *Istoricheski pregled* 4–5 (1974): 160–88.

——. "Revoliutsionniiat protses i politicheskata sistema na narodnata demokratsiia v Bulgariia (1944–1948)." *Istoricheski pregled* 4–5 (1979): 83–113.

Isusov, Mito. "Stopanski yazkhodi no Bulgariia v otechestvenota voina 1944–1945," Istoricheski pregled 25 (January–February 1969): 42–59.

———. "Vasil Kolarov's Mission in Europe in 1946." *Bulgarian Historical Review* 4 (1977): 3–23.

Ivanov, Colonel Ivan T. "Angliiskata i severoamerikanskata strategiia na Balkanite prez liatoto na 1944 g. i opitite na Bulgarskata burzhoaziia za izlizane ot voinata." *Voennoistoricheski sbornik* 37 (Sept.–Oct) (1968): 3–19.

Khakov, Dimitur. "Osnovni nasoki na vunshnata politika na Turtsiia prez vtorate svetovna voina." *Istoricheski pregled* 6 (1967): 3–33.

Khristov, Filo. "Deveti septemvri i Bulgarskata narodna armiia." *Istoricheski pregled* 25 (March–June 1969): 172–93.

———. "Kum vuprosa za organizatsionnite formi na BKP v armiiata (1944–1949g.)." *Voennoistoricheski sbornik* 4 (1965): 37–47.

———. "Pobedite na suvetskata armiia i tiakhnoto znachenie za razmakha na vuoruzhenata borba i uspekha na devetoseptemvriiskato narodno anti-fashistko vustanie." *Voennoistoricheski sbornik* 34 (March–April 1965): 3–15.

Khristov, Khristo "Devetoseptemvriiskata sotsialisticheska revoliutsiia i Bulgarskata istoricheska nauka." *Istoricheski pregled* 25 (March–June 1969): 5–17.

Kinov, Ivan. "Znachenieto na pobedite na Suvetskata armiia za uspekha na devetoseptemvriiskoto vustania i pomoshta na Suvetskiia suiuz za otbranata na narodna republika Bulgariia." *Voennoistoricheski sbornik* 33 (September–October 1964): 33–39.

Kolonkin, M. "Suzdavane, razvitie i ukrepvana na pomoshtnik—komandirskii institut v Bulgarskata narodna armiia." *Voennoistoricheski sbornik* 47 (March–April 1978): 37–49.

Kostova, Emilio. "Bulgarskata istoriopis za devetoseptemvriiskoto vuoruzheno vustania prez 1944 g." *Izvestiia na instituta po istoriia na BKP* 31 (1974): 163–88.

Kukov, Kol'o. "Borbata na BKP za preodoliavane porazhenskata deinost na Gemeto i negovata grupa po vreme na otechestvenata voina." *Voennoistoricheski sbornik* 34 (January–February 1965): 17–29.

Kuneva, Kera. "Putiat na Suvetskata armiia prez Bulgariia." *Vekove* 3 (July–October 1974): 42–57.

Lazarov, Kiril. "Obaianie i ocharovanie." In *Spomeni za Georgi Dimitrov,* 2: 401–13. Sofia, 1971.

MacKintosh, Malcolm. "Stalin's Policies toward Eastern Europe, 1939–1948: The General Picture." In Thomas T. Hammond, *The Anatomy of Communist Takeovers,* pp. 229–43. New Haven, 1975.

Maddox, Robert James. "Atomic Diplomacy: A Study in Creative Writing." *Journal of American History* 59 (March 1973): 925–34.

Manov, Kiril. "Maior Tompsun." in Ivan Kozarov, ed., *Za svobodate na Bulgarskiia narod,* pp. 268–80. Sofia, 1967.

Marinov, Ivan "Pet dni v pravitelstvo na K. Muraviev." *Istoricheski pregled* 24 (May–June 1968): 81–102.

Mark, Eduard, "American Policy toward Eastern Europe and the Origins of the Cold War, 1941–1946: An Alternative Interpretation." *Journal of American History* 68 (September 1981): 313–36.

Mastny, Vojtech. "The Cassandra in the Foreign Commissariat: Maxim Litvinov and the Cold War." *Foreign Affairs* 59 (January 1976): 366–76.

———. "Soviet War Aims at the Moscow and Teheran Conferences of 1943." *Journal of Modern European History* 47 (1975): 481–504.

Mateev, Boris. "Za glavniia udar devetoseptemvriiskoto vuoruzheno vustanie." *Istoricheski pregled* 25 (March–June 1969): 82–105.

Melamed, A. "Preustroistvoto na otechestveniia front v edinna obshtestveno-politicheska organizatsiia." *Istoricheski pregled* 34 (November–December 1978): 3–21.

Mosely, Philip E. "Hopes and Failures: American Policy toward East Central Europe, 1941–1947," in Stephen D. Kertesz (ed.), *The Fate of East Central Europe,* Notre Dame, 1956, pp. 51–74.

Nakov, Angel. "Antisovetskaia politika Bolgarskikh pravitel'stva nakanune deviatogo sentiabria 1944 g." *Etudes Historiques* 2 (1970): 565–87.

Nekrich, A. "Balkanskii variant." *Mezhdunarodnaia zhizn'* 6 (August 1959): 87–96.

Nenchovski, G. "Bulgarskata selo po putia na sotsializma (1944–1947)." *Istoricheski pregled* 30 (July–October 1974): 103–20.

———. "Ideologicheskata i politicheskata rabota na partiiata v period na podgotovkata za masovo kooperirane na zemiata (1944–1948)." *Izvestiia na instituta po istoriia na BKP* 31 (1974): 189–229.

"Nepublikuvani radiogrami na Georgi Dimitrov i TsK na BRP(k) (avgust–dekemvri 1944 g.)." *Izvestiia na instituta po istoriia na BKP* 32 (1975): 61.

Nestorov, Khristo. "Antikhitleristkata koalitsiia i devetoseptemvriiskata revoliutsiia v Bulgariia." *Vekove* 3 (July–October 1974): 16–30.

Ostoich, Peter. "BRSDP (avgust 1945–avgust 1948g.)." *Izvestiia na instituta po istoriia na BKP* 26 (1971): 181–246.

Peikov, Ivan. "Smazvane na konspirativno-vooruzhenata suprotiva na suborenata burzhoaziia. *Voennoistoricheski sbornik* 34 (November–December 1965): 18–32.

Peshleevski, Krust'o. "Tvorcheskiiat podkhod na partiiata pri izgrazhdaneto na Bulgarskata narodna armiia." *Voennoistoricheski sbornik* 33 (September–October 1964): 121–30.

Petroff, Dimitar R. "The Bagrianov Cabinet." *Bulgarian Review* 4 (December 1964): 52–54.

———. "The Mouraviev Cabinet 2–9/IX/1944." *Bulgarian Review* 3 (November 1963): 28–31.

Petrova, Slavka. "Podgotovka i provezhdanie na devetoseptemvriiskoto narodno vustanii v Sofiia." *Izvestiia na instituta po istoriia na BKP* 1–2 (1957): 255–88.

———. "Vuzmozhen li be mirniiat put kum vlastta prez 1944g." *Vekove* 2 (March–April 1973): 5–11.

Pinter, Stoian. "Angliia i Bulgaro-Iugoslavskoto sblizhenie v kraia na 1944 g. i nachaloto na 1945 g." *Vekove* 8 (November–December 1979): 15–25.

———. "Nachalna deinost na suiuznata kontrolna komisiia v Bulgariia (oktomvri 1944–ianuare 1945 g.)." *Istoricheski pregled* 35 (July–October 1979): 196–203.

Pulova, V. "Arkhiven fond Bulgarska rabotnicheska sotsialdemokraticheska partiia (1944–1948g.)." *Izvestiia na instituta po istoriia na BKP* 25 (1971): 349–58.

Rachev, Stoian. "Otnoshenieto na Angliia kum partizanskoto dvizhenie na Balkanata prez vtorata svetuvna voina (1941–1945)." *Voennoistoricheski sbornik* 39 (July–August 1970): 17–39.

Radkov, Ivan. "Aktsiiata za otmeniavane na chetvurtoto postanovlenie na ministerskiia suvet ot 23/XI, 1944." *Istoricheski pregled* 20 (March–June 1964): 171–83.

———. "Komitetite na otechestveniia front—fakticheski organi na mestnata vlast neposredstveno sled 9 septemvri, 1944 g." *Istoricheski pregled* 19 (March–April 1963): 3–22.

———. "Suzdavane na TKZS v Rusenska oblast (1944–1948)." *Istoricheski pregled,* 27 (July–August 1971): 74–86.

Radulov, Dimitur. "Koga i kak zapochna vustanieto na 9 septemvri 1944 g. *Voennoistoricheski sbornik* 33 (July–August 1964): 85–88.

Resis, Albert. "The Churchill-Stalin 'Percentages' Agreement on the Balkans, Moscow, October 1944." *American Historical Review* 8 (April 1978): 368–87.

Schlesinger, Arthur, Jr. "Origins of the Cold War." *Foreign Affairs* 46 (October 1967): 22–52.

Sharlanov, Diniu. "G. Dimitrov za sotsialnata priroda na otechestveniia front." *Istoricheski pregled* 28 (March–April 1972): 18–37.

Shinkarev, Ivan. "Osvobozhdinieto na Bulgariia ot Suvetskata armiia prez septemvri 1944." *Voennoistoricheski sbornik* 38 (July–August 1969): 3–14.

Sosnovikov, General-Major V. V. "Obiknakn tazi strana." In Ignat Lalov, *Ot Volga do Balkana,* pp. 95–104. Sofia, 1967.

Suchkov, A. I. "Iz moite spomena za Bulgariia." In Ignat Lalov, *Ot Volga do Balkana,* pp. 159–75. Sofia, 1967.

Tanev, Stoian. "Pomoshtta na Suvetskota voenno komanduvane za politscheskoto ukrepvane na narodnodemokratichnota vlast v Bulgariia (septemvri 1944–1947 g.)." *Voennoistoricheski sbornik* 40 (July–August 1971): 65–81.

———. "Pomoshtta na Suvetskite voiski za ukrepvaneto i razvitieto na purvite kooperativni stopanstva v Bulgariia (septemvri 1944–1947g.)." *Voennoistoricheski sbornik* 43 (March–April 1974): 74–84.

———. "Reshavashtata rolia na Suvetskata armiia za pobeda na narodnoto anti-fashistika vustanie prez septemvri 1944." *Voennoistoricheski sbornik* 43 (May–June 1974): 82–93.

Toshev, Todor. "Rabotata na BKP sred komandniia kadur na fashistkata voiska za podgotovka na devetoseptemvriiskoto vustanie." *Voennoistoricheski sbornik* 33 (September–October 1964): 131–33.

Toshkova, Vitka. "Bulgariia v Balkanskata politika SASht (septemvri 1943–iuni 1944 g.)," *Istoricheski pregled* 35 (January–February 1979): 27–49.

———. "Khitleristkata diplomatsiia i Bulgaro-Suvetskite otnosheniia." *Vekove* 1 (November–December 1972): 3–12.

———. "Khitleristki planove za prevrat v Bulgariia (avgust–septemvri 1944 g.)." *Vekove* 3 (July–October 1974): 30–41.

———. "The Policy of the United States towards the Axis Satellites (1943–1944)." *Bulgarian Historical Review* 7, no. 2 (1979): 3–25.

———. "Politikata na SASht kum Bulgariia (septemvri 1939–septemvri 1944)." In *Bulgariia v sveta ot drevnotta do nashe dni,* 2: 258–75. Sofia, 1979.

———. "Prisuediniavaneto na Bulgariia kum tristranniia pakt." *Istoricheski pregled* 25 (July–August 1969): 56–72.

———. "SASht i izlizaneto na Bulgariia ot tristranniia pakt (iune–septemvri 1944 g.)." *Istoricheski pregled* 35 (July–October 1979): 204–17.

———. "Vunshnata politika na pravitelstvo na Dobri Bozhilov (septemvri–mai 1944 g.)." *Istoricheski pregled* 30 (March–April 1974): 3–34.

USSR. "Apeli na komanduvanete na Suvetskata armiia, otpraveni kum Bulgarskiia narod prez septemvri 1944 g." *Voennoistoricheski sbornik* 39 (May–June 1970): 71–82.

Voznesenskii, V. D. "Deviatoe sentiabria 1944 g. v Bolgarii." *Novaia i noveishaia istoriia* 3 (1974: 94–117; 18 (July–August 1974): 111–36.

———. "SShA, Angliia i vykhod Bolgarii iz voiny v 1944 godu." *Novaia i noveishaia istoriia* 12 (July–August 1968): 98–107.

———. "Zakliuchitel'nye etap politicheskogo krizisa v Bolgarii (aprel'–9 sentiabriia 1944 g.)." *Novaia i noveishaia istoriia* 8 (July–August 1964): 29–49.

Walker, Richard L. "E. R. Stettinius, Jr.," In *The American Secretaries of State and Their Diplomacy,* ed. Robert H. Ferrell and Samuel Flagg Bemis, 14: 1–83. New York, 1965.

Williams, William A. "A Historian's Perspective." *Prologue* 6 (Fall 1974): 200–203.

Zheltov, A. S. "Osvobozhdenia Bolgarii." *Voennoistoricheskio zhurnal* 14 (September 1969): 59–70.

———. "Vinage zaedno." In Ignat Lalov, *Ot Volga do Balkana,* pp. 48–57. Sofia, 1967.

Index

Acheson, Dean: advises postponement of peace treaties, 175–76
Allied Control Commission, Bulgaria, 3, 63, 64; suggested by U.S. and U.K., 33, 47–48; U.S.S.R. objects to tripartite control of, 48; as established at Moscow Conference, 49–50; Barnes' initial complaints about, 65; restrictions on western representatives, 68, 121–22, 125; first three meetings, 69; meetings of sections, 105; considers economic issues, 106; U.S. and U.K. requests for reform of, 113, 114–15, 117; U.S.S.R. accepts reform of, 118; reformed at Potsdam, 120–21; meetings of, 120–26; policy of censorship, 124; discusses postponement of 1945 elections, 144–46; last meeting of, 184, 187
American Military Mission, Bulgaria: size of, 64; history and functions, 103; sections of, 103–06; intelligence functions of, 104; constructs orders of battle, 105; changing views of Bulgaria, 106; restrictions on activities, 106–07; quarters of, 107; watched by Bulgarian militia, 176, 177
Antonov, General A. I., 57
Arnold, General Henry H., 12
Austria: U.S. worries over Soviet domination of, 124

Bagrianov, Ivan, 38; surrender conditions of, 39, 42; rivalry with regents, 43; discovers pro-German coup plot, 44; withdraws troops from Macedonia, 45; negotiates with Fatherland Front, 54; orders withdrawal from occupied lands, 200 n.79
Bakeless, Colonel John, 103–04
Balabanov, Nicolas, 42; meets Kouyoumdjisky, 20, 22; reports Kouyoumdjisky's peace plan to Sofia, 21
Barnes, Maynard B.: views on Fatherland Front, 53, 65, 70, 76; career prior to 1944, 62; negative views of U.S.S.R., 62–63, 77, 78, 97; position in Bulgaria, 63, 121; complains Allied Control Commission misfunctioning, 68; discovers spheres of influence agreement for Bulgaria, 70; complains of purges in Bulgarian army, 74; inquires as to U.S. policy in Eastern Europe, 82, 95; tells

Bulgarian government America supports Yalta accords, 83; believes Agrarians would win free elections, 92; objects to single-list elections, 92, 135; wishes to invoke Yalta accords, 93–95, 118; meets with Petkov, 100, 141; suggests five-point reform of Allied Control Commission, 104; sees problems in Soviet reform draft for Control Commission, 119; letters to Bulgarian press censored, 124; supports U.S. policy of nonrecognition, 134; suggests 1945 elections be postponed, 137, 145, 161; delight over Potsdam results, 140–41; criticized by Byrnes for election postponement efforts, 150; reports unrest in Zveno, 161, 173; assesses failure of Moscow Foreign Ministers Conference, 167–68; accused by Vyshensky of sabotage, 169; assesses situation after 1946 elections, 183; refuses post in Bulgaria, 184; uncertain as to Bulgaria's future, 184–85; activities in Bulgaria assessed, 191
Beckerle, Adolf-Heinz, 25; advises against new Soviet consulates, 39
Berry, Burton: reports 1943 contact with Kiselov, 10; and Kiselov visit of 1944, 26; talks with Bulgarian officials, 42
Beshkov, Ivan, 38
Bessarabia, 36
Biriuzov, General Sergei: inability to defend Sofia, 60; liaison between Bulgarian and Soviet armies, 61; lectured by Barnes, 62–63; views of Barnes, 63; career prior to 1944, 64; made head of Allied Control Commission, Bulgaria, 66; discusses goals in Bulgaria, 66–67; retains command of thirty-seventh army, 66; forbids contact between western representatives and Bulgarian government, 67–68; discusses Control Commission with Crane and Barnes, 69; decides to terminate Control Commission meetings, 69; demands revocation of Order Number Four, 75; demands Gemeto's resignation, 91; interferes in Bulgarian internal affairs, 111; discusses postponement of 1945 elections, 144–49
Bohlen, Charles (Chip): and Emergency High Commission for Liberated Europe,